AO 0 1429

K4. 4   HUD

AV 112 HUD .

D0431636

1977

Time-Limited Th
General P

Time-Limited Therapy in a General Practice Setting

How to Help Within Six Sessions

GLYN HUDSON-ALLEZ

MEDICAL LIBRARY
AILSA HOSPITAL
DALMELLINGTON ROAD
AYR KA6 6AB

SAGE Publications
London • Thousand Oaks • New Delhi

© Glyn Hudson-Allez 1997

First published 1997

All rights reserved. No part of this publication may be
reproduced, stored in a retrieval system, transmitted or utilized
in any form or by any means, electronic, mechanical,
photocopying, recording or otherwise, without permission in
writing from the Publishers.

 SAGE Publications Ltd
6 Bonhill Street
London EC2A 4PU

SAGE Publications Inc.
2455 Teller Road
Thousand Oaks, California 91320

SAGE Publications India Pvt Ltd
32, M-Block Market
Greater Kailash – I
New Delhi 110 048

British Library Cataloguing in Publication data

A catalogue record for this book is available
from the British Library

ISBN 0 7619 5656 5
ISBN 0 7619 5657 3 (pbk)

Library of Congress catalog card number 97–068970

Typeset by Mayhew Typesetting, Rhayader, Powys
Printed in Great Britain by Biddles Ltd, Guildford, Surrey

*To my GP colleagues and friends,
without whose support and trust, this
book could not have been written*

Contents

Preface

Counselling has become a boom industry with many counsellors coming out of the training-course pipeline with basic skills. Counselling in General Practice has become a popular goal for counsellors, and it is now considered that nearly a half of all surgeries offer some form of counselling service. However, GPs have increasingly set a limit to the number of counselling sessions they are prepared to offer to their patients; most commonly six, ten or twelve sessions. Yet counsellors are trained to work in an open-ended way, and may not have the skills required to work within a time limit. With the large number of referrals a counsellor receives in primary care, the counsellor needs not only the counselling skills acquired during their training, but also a psychological knowledge of the human process.

Time-limited therapy is not long-term counselling cut short, but a specific set of skills enabling the counsellor to deal with the vast range of difficulties presented in a short space of time. It is not just about counselling skills, which is why it is called time-limited *therapy*. It is also about other skills that can enhance the counsellor's role in primary care. These skills include teaching, guiding, administering, and even (dare I say it?!) advising. It is essentially a skills book for the counsellor that integrates counselling skills with psychological knowledge. It aims to fill a training gap by providing an overview of how to develop a primary care counselling service, teach the underpinning required to work within a time limit, and then offering skills and tips for the counsellor to use. It will be of interest to student counsellors, newly qualified counsellors, and any counsellor planning to work within primary care who has hitherto worked in an open-ended way. GPs interested in the counselling service offered by their practice might also find it of value.

The reader will note that the topic of psychotherapeutic groups has not been covered in the text. This is not because I feel groups have no value. Indeed, much developmental work can be undertaken in a group, which can be considered as more cost-effective in terms of therapist hours. However, this book is about the one-to-one skills that can reduce a client's presenting distress in the shortest time possible.

The book is divided into two parts. Part I is about the management and administration of a counselling service within primary care, and discusses the political side of working within a time limit. It provides a brief evaluation of a time-limited service in Chapter 2, and in Chapter 3 elaborates the integrated psychotherapeutic skills used to make the therapy shorter and more focused. Part II applies the theories of Part I to specific client presentations. It provides an outline of the psychological and physical aspects of each presentation, and then offers tips on how the therapy can be more efficient. The skills elaborated in the earlier chapters will be of equal relevance to the later ones, but are not reiterated, for the sake of brevity. So if you skip to later chapters (as I often do in books like this!) you will miss some of the skills proposed. I hope you will find something of use to you in the following pages.

I would like to express my grateful thanks to Graham Curtis Jenkins, Director of the Counselling in Primary Health Care Trust for his advice and support in the preparation of this book.

Glyn Hudson-Allez
April, 1997

PART I

1

The Management of a Counselling Service in General Practice

Ten years ago, I was involved in a research project looking at preventative health care in General Practice in the Bristol area. Principal GPs were interviewed, elaborating on their practice's preventative health care measures. Some of the questions asked related to the prescription of psychotropic drugs and counselling services within the practice. One particular question required the respondents to assess what proportion of their patients attended their surgery for psychological or social reasons. The doctors responded that only 53 per cent of patients attended purely with a physical illness. And it emerged that in some of the poorer, working-class areas of the city, GPs reported that up to 75 per cent of presentations had a psychological or social underpinning (Hudson, 1988). Parenthetically, this is consistent with other research which found that 60 per cent of patients presented with illness but no disease (Shapiro, 1971). Of course, there were variations in the perception of these patient presentations. Some doctors suggested that virtually all the ailments presented to them had some form of psychological underpinning. Others felt that even psychological problems cause illnesses and should therefore be considered physical. What became clear was that approximately half of a GP's patient presentations had a psychological element. The doctors themselves said that they had little or no psychological training, and often felt inadequate to deal with such a large psychological caseload.

The GPs interviewed were aware of, and predominantly frustrated by, their inability to tackle these issues within the space of their 6–10 minute consultation time (Noon, 1992). Counsellors in primary care were rare at this time, often working for nothing, and anyway there was a distrust of what were seen as well-meaning, non-professional do-gooders. Only patients with more serious problems manifesting severe physical or psychiatric illnesses could be referred to the secondary mental health teams. So that left a large number of patients who were finding it difficult to cope with life, being maintained pharmacologically on repeat prescriptions of psychotropic drugs. These patients became the GPs' 'heartsinks', often referred to as the 'worried well' or the 'walking worried'. This was a large proportion of the patient population, as one in 50 adults takes mood-altering drugs permanently, and one in ten men and one in five women will take them at some time in their lives (Mitchell, 1984).

Nearly a decade later, it is considered that a half of all fundholding practices and a third of non-fundholding practices offer a counselling service. Fundholding in General Practice has given doctors the freedom (and the money) to widen the services offered to their patients. GPs knew what the patients needed (Kriesel and Rosenthal, 1986; Small and Conlon, 1988); but they had been unable to persuade those holding the purse-strings that non-medically qualified staff might have something to offer. Once GPs had the financial freedom to employ counsellors, the introduction of counsellors into the primary health care team mushroomed (Sibbald et al., 1993). And, once installed within the system, counsellors became their own best advocates, with GPs and patients alike wondering how they ever managed without them. GPs know that caring for people is labour-intensive. As Mitchell (1984) argued, machines cannot do it and it cannot be done against the clock. Yet GPs have only 10 minutes to offer for each consultation (some appointments are only five minutes apart). The great medical writer Balint (1964) agreed: if patients need something special, like time, only time will do. One of the contributions that a counsellor gives to a client is time. Even time-limited therapy offers a client abundantly more time than the doctor can give. Balint continued that the more one knows of the problems in General Practice, the more impressed one becomes by the immediate need for psychotherapy. Thirty years later, it is still not a universal service.

Advantages and disadvantages of primary care counselling

What are the benefits in having a counsellor in General Practice? For the GPs, outcome research indicates a reduction in psychotropic drug prescribing (Ives, 1979; Gath and Catalan, 1986; Spiers and Newell, 1995) and a reduction in patient presentations with numerous minor physical ailments (Marsh and Barr, 1975). GPs can refer early to someone they know and trust, and receive direct feedback from their patients and their counsellors. Having a counsellor liaising within a primary health care team introduces a person experienced in interpersonal relationships, with more time to listen and to hear the full extent of the patient's difficulties, thus reducing the tendency to medicalise the patient's problem. This also makes the other team members more aware of an alternative non-medical approach.

For the patient, there is an opportunity to unload and be heard in familiar, safe surroundings, without the fear of stigmatisation that secondary referral can bring. Secondary referral can take months of anxious waiting, and may not necessarily be taken up even when the person reaches the top of the waiting list. Mental health teams are so under-resourced that they are selective in the referrals they receive and only take what they consider to be the more severe cases.

A counsellor can normalise many of the client's difficulties rather than exaggerating them into 'mental health problems'. Much has been written on the tendency to prescribe psychotropic drugs to change the way patients feel about a situation, rather than helping them deal with their problems (Parish, 1971; Gravelle, 1980; Wells, Goldberg and Brook, 1986). This has led to widespread addiction and in some cases permanent physical damage from prescribed psychotropic drugs (Johnstone, 1989; Breggin, 1991). Now, patients are more likely to end pharmacological interventions when they have been counselled than when they have not been counselled (Ashurst and Ward, 1983). Plus GPs are less likely to reach auto-matically for the prescription pad when a counselling alternative may be considered more appropriate.

For the counsellors, the advantages are that they receive a challenging and interesting caseload of regularly referred clients, a regular income, a consulting room, and the benefit of reception and secretarial facilities. Working within a team is less isolating than working in private practice, usually from home.

What are the disadvantages of having a counsellor in primary care? Well, cost is always a consideration of services provided in the 1990s. Gone are the days when counsellors chose to work for nothing, and rightly so. As the discipline has become professiona-lised, counsellors have demanded a fair remuneration commensurate with their qualifications and experience. Equally this has ensured that only appropriately qualified counsellors are employed in the capacity, rather than interested health visitors or the GP's wife. However, the cost has to be met either by the patient (soon to become the counsellor's client) or from the practice budget.

There is also the ubiquitous criticism of the lack of evidence that talking therapy actually works, especially given the knowledge that some patients spontaneously recover. Evaluation of the service is covered in more depth in the next chapter. Some argue that having an in-house counsellor encourages patients to go to the doctors even when they are not 'ill'. There are also fears from the psychotherapeutic profession that confidentiality may be compromised in a team setting. This concept will be addressed more fully later on in this chapter.

Finally, because of cost restrictions, there is usually a limit on the number of sessions offered for each client. You will notice that I have placed this in the disadvantages section. Some people strongly believe that placing limits on therapy inhibits the process. I have written this book because I disagree. Thus, the ability to undertake brief therapeutic work is the focus for this book. Arguments for and against time-limited therapy will be addressed in Chapter 3.

Funding the service

FHSAs vary in their approaches to counselling services. Some promote the idea of an 'in-house' counsellor by offering GPs reimbursement of up to 70 per cent of the cost of employing one under the ancillary staff scheme. However, when the range of trained staff eligible for reimbursement was extended in the GP contract in 1990, some FHSAs withdrew this benefit under the ancillary staff scheme. Other practices have employed a counsellor under the scheme for health promotion clinics, but this tends to be unsatisfactory as it is likely to be the first resource cut if the books are not balancing towards the end of the financial year.

Fundholding or non-fundholding practices will invoke different methods of employing counsellors. In order for non-fundholding practices to offer a counselling service when they have not got an interested FHSA, some practice managers have made a room available in the surgery for the counsellor to use. The counsellor and client make their own arrangements for the payment of a fee. Some practices charge the counsellor a nominal fee for the use of the room; others do not. The counsellor pays for his or her own supervision and professional liability insurance. The advantage of this method is that the counselling service is offered to patients at no cost to the practice. The disadvantages are that the patient has to pay, and not all patients in need can afford to do so. Thus the counselling service will not be as well used as in fundholding practices. Plus the practice partners have very little say in how the counselling service *per se* is organised, especially with regard to the quality of service.

Fundholding practices are more likely to employ their own counsellor directly, offering the service to their patients free of charge.

The counsellor's salary, or fee if employed on a contract basis, can be taken from either the mental health budget, hospital services budget, or from savings made from the FHSA allowance. Under these arrangements counsellors may receive financial assistance for their supervision and insurance commitments. The disadvantage of this approach, for the counsellor, is that job security exists only as long as fundholding is maintained by the government of the day. For the practice partners the service is expensive in an already tight budget, and can be frustrating when patients fail to attend for appointments that have been paid for. Advantages of this approach are that the patients get the service free, thus it is available to all who need it, and the practice partners can monitor, evaluate, and generally participate in the service they are providing.[1]

Qualifications and training of the counsellor

Counsellors are now coming off the training course conveyor-belt in large numbers; it is a boom industry (Hudson-Allez, 1994). GPs are frequently petitioned as to their willingness to employ counsellors, or to refer to the counsellor practising around the corner. Yet how do doctors know that they are getting someone suitably qualified for the job? One practice I know advertised in the local press for a counsellor. Amongst the numerous applications received, the partners had to consider applicants who did not have any paper qualifications but 'people enjoy talking to me', an astrologer who had to counsel in the course of giving horoscopes, nurses trying to escape from the hospital regime, community psychiatric nurses and newly qualified counsellors with shining new certificates but no working experience.

The British Association for Counselling (BAC) and Counselling in Primary Care Trust have been working hard to try to establish specific criteria which doctors can look for when employing counsellors, and have published guidelines (BAC, 1993) to help them do so. The BAC has recommended that GPs only employ counsellors accredited by their organisation (Curtis Jenkins, 1993b). This accreditation procedure applies rigorous training and experience criteria. However, there are comparatively few accredited counsellors, as the accreditation procedure has many critics from within the discipline – especially from those who do not meet the accreditation regulations. With all this controversy within the discipline, we can hardly expect outside professionals to have confidence in the standards that are being set.

Working in General Practice, although very rewarding, is also very demanding. As it is the first port of call for most people with any sort of difficulty, it produces a large number of clients with a wide range of difficulties. It therefore needs a very experienced and very emotionally stable counsellor to tackle such case-loads. As Curtis Jenkins (1996) argues, it is no good employing a Relate counsellor trained only in relationships and expecting them to be able to treat people with post traumatic stress, anxiety and depression. Controversially, I believe that the job also needs a substantial amount of psychological knowledge; that counsellors who have been trained only in counselling skills are probably underqualified for this work. The reason I hold this view is that time-limited therapy requires good early assessment skills. The ability to assess appropriately in a short space of time requires more than just listening skills; it requires a psychological understanding of the dynamics of presenting problems and what may underpin them. It is also equally important that the counsellor have knowledge and understanding of people with mental health problems, and that they do not, naively, embark on trying to counsel people who are mentally ill. Part II of this book brings together psychological underpinning and counselling skills to aid people when working in a time-limited way.

Once a counsellor is in post in primary care, it is important for both counsellors and GPs to remember that training for the job does not end there. It is part of counsellors' professional working ethic that they continue with personal and professional development. This means continuing to attend training and therapeutic workshops to keep abreast of new techniques and theoretical research. A counsellor's supervisor, and line manager if appropriate, should monitor the continuing professional development of her supervisee.

Referrals to the counsellor

Counsellors need to be aware of the mixture of emotions that referrals to the counsellor elicit, both in the client and the GP. Counsellors also need to be aware of the effect of this referral in terms of the triangular relationship (i.e. client, GP, counsellor) on the therapy (Palazzoli et al., 1980). If you are a new counsellor within the practice, the GP may feel a little unsure about referring a patient for whom s/he has hitherto had sole responsibility. Delegating the work while maintaining that responsibility is difficult. Younger and newly trained GPs tend to find it easier to refer to a counsellor than older doctors do (Neilson and Knox, 1975; Waydenfeld and Waydenfeld, 1980). But whatever the age of the GP, it is important to keep the channels of communication open. As discussed later, in the confidentiality section, the way to alleviate nervousness and anxiety about the counselling service, and to promote trust and confidence in your skills as a counsellor, is to be open with the others in the team about what you are doing. Cloaking the counselling process with a mysterious veil on the grounds of confidentiality inhibits the team relationship.

If you are the first counsellor to work within a certain primary health care team, it is useful to write a memo to the GPs as to the type of referral that you feel is appropriate for you to receive. GPs need to be made aware that it is fruitless to send their 'heartsink' patients to the counsellor as a means of getting the patients off their backs for a few weeks. There is a limit to what a counsellor can do, especially in time-limited therapy, and it is up to the counsellor to reinforce these types of boundaries (Curtis Jenkins, 1993c). Inappropriate referrals reduce the cost-effectiveness and efficiency of the counselling service. Having said that, small but significant changes can occur with some of these patients simply because the quality of the listening service has been enhanced (i.e. 6 to 10 minutes of GP time is increased to 50 minutes of counsellor time). Maybe for the first time, the patient has felt heard and their feelings acknowledged.

Patients who become the counsellor's clients will also be feeling nervous. They may have known their GP for years, and feel safe and confident in his abilities. Now the patient is being asked to see someone new, who is not a doctor. In this referral, the message being transmitted is that the patient is not really ill, but has something wrong in their head. Words like 'psychiatrist', 'shrink' and 'mad' fly around in their minds, producing feelings of anxiety and fear. It feels safer to have an illness that can be labelled, like 'nervous debility', 'irritable bowel syndrome' or 'stress', than to admit both to oneself and to others that one cannot cope with life. It is not enough for the counsellor to understand these feelings of the client. The counsellor needs to convey this to the GPs too, so they can be more sensitive when discussing the referral with their patients. For an outline of the sort of person who is referred to the counsellor, see the next chapter.

Having accepted a referral from the GP, it is important for counsellors to feed back progress of the counselling process to the referring doctor. This feedback may be in two forms. First, there is the informal conversation. It is this kind of discussion that some counsellors are so vehemently opposed to. It is interpreted as coffee-room gossip, and is considered demeaning to the client. Yet this sharing is as important for the counsellor as it is for the doctor. Clients are selective as to the information they convey between the two helpers. They often also have implicit assumptions about the counsellor and GP discussing their case, and about the counsellor having read the medical notes. They expect the counsellor to know why they have come and to know about the major events in their lives. Clients frequently express surprise when I tell them after I have introduced myself at an assessment session that I know nothing about them. If the counsellor and doctor are used to liaising informally, it can relieve a lot of pressure for them both. Saying, 'I am not really sure what is going on here' becomes easier on both sides. Difficulties can be shared, and appropriateness of referral can be questioned. Differences in philosophy can be discussed, e.g. the medical versus the humanistic model, thus allowing for a deeper understanding of different perspectives. Remember that keeping the content of the client's sessions to oneself can still preserve confidentiality. What may be shared, however, is the process, and this sharing is too valuable to lose.

The second form of feedback is the counselling formulation. At the end of the counselling contract, a formal acknowledgement of the termination of that contract is appropriate. A formulation of the counselling process and progress made will inform the GP of the current situation. This is important, not only because counsellors should be seen to be working in a professional manner, but because GPs are entitled to know of the outcome of the service for which they have paid. The formulation should include the counsellor's evaluation of the counselling process, an assessment of the progress made, and any recommendations the counsellor may wish to make for consideration in future dealings with the client. This formulation should not be filed in the patient's medical notes, but in a separate locked place without any identification of the person on it. Formulations can be identified by client number, which the counsellor will allocate at the assessment session. When a formulation is sent to a GP, patient identification should be detachable. The GP can note its contents, detach the identification label, and the formulation can then be filed away safe from curious eyes. Medical case notes may be marked discreetly with the formulation number to refer back to at a later date, if appropriate.

Reception facilities for the client

As mentioned, being referred to a counsellor for the first time may be scary. And the patient, soon to become the client, does not wish to be distinguished from the other patients in the doctor's waiting room. It is important, therefore, that receptionists are briefed as to the sensitivity of this situation. Stories abound of unthinking receptionists who have boomed across crowded waiting rooms, 'Mrs Jones, you're next for the counsellor. Go to room six!'

Very often doctors in group practices use an intercom system to summon patients from the waiting room to the consulting room. Counsellors, however, prefer to greet a client personally, and may choose to fetch the client from the waiting room and take him or her to the consulting room. But this immediately distinguishes this client from the other patients. Patients in waiting rooms talk to one another, and if something different is noticed, it is commented on. It is preferable that clients are summoned to the consulting room in exactly the same way as other patients, in order to preserve the anonymity of the consultation.

Leaflets should be available at the surgery to explain to the client what to expect when being referred to the counsellor. Clients should be made aware of the qualifications of the counsellor, what to expect in terms of a time-limited contract, and what the confidentiality boundaries are. Ideally, these leaflets should be handed to the patient when the doctor first makes the referral to the counsellor, but it would also be helpful to have the leaflets available in the waiting room, so that other patients can read about the service being offered. An example of such a leaflet can be found in Appendix 1.

It is very difficult to de-medicalise a medical setting, especially if the counsellor is receiving clients in one of the doctor's consulting rooms. Yet it is important for the clients to feel, as soon as they walk through the counsellor's door, that this is a different form of consultation. Attention must be given to the detail of the room structure. If the counsellor is in a special room for the purpose, then it is easy to place comfortable chairs at non-threatening angles, to have pictures and plants to soften the room, and to have an occasional table with the necessary tools of water, paper, tissues and a well-positioned clock.

If the counsellor is seeing clients in a medical consulting room, it is much harder to soften the atmosphere. It is common for GPs to have high swivel chairs positioned at a desk, while the patient sits in a small, hard dining-chair perched at the corner of the desk. Of course, these are not appropriate for a counselling setting, so two (or three, if seeing couples) soft armchairs of equal height will need to be transported in from another room. The curtains can be drawn around the examination couch and the computer monitor should be placed well out of view of both the client and counsellor, to avoid distractions.

The counsellor should never fall into the habit that some GPs have, of not greeting the client appropriately. Patients frequently lament that when they enter the consulting room the doctor asks what the problem is before even looking up from completing the previous patient's notes. This makes the patient feel small, undervalued and often angry. The relationship between client and counsellor is very important in a counselling interview. It is even more so in time-limited therapy, where there is not the luxury of additional time to be spent on enhancing the relationship and checking out its progress as in other therapeutic interventions. The counsellor should have read any previous notes before a client enters the room, and should greet the person in a warm, friendly and informal manner.

Confidentiality

I feel very strongly that counsellors working within primary care lose an essential benefit of team-work when they adhere to a very strict code of confidentiality (Hudson-Allez, 1995), to the extent that they refuse to share the process of their work with other professionals within the team. This is one of the most common criticisms of counsellors from the medical discipline. Doctors are used to working in team settings, and are trained to make comprehensive notes to which colleagues can refer. They share case histories and bounce ideas between each other. Doctors treat the counsellor's unwilling-ness to share with suspicion, making them reluctant to refer if they cannot keep abreast of what is going on. It must be remembered that GPs have a confidentiality ethic, too.

Counsellors are also trained to adhere to a strict code of confi-dentiality (BAC, 1992). The BAC reinforces that the counselling relationship is, by its nature, confidential, and we are aware that many clients would not open up as they do if they were not assured of this confidentiality. But strict adherence to the rule can isolate the counsellor from the rest of the primary health care team, causing distrust and resentment, and the loss of a lot of important sharing. And it has to be remembered that the persona presented by the client to each member of the team is different. If the professionals share with each other their impressions of the work that needs to be done with a client, a much clearer, holistic view is built up, enhancing the service that the client receives.

So how can this bipolar approach to confidentiality be resolved? Counsellors can never assure clients of absolute confidentiality: the Children's Act and Prevention of Terrorism Act prohibit us from doing so. But there are also personal moral boundaries that may encourage counsellors to break the confidentiality code. For example, suppose your client tells you that she sells illegal drugs outside the local primary school, or that he is sexually abusing an adult with learning difficulties? These are the cases that we take to our supervisor before deciding what to do. We will probably discuss with our client our intention to break confidentiality, and suggest that it would be better if he or she does so. But the client can still refuse, and demand that we keep the secret. When working in primary care, it may be valuable in such cases to discuss difficulties with the GP. The GP usually knows the family well, and can not only offer a clearer insight into the dynamics of the person, but can also provide the counsellor with professional back-up if the situation becomes difficult.

Another grey area in our confidentiality code is when the client expresses serious suicidal intentions. Medical staff are trained to interpret this as a severe psychiatric disturbance which needs medical intervention. Counsellors are more likely to consider that, although some clients may be severely psychologically disturbed, they are still autonomous individuals who have the right to make their own choices. Bond (1993) suggests that legally it is doubtful that being suicidal is sufficient grounds for breaking confidentiality. But when the counsellor is working in a team setting, there is more than just the client to consider. If a client takes at once all the medication prescribed by the GP for a month, and the counsellor who had been seeing that person in parallel knew this was very likely to happen but kept it confidential, how would that GP feel about that counsellor? What would it do for the trust and confidence of working within a team?

In practices where I work, we have discussed this at length. Our way around this problem is to annotate the medical notes 'at risk' following the counselling endorsement. Confidentiality boundaries are protected as no further information is provided. But the doctors and nurses are alerted to distress calls when in attendance or when prescribing. A similar annotation can be used when a counsellor is concerned that a child or an elderly person may be in danger, but has insufficient information or evidence to warrant social services intervention. Thus doctors can be alerted and be vigilant when these people attend the surgery. Here again, confidentiality is not broken, yet vulnerable people are protected.

What does the client feel about confidentiality in the doctor's surgery? In my experience the client comes with an implicit assumption that the doctor, who may be in the next room or down the corridor, will know some of our conversation, despite my explaining the confidential nature of our relationship when we first meet. As I have said, clients often express surprise when I say that I do not know why they have attended, or what their difficulties are. Sometimes this prior assumption is made explicit as the doctor has told the client that she will talk to me to see how they are getting on. If clients felt unhappy or uncomfortable with this, they would not attend the sessions. Yet they do, and they still pour out all their unhappiness and reveal things in complete trust and confidence that they have never told anyone else, even the doctor. Their assumptions are highlighted by the comments they make, like 'Did the doctor tell you this. . .?' It is true that clients tell the counsellor things that they do not want their GP to know. However, they highlight these points by saying, 'This is one thing I would not want the doctor to know, but. . .' or 'I have never told anyone this, and I wouldn't want anyone else to know. . . .'. Such cues are important as they confirm the trusting nature of the relationship, but they also confirm that the clients are not assuming that confidentiality is absolute. This assumption should be acknowledged either verbally or in the patient leaflet.

Clients may also use the counsellor to complain about their doctor. Not all patients are happy with the service they receive and like to tell someone within the team of their disquiet. Others may wish to tell you things that they want you to convey to the GP but have been unable to express themselves, either because of time pressures or because of embarrassment. One example is of a middle-aged man referred to me because of his depression due to loneliness. At our second meeting, he brought with him a letter that he had written to me and asked me to read it in his presence. In this letter he described impotence difficulties that he had experienced for the previous 15 years, that had led to the loss of his last relationship, and his fear of forming a new one. Although he had known his GP well for over 30 years, he was too embarrassed to tell him of his problem. It was probably because he knew him well that he could not tell him. I asked the client if I could show the GP his letter, and with great relief he agreed. The GP read the letter, expressed his astonishment and shredded the letter at my request (otherwise, like everything else, it would have ended up filed in the case notes). The client has now been successfully treated for his physical dysfunction.

What about the confidentiality of the counsellor's notes? In my experience, GPs are not interested in seeing them, and would prefer a short conversation rather than ploughing through written ideas that may be incomprehensible to them. Counsellors' notes and formulations of the progress of the contract, as I have previously mentioned, should always be filed separately and anonymously away from medical records.

Another aspect of sharing that is required within the primary care team is when the counsellor needs to refer on to the secondary mental health care teams. As counsellors, we must all recognise our limitations, and there are some problems that are not appropriate for brief therapy, so secondary referral is appropriate. At present, it is not considered politically correct for a counsellor in primary care to refer direct to a consultant psychiatrist or clinical psychologist; this has to be done by the GP. This means that the counsellor is required to share with the GP sufficient detail of the presenting problem in order to justify the referral, otherwise it will not be taken up by the under-resourced secondary team. Of course, our confidentiality boundaries are protected in the sense that we can discuss with the client the need to convey this information to the GP in order to make a referral. Where it leaves the counsellor's control, however, is when the GP's secretary types up the referral letter which is later filed by someone else in the medical notes and is then accessible to anyone working within the confines of the practice. It should also be said that once a secondary referral has been accepted by a mental health team, the consulting physician sends the GP a detailed summary of all the client's presenting problems, past history, medication pre- scribed, etc., after the initial consultation, followed by detailed letters after every consultation thereafter until discharge. All of these are filed in the medical notes to be accessed by doctors, nurses, receptionists, secretaries and office staff.

So what information should counsellors give to GPs? Well, I feel a distinction should be made between process and content. In supervision, one can scratch the surface of the content to discuss the progress of the counselling process a client is undertaking. Similarly, when a GP asks, 'How is Joe Bloggs getting on?', this is not an opening for gossip, but a need to know how the counselling is going. Indeed, it is especially important for the GP to know when he is seeing the person in parallel and may need to review medication. What the GP wants is for he and the counsellor to work together in patient care, not as isolated units. What must not be forgotten is that the person with prime responsibility for that patient is the GP. He will ultimately direct the course of care for his patient. But if the GP has a good and trusting relationship with the counsellor (and other members of his team), the GP will be open for discussion, advice and even challenges of alternative viewpoints from the counsellor. Thus a counsellor who is open and sharing is likely to have greater influence within the team than one who is closed and aloof.

Administration

Taking notes in the 10 minutes between sessions (assuming a 50-minute session) is vital for the continuity between sessions. A paragraph outlining how the session progressed, what aspects were covered and what was left undone, any items to be taken to supervision, and any tasks set or recommendations for the next session are a vital *aide-mémoire* which will be re-read before the client's next session. With the numbers of clients that attend in General Practice, committing such things to memory is a mistake. It is also worth noting details that are vital to the client, e.g., names of spouse or children, significant dates or places. These fine details enhance the counsellor–client relationship. Unlike a psychiatric consultation, the client does not see the counsellor take any notes. So when fine details are mentioned they feel valued, and often remark how essential such attention to detail is to them. It is, for them, an overt demonstration that they have been listened to, and heard.

Counsellor notes should not be incorporated into the client's medical notes, or even be kept as an addendum to them. This would breach confidentiality, as these notes are only for the eyes of the counsellor, and perhaps the counsellor's supervisor. The medical records, whether handwritten or computerised, should however be inscribed with a note of the person's attendance for counselling, and the sessions could perhaps be numbered to help the doctor to assess how far the counselling has got. It is equally necessary for the doctor to know if the client did not turn up for a counselling session, so that should be annotated on the medical notes as well.

Sometimes the counsellor will be required to write a report to a solicitor or a tribunal giving an outline of the counselling work undertaken. This commonly occurs in cases of road traffic accidents, industrial injuries or claims for unfair or constructive dismissal. It is essential not to write anything without the written consent of the client, as some solicitors adopt bombastic attitudes insisting on immediate reports which may make the counsellor feel pressurised. Of course, courts may subpoena copies of documents and even counsellors' notes in certain situations, so care needs to be taken even in writing notes to oneself. In general, GPs are often happy to do the reports themselves, and already have a fee structure in place for doing so. However, solicitors are very keen to encourage their clients to be assessed for post traumatic stress following accidents of various kinds, so they prefer a psychological assessment of the client in addition to the medical assessment.

Another administrative responsibility may be to liaise with occupational health services or employers direct. Once again, this can only be done with the written consent of the client. Although most occupational health workers are objective, for some their allegiance is to the employer rather than the client. It is therefore necessary to be guarded as to the information conveyed.

There will also be clients who will wish to discuss the appropriateness of time off work, and may even expect that the counsellor will write the sick note. This demonstrates how the client sees the counsellor as a medical auxiliary within the team. Although the counsellor may give an opinion as to the client's ability to work, it should be made clear to the client that this is a matter of judgement for the GP, not the counsellor.

These administrative duties – writing notes, counselling formulations, referral letters, and liaison with outside agencies – all take time, and space needs to be allocated within the worked contract for them. I am aware that some counsellors insist on making their own appointments. I feel this is unnecessarily pedantic, as the receptionists are trained and do a very good job.

Counsellor supervision

It is a professional working ethic that counsellors cannot counsel without receiving ongoing counselling supervision. Similarly, counsellors cannot supervise working counsellors without ongoing supervision. At the moment the requirement for BAC accredited counsellors is a minimum of an hour and a half counselling supervision per month, although discussions are now taking place within the BAC concerning the introduction of supervision requirements linked to client caseload. Thus an experienced counsellor would need one hour's supervision for every 25 clients seen. This requirement will have greater implications for counsellors working in medical settings as opposed to those working in private practice, as the caseloads of the former are higher. Thus the expense of supervision will be greater, unless the employer provides it. Counselling Psychologists are also required by the British Psychological Society to undertake personal therapy in addition to their supervision, which is also expensive. The Counselling in Primary Care Trust recommends personal therapy for counsellors, although it is not a requirement.

Other caring professions, including GPs, do not have the luxury of such safeguards as supervision. Working with a team of caring professionals in primary care, the counsellor may be the only one who gets a back-up service. Colleagues who understand the concept of counselling supervision are often envious of the support provided, although unwilling to pay for the service themselves, as the counsellors are required to do. Colleagues who do not understand the nature of supervision may misunderstand the word and may feel the counsellor is underqualified to work alone, as the word 'supervision' suggests inexperience.

Counsellors working in primary care need to choose a supervisor who understands the pressures placed on a counsellor within a medical setting. That supervisor should also understand and approve of the concept of working in time-limited therapy. Recently I met an experienced counsellor and supervisor who was vehemently opposed to time-limited therapy, and admitted to having little understanding of how the process worked. Yet she supervised a counsellor working in General Practice with a six-session contract. That counsellor could not get the support and understanding that she deserves (and is paying for) if her supervisor had no empathy with the philosophy in which she works. Feltham (1997) had similar experiences and suggests that the supervision of time-limited counselling presents a challenge to supervisors. However, he is making the assumption that time-limited counselling is over in a short period of time, whereas the method to be proposed here is few sessions over a longer expanse of time. Nevertheless, counsellors working in primary care need to give careful consideration to the professional orientation and belief system of their supervisors.

Referrals by the counsellor

Secondary mental health teams in the NHS are in serious financial crisis. They have insufficient finances and insufficient staff to cope with very large caseloads. They are therefore placing restrictions on the quantity and quality of the referrals they accept from primary care. Initially, these mental health teams greeted the employment of counsellors in primary care with suspicion. They feared further cuts in their budgets, and feared having to deal with the consequences of the mistakes that poorly trained counsellors would make. They were initially quite resistant to the idea of accepting a primary care counsellor as an addendum to their own service. This attitude is now improving as time has progressed. It has been found that although practices who employ counsellors reduce their referrals to secondary care (Corney, 1987), the referrals they do make are more appropriate. As such, their budgets have not been substantially reduced. What the counsellors are doing, then, is providing a filtering service whereby life events and short-term crises are dealt with at primary care level, and only the more serious psychological distress requiring more in-depth care is referred on to the mental health teams. Essentially, the counsellor in primary care is dealing with a different client caseload than has always been handled by the secondary mental health teams, although there will be some small overlap.

What alternative services are available for counsellors to refer clients on to? Well, different Health Trusts provide different services, but there are some generalisations that can be made. People with mental ill-health problems, who may be a danger to themselves or to others, can be referred to the psychiatric service. People with serious long-standing phobias, or obsessive-compulsive behaviours, can be referred to the psychology service for cognitive-behavioural therapy. It is not appropriate for counsellors to try and resolve deeply entrenched personality difficulties within the space of a six-session contract. But some useful work can be undertaken with these clients while referral is being put into operation. This will be elaborated in Chapter 13. However, counsellors can face an ethical and moral dilemma. Where do you refer clients who patently need longer therapy than six sessions, yet are unlikely to be accepted by the psychiatric service? People with long-standing eating disorders or people who were sexually abused as children tend to fall into this category. These clients are not considered by the secondary care teams to be 'ill' enough to require the referral. They tend to function on a day-to-day level, yet they exhibit genuine distress. Drugs prescribed by their GP are effective to a certain degree, and may suppress some of the symptoms, but that, as we know, is not dealing with the cause of the problem. These people need long-term psychotherapy, yet few Regional Health Care Trusts offer this service to the public, and when they do they are usually very over-subscribed, with long waiting lists.

It is necessary in such cases for the counsellor to refer the client on to the private or voluntary sector. A good knowledge of other local agencies, what their referral criteria are, costs, etc., is important to have to hand. We have already discussed how it feels for the client to be referred from the GP to the counsellor. If, then, the counsellor points out that yet another referral is appropriate, the client is going to feel anxious again, and may identify with previously held feelings of rejection and abandonment. If the counsellor is confident in the knowledge of the referred agency, some of these anxieties can be allayed. I keep a box file with details of agencies and support groups for all sorts of difficulties and physical complaints, together with up-to-date telephone numbers and easy-to-read books. This encourages clients to start taking control of their own difficulty rather than looking for others to do it for them.

Counsellors should be aware of the problem of suggesting that clients should continue to see them on a private basis following the end of a time-limited contract. This may have some ethical issues, as the counsellor is in a position of power whereas the client is

2

Evaluation of the Service

Evaluation of psychotherapeutic services is fraught with difficulties (Aebi, 1993; Martin and Mitchell, 1983; Trepka and Griffiths, 1987; Waydenfeld and Waydenfeld, 1980), but numerous clinically controlled trials now demonstrate the efficacy of counselling in primary care: see Balestrieri, Williams and Wilkinson, (1988), Karasu (1986) or Smith, Glass and Miller (1980) for meta-analyses of studies which suggest that people having some form of psychotherapy do better than 85 per cent of control participants (Holmes, 1994). There are many factors that confound any analysis of a counselling service, besides the obvious one of trying to make an objective study out of a subjective process. How do we know that people are 'better'? Who can decide that it has 'worked'? What justifications do we use; is it people's well-being according to their own subjective assessment, or is it what is more economically viable that is important? Spontaneous recovery, which occurs in all therapeutic situations, both medical and psychological, also confounds comparison (Corney, 1992; Schachter, 1982).

Because counselling is a subjective process, scientific evaluation cannot address its quality, it can only reduce it to an activity and look at various forms of overt outcomes. Rowan (1992) argues for a new research paradigm that talks about people rather than variables. Rennie (1994) agrees and calls for a more phenomenological form of investigation which he calls human science research.

The quality of the counselling service will be dependent on the quality of the counsellor's skills (Balestrieri et al., 1988; Orlinsky and Howard, 1986). Outcome research has shown that a crucial factor in effective therapy is the relationship or bond between the therapist and the client (Bordin, 1979; Goldstein, 1962; Spinelli, 1996). Counsellors are suspicious of some outcome studies which have held that counselling does not benefit the primary health care team (Pringle and Laverty, 1993), because the quality of the counselling has not been assessed or because the counselling has not been done by appropriately trained counsellors, but by nurses, health visitors, CPNs and the like (Corney, 1993).

All too often, some people (particularly purchasing managers with an eye to a financial budget) have seized upon negative outcome studies as proof that the service is not worth the financial input. And, as Curtis Jenkins (1992) emphasised, providers will exploit the situation to slash costs by allowing incompetent staff to offer inadequate services. Counselling is not a cheap option if compared to pharmacology in the short term, and one can only surmise how long medication would have to be taken if counselling had not taken place. Holmes (1994) argued that, following all the outcome research, it could be considered unethical to try to save money in the short term by not offering a counselling service as a necessary and ordinary part of medical practice; that it is unethical to consider primary care counselling a luxury.

For people who take an unbiased view of the outcome studies, the issue has moved on from one of 'is counselling effective?' to one of 'which psychotherapeutic treatments are most effective' (Stiles, Shapiro and Elliott, 1986)? As Spinelli (1996) has said, whilst research demonstrates that psychotherapy is beneficial, there is a distinct lack of evidence that one form of psychotherapy or counselling is superior or is more likely to produce beneficial outcomes than another. Clinical trials have produced ambiguous results, most commonly because controls are matched in terms of age and sex and not on psychosocial problems (Corney, 1992), psychosomatic illnesses or coping resilience. Psychotherapeutic data is anyway so inhomogeneous that research studies cannot be compared with any true validity (Paul, 1967).

Evaluative procedures

There are basic techniques that the counsellor or practice partners can employ to monitor the quality of the service being provided. The simplest method is to survey the users. Woolfe (1996) has argued that all too often when 'the state' has sought to identify client need, it has turned to professional practitioners for the answers, instead of the customer or user. Here again, purchasing managers are often interested not in what the client wants, but in whether scientific research can be converted into financial considerations. Funders want to know whether counselling is value for money; planners want to know if the continuation or expansion of the service is justified.

Yet a simple anonymous questionnaire (see Appendix 2 for a copy of the one I use, or examples in Corney, 1993) sent to clients when they have finished their contract can be very informative. It can tell whether the standards of the service are consistently high (which monitors quality assurance); it can determine how effective the service is according to the client's subjective interpretation; and it can monitor how the service is being used. This information will assist in planning and decision-making as to the extent of the service being offered.

It is also useful to do a follow-up questionnaire some six months to a year after the end of the contract to determine whether any progress reported has been maintained. Care must be taken when posting questionnaires, however, as some clients see the counsellor without other members of the family knowing, and may wish to maintain that confidence. Having a questionnaire arriving in the post which, say, a spouse may open, betrays client confidentiality. The counsellor, or better still the counsellor's secretary/receptionist, should mention the likelihood of a postal communication at the closing session, and ascertain the client's consent before this occurs. The client needs to feel that the questionnaire is returning to the practice, not to the counsellor, as this may affect the kind of response that is given.

Another method of evaluating the service is by utilising computerised consultation records. Most larger practices now record consultations and prescriptions on computer. An experienced computer operator would be able to extract information on patient presentation rates both before and after the counselling contract, and any changes in prescribing. These can then be changed into financial costs if that is considered to be an important consideration (McGrath and Lowson, 1986; Menzies, Dolan and Norton, 1993). For a full review of how to evaluate the cost-effectiveness of a counselling service, see Tolland and Rowland (1995).

Fundholding GPs need to review their budgets on a regular basis, so it is necessary for the counsellor to provide an audit of work conducted, preferably on a six-monthly basis. This audit needs to cover the number of referrals (and it is also useful for the GPs in a partnership to know the number of referrals per GP), reasons for referral, non-attendance percentage, number of contract completions, and the size of the current counsellor caseload. This allows the GPs to assess whether the number of counsellor hours currently being worked meets the demand. This is difficult to judge, but a common rule of thumb proposed by Jewell (1992) is one hour's counselling for 1,000 patients. Thus a surgery with 12,000 patients should consider employing a counsellor for 12 hours per week. However, the Counselling in Primary Care Trust considers a greater commitment, of 22 hours' one-to-one counselling per 7–9,000 patients, to be more appropriate (Curtis Jenkins, 1993a).

Overview of a time-limited service

The following sections of this chapter examine a primary care service using the time-limited therapy described in detail in the next chapter. The evaluation looks at data acquired over a two-year period from two surgeries in the Bristol area, approximately one mile apart, which share the same counsellor. Each practice has an approximate patient capacity of about 12,000 and covers both private housing and council housing estates in both urban and semi-rural areas. Each practice is fundholding, has five GPs, and each practice sets a time limit on the counselling of a six-session maximum.

Over the two-year period, 612 people were referred to the counsellor, two-thirds of whom were women. Referrals to the secondary mental health teams were concomitantly reduced by 50 per cent. The spread of referrals between GPs proved interesting. In each practice, one GP referred nearly one-third of the clients. There was also one GP in each practice who referred very few clients. This reflects the differing interests of the GPs in dealing with psychological problems, the differing levels of trust placed in the counsellor's abilities, and the selectivity of the patients themselves who choose GPs who are more receptive to hearing about their psychological or social problems.

The age range of these prospective clients was distributed as shown in Figure 2.1.

You will notice that the greatest age distributions are for people between 20 and 50, which may be the result of modern-day pressures of working and maintaining relationships.

The most common reasons for referral to the counsellor can be seen in Table 2.1.

One must remember, of course, that these presenting difficulties are often interrelated. For example, a woman may present with depression because she has marital difficulties, or because she is stressed at work; a man may present with sexual dysfunction because he is depressed. So many of these presenting difficulties are not as clear-cut as shown in the table, but it does give an indication of the kinds of referrals received, and therefore the quality of the counsellor required. It is not sufficient for a counsellor presented with this range of difficulties to have just good counselling skills when nearly a quarter of the referrals require, for example, stress management training skills (Spiers and Newell, 1995). With such a wide range of difficulties, and such a large caseload, the counsellor needs to be very qualified, very experienced, and very well supervised (CPCT, 1993). This, again, shows that any outcome evaluation must consider the quality and the appropriateness of the counsellor

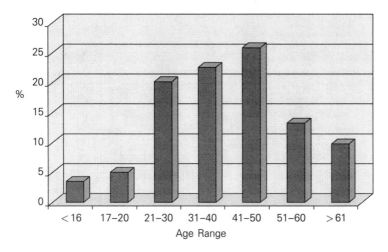

Figure 2.1   *Percentage age range*

Table 2.1   *Most common presenting problems of clients referred to the counsellor*[1]

Presenting problem	Number	Percentage
Anxiety	76	12.41
Stress	129	21.07
Bereavement	70	11.44
Depression	134	21.89
Marriage problems	97	15.85
PTSD	14	2.29
Eating disorder	12	1.96
Sexuality	7	1.14
Substance abuse	6	0.98
Family difficulties	16	2.61
Sexual abuse	18	2.94

[1] The remaining 5.42% are the less common presentation difficulties.

before judgements can be made as to the effectiveness of the service. Trainee or inexperienced counsellors simply will not do unless they are working alongside, and are supervised by, an experienced and fully qualified counsellor.

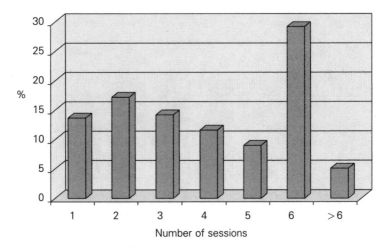

Figure 2.2   *Percentage number of sessions*

Audit of time-limited service usage

The ongoing audit of client usage of the counsellor's time provided interesting information, which, in essence, challenges the counsellor's basic training. Figure 2.2 shows the breakdown of the number of sessions each client had received when the counselling was formally ended.

Only 38 per cent of clients had formal endings; the rest ended the counselling by not attending a booked session (DNAs). This is an interesting phenomenon, as counsellors are trained about process. Process has a beginning, middle and an end. Endings to the counsellor are extremely important and require attention (over several sessions for long-term therapy). Here, however, clients are ending when they feel better, and are not concerned with the formality; they just want to stop. At first it was wondered whether clients were voting with their feet, and not attending through dissatisfaction. But selecting DNAs from the survey sample discussed in detail in the next section revealed no differences in levels of satisfaction. Counsellors would have encouraged clients to extend the number of sessions in order to formalise the process, yet here was an indication that people wanted just a couple of sessions, and then wanted to get on with their lives. Budman (1990) similarly found in the United States that nearly 70 per cent of individuals visiting outpatient mental health centres had six sessions or fewer. This was referred to as brief therapy by default (Budman and Gurman, 1988).

The other important feature shown in Figure 2.2 is that only 29.2 per cent of clients needed the full six sessions or more. The remainder, a total of 532 clients (66 per cent of those with endings and the DNAs) from the original 612, ended their counselling before the sixth session. Indeed, the mean number of sessions was four. This was consistent with other outcome research findings of primary care counselling (Davies, 1993; Spiers and Newell, 1995). Time-limited therapy, therefore, appears to be what the client wants.

Questionnaires

When the service commenced at the beginning of the two-year period, the practices obviously wanted some form of evaluation of it. They therefore sent out 342 questionnaires, as in Appendix 2, over a period of 18 months. The allocation of the questionnaire was not totally at random because of the confidentiality aspects described earlier. It was more likely to be sent to clients who indicated their willingness to receive one. One hundred and fifty-two questionnaires were returned, providing a response rate of 44.4 per cent.

You will notice that the questionnaire commences with an overview of the facilities offered, and then looks in more detail at whether and how the service helped, anything that was unhelpful, and any suggestions for modification or change.

Interestingly, 73 per cent of respondents felt that they would prefer a female counsellor, even if the client was male; 25 per cent expressed no preference, whereas the remaining 2 per cent (only three people, in fact) would have preferred a male counsellor. Some respondents elaborated on their preference:

'I would have declined to see a male counsellor.'

'I suppose that a male patient may like the opportunity of talking with a man (I am female and felt it was right to speak with another woman).'

'Even though I am male, I do not think I could talk about my problems with a strange male person.'

'The personality of the counsellor is more important than the gender.'

For the greater majority of clients, however, the gender of the counsellor was shown to be an important criterion. This is interesting, as in Thomas's (1993) survey, the counsellor was a woman and 37 per cent said they would have preferred to see a counsellor of the same sex. What he did not consider was that men might actually rather see a woman. There are implications here for the therapeutic alliance. What if the gender choice is not available? What if the counsellor in the surgery is a man when the majority of clients want to see a woman?

How about time-limiting the counselling; did respondents' feel they had enough sessions, too few, or too many? Eighty-six per cent of clients felt that the number of sessions they had was about right, justifying the use of time-limited therapy. The remaining 14 per cent said they had too few sessions. Presumably this 14 per cent is a proportion of the 34 per cent who had six sessions or more. However, this still leaves approximately 20 per cent of clients who had six sessions and were satisfied with that number. A few respondents commented on the number:

> 'Remove the statutory limit of six. I was helped by only four, but doubtless other people would need more and might be afraid to ask.'

> 'I would like personal development and also the sessions to go on for as long as you need help not just six sessions.'

> 'I did not attend the full course – I stopped going.'

> 'I had one session which proved beneficial. As a result of that meeting, I structured my objectives for 1–3 years realistically.'

> 'I had three sessions with the counsellor and really found little to complain about.'

> 'I felt loads better even after the first meeting. It helps to talk to someone outside of the family who is non-judgmental. I only attended for two sessions as I felt "normal" again!'

However, those clients who wanted more than six sessions were clearly in the minority.

The next question was an open one asking respondents to say in what way the counsellor helped them. It provided the same sort of replies as any psychotherapeutic helping:

> 'She let me talk about my feelings without passing judgement. I could have a good cry without feeling I shouldn't be showing any strong emotions after such a time after my loss. I could get out a lot of anger and confusion over my feelings and other people's reactions to me.'

> 'She allowed me to express a lot of hidden anger about my past and present and thereby come to terms with my situation and allow me to view life more positively.'

> 'She made me feel a whole person. At last I am an individual who has a right to say NO to other's demands. I have never been happier.'

> 'Helped me to regain control and confidence. Enabled me to unload a lot of thoughts and feelings that I would have just carried around with me –

and would probably have lengthened my recovery. Helped me to understand I was not going "mad", that my reactions were normal, and it was OK to react the way I did. Helped me to understand my feelings.'

There were also comments more specifically about the skills of time-limited therapy which encourage the client's self-understanding and self-help (to be elaborated upon in the next chapter):

'The counsellor helped me to express my feelings of anger and sadness due to losses in the past/childhood/adulthood and more recently. Feelings which I was not aware I had repressed, and allowed me to feel that I had a right to express them. These feelings had caused my depression. Therefore, by coming to terms with my past, this enabled me to move on, and look forward to the future. Also, showing me that my politeness was covering up a certain amount of anger and I was given a leaflet on assertion, which I found very helpful.'

'She helped me to help myself, to understand my patterns and educate me in the field of childhood sexual abuse and its patterns. Helped me and advised me on seeking a food allergy test, which in turn is helping with my migraines and helped me to learn how to relax. In fact the list is endless!'

'She helped me to see what my real problem was, I came to her for help with stress at work. She made me realise that with correct diet and exercise, I could overcome the stress. She also helped me to come to terms with my wife's breast cancer.'

'She gave me tasks to do and I tried making myself do them before I seen here [*sic*] next (some I done some I never) but I have to see her in six months time so I hope I would of done it. Also with having someone to listen and understood me.'

'To see that there are reasons from childhood why I felt like I did and that it was not unreasonable. Also that maybe I had an unused brain and could cope if I had to. It was also pointed out to my husband that he might be at fault sometimes.'

These comments show that clients can learn to help themselves and can understand what happens to them in order to take control of their own lives. Has this time-limited therapy enabled them to make any permanent changes to their lives?

'Yes, my approach to my work has altered in subtle ways and has assumed its proper place *vis-à-vis* family life. I now do not feel guilty that I cannot "relax" by doing nothing. I and my family understand my personality type relaxes by doing something different but still active.'

'Many: – trying to adopt a more positive attitude to men, being more assertive in a relationship, to relax more, be healthier in my mental and physical state. Listen more to people.'

'Yes I will try to talk to my partner, without getting violent with him.'

'Yes: I have recognised the need for me to make time for my own needs and not feel guilty when I am looking after myself rather than others.'

'1. Slowing down/cutting down – hours at work and putting family first as much as possible. 2. Eating proper meals at regular times.'

'Yes I am a stronger person now and like to have my feelings considered they [*sic*] same as I would consider other people.'

'The future is now very clear and I know that towards personal relation-ships I am now on the right path.'

This shows, then, that clients can adopt life-changing strategies following time-limited therapy.

Very little negative feedback about the counselling was received, although one respondent felt:

'The counsellor was a little naive and not cynical enough perhaps. Tended to see the good in other people's behaviour too readily. Not sceptical enough.'

More commonly, comments about the counsellor's skills were positive:

'The counsellor kept a correct professional distance but somehow had the knack of getting me to talk to her as if she was an old involved friend. I told her some things that I have never told anyone else in my life and she gave me a better understanding of my own feelings and personality.'

'I found the counsellor absolutely excellent. Her skills of listening were superb – perceptive and accurate and she remembered every small detail from week to week. I am very grateful for this service at your surgery.'

Did the respondents have any suggestions as to how the service could be improved? Half a dozen or so suggested that some form of refreshments would help, like tea or coffee, which are not provided at present. Other suggestions were:

'I appreciate that resources are finite and one counsellor can only deal with a limited number of cases. However, I would like to see the service expanded, and perhaps separate entrance/exit, to maintain confidentiality. A doctors waiting room is such a public place!'

'It would be most useful to have evening sessions as my husband came for one session early evening and it was most difficult for him to get an appointment before 7.00pm, as a result his counselling did not continue.'

'It would help if useful reading material was available to borrow. It took me 3+ weeks to obtain a recommended book, which proved invaluable.'

'Make it more readily available without consulting the GP first.'

All these suggestions have merit, but their implementation has ramifications for staffing and expenditure.

We now know that time-limited therapy can and does work. We know that clients like the service they get, and it can produce life changes, very often with fewer than six sessions. It is cost effective compared to other psychotherapeutic procedures because it can produce the same results in a shorter time. The next chapter will describe how time-limited therapy works. This chapter will end with the clients' opinions of their new counselling service:

'You are to be commended for offering the service. It worked for me.'

'I feel extremely privileged to be a patient on the list of a General Practice which offers this type of service, especially in the hands of such a competent counsellor.'

'Being able to use the surgery and arrangements made by the doctor made things much easier.'

'I think this is a valuable service with the surgery. Long may it continue!'

'I think the counselling service is a great idea, especially to the people like myself who are embarrassed to seek outside help. It is friendly, and comforting, and is a good way to offload problems, stress, etc.'

'I think this is a positive and helpful asset for the practice, probably because of the high calibre of the counsellor! I hope that the practice will feel they can retain this service so that others can benefit.'

'Don't for goodness sake ever stop this service because remember this STRESS KILLS.'

3
Time-Limited Therapy

Most General Practices employing a counsellor impose a time limit on the counselling contract; most commonly six, eight or twelve sessions. Therapists trained in the traditional psychodynamic or humanistic schools of therapy would argue that such short interventions are worthless; that the only good therapy is long-term which gets to the deep-seated root of the problems. More cognitive and behavioural orientated therapists may not agree with this premise and will be used to working in a briefer way. This chapter looks at time-limited therapy (TLT) in more detail and examines the similarities and differences with more traditional long-term approaches. It then goes on to highlight the common techniques that counsellors working with TLT can employ.

What are the reasons for considering time-limited therapy?

GPs have been aware for years of the difficulties they face in their day-to-day workload. The increase of consumerism in our society and the Patient's Charter has changed the concepts of how the public view their doctor. Once considered a person to be admired and even revered, the GP is now faced with demands for improvement in the service, numerous inappropriate out-of-hours calls, complaints about delays and unsatisfactory treatment, and is overshadowed by a fear of litigation.

As the demand for improvement has increased, GPs have been forced to look closely at the service they offer. It has long been established that a large proportion of patient presentations are not underpinned by medical problems (as discussed in Chapter 1), but have a more social or psychological orientation. Lacking the time, training and very often the inclination to deal with these issues, GPs have reached for the prescription pad as the only means of helping those who presented to them with emotional distress. More enlightened GPs would refer to outside counselling agencies, but there was always the fear that if the result was ineffective for some, the GP might be held responsible for making the referral in the first place. Thus a reluctance to trust someone outside the medical arena was common.

By bringing counsellors into their work-place, GPs can monitor the service that is being provided to their patients. But why limit the sessions at all? Why not let the counselling take its natural course as it does in other settings? What needs to be remembered in answer to these questions is that the counselling service being offered in General Practice is not personal development for the benefit of their patient's psychological well-being; people can pay for that privately if that is what they want. In this case, patients have presented to their GP with a crisis, conflict or confusion in their personal lives which is causing them emotional and/or physical distress; they are asking the GP for help. The public are becoming more aware of the role of counselling, and when they go to their doctors, what they are often asking for is not medication but someone to talk to. A time-limited service not only offers immediate help when it is needed, it allows for people to choose to move in and out of therapy as they wish (Curtis Jenkins, 1996).

By referring to an in-house counsellor, GPs are offering to their patients the opportunity to deal with the issues that are causing the presenting distress. It is not the role of the practice counsellor to delve into other material that may be lurking in the client's psyche that could be dealt with but is not really relevant to the presenting issue. Once again, it is the prerogative of the client to sort that out at another time, and in another place, should the client so wish. It is also not for the counsellor to insist that the difficulty ought to be dealt with. Sifneos (1992) insists that it is insulting to suggest that human beings are so rigid, so inflexible and so unyielding that they require a great deal of time to learn and change. Why does therapy have to be a long and painful journey? It seems that, at the moment, therapy is too much determined by the therapist, not by the client. As O'Hanlon (1989) and Curtis Jenkins (1992) have argued, too often the client receives the counselling offered by the counsellor, but may not necessarily be needed by the client. So Freudian therapists offer analysis, Jungian therapists offer art therapy, and behaviourists offer desensitisation. And although these have all been shown to work, they are often inefficient and take far too long (Curtis Jenkins, 1992). By limiting the time given for therapy, there-fore, the GP and the client stay more in control of the treatment/ counselling work, which also helps avoid dependency difficulties. Clients know they have a short time to resolve their problems, and they usually make a conscious effort to make the most of the time they have available.

Many therapists are against time-limiting therapy, arguing that it is dictated on the grounds of cost rather than client need. Yes, of course financial restrictions have something to do with it. There has to be a limit to how much money GPs can pay out for their patients' counselling, otherwise resources would have to be taken from other forms of patient treatment. In the real world, resources are finite, unlike the demand on them. But what this objection is overlooking is that GPs are now putting considerable resources into a service that was not provided before, out of a very tight budget. The costs of providing no-limit therapy to anyone who wanted it would be prohibitive. Providing a time-limited service is infinitely better than providing no service at all and is an effective use of scarce resources. Certainly in my experience, GPs are not looking for the cheapest option, but one that is the most cost-effective in terms of patient care and outcome. As Cummings (1977) highlighted, the choice is not about long-term versus short-term therapy, but short-term versus no therapy at all.

Time-limited brief therapy has been well researched (Mynor Wallis and Gath, 1992; Sabin 1992; Cade and O'Hanlon, 1993) and, as discussed in the last chapter, has been proven to be no worse, and no more effective, than long-term therapy. Indeed, according to Malan (1976), the evidence shows that radical techniques of brief, focused therapy produce lasting results because they get to the root of the problem. Cade and O'Hanlon (1993) agreed that more is not necessarily better. Research also demonstrates that some clients do very well with only one session (Talmon, 1990; Budman, Hoyt and Friedman, 1992; Hoyt, 1995). That being the case, if outcome research indicates little difference, then, given financial considerations, it is more cost-effective.

Limiting the number of sessions offered seems to fit in with what the patient/client wants (Earll and Kincey, 1982; Hudson-Allez, 1994). TLT can be less intimidating for clients. At times of need like a major life change, desperation or crisis, clients often feel they need some temporary source of help or support. Embarking on long-term therapy can be a daunting decision in terms of emotion, time and cost. TLT provides interventions as and when they are needed, allowing clients to then get on with their lives, leaving their difficulties behind them. As Cummings (1988) reminds us, clients are entitled to relief from pain, anxiety and depression in the shortest time possible with the least intrusive interventions.

For the counsellor, too, TLT can be very satisfying as process and progress are expedited, and dependency issues are usually avoided. In terms of cost to the provider, and cost to the client, TLT is an effective use of scarce resources, and as we have already seen the treatment of choice for 86 per cent of clients.

Can anything be resolved in such a short space of time?

A six-session contract does not imply six weeks. In most cases the six sessions together with an initial assessment session may span three to six months. Flexibility in between-session duration has contributed to the success of the therapy. Many clients have no wish to be seen on a weekly basis; that is too disruptive in their lives. Plus they say they want more time to think about the session, to practise tasks they have been given, or to wait for an event or anniversary to pass. More distressed clients can be seen weekly or fortnightly for the first two or three sessions. Then, as their confidence both in themselves and in their counsellor grows, they are content to have longer periods between sessions.

One must not overlook the importance of between-session work, and clients must be given the time and space to do that work at their own pace. Although several weeks may have elapsed between client–counsellor sessions, the client still feels held, or contained, by the awareness of their forthcoming appointment, and a lot of self-therapy occurs as time progresses. If, however, a crisis does occur and the client needs to see the counsellor urgently, taking cancellation appointments usually means that the client can be seen within a few days at short notice.

What are the counsellor's fears about TLT?

The biggest difficulty counsellors experience is a philosophical dilemma. Counsellors who are trained in (especially) psychodynamic or humanistic, person-centred traditions are trained to give clients space and time to work through their issues at their own pace. The external limitations of a fixed-session contract require adaptation of the basic counselling skills used. Some argue that this devalues the training they have received. On the contrary, good time-limited therapists can only practise the way they do because they have had a solid background of appropriate training and experience in long-term therapy (Mann, 1981). As with all skills, one cannot start making adaptations and taking short-cuts unless one knows the skill intimately. Elton Wilson (1996) does not agree, however, and points out that many less experienced practitioners do work within time-limited parameters.

When a counsellor first starts practising TLT, it can be a little scary. Maybe two sessions into the process, and the client (as often happens) has got worse not better. The counsellor rushes off to his or her supervisor with the cry, 'Have I got this wrong? Will there be enough time?' Here, again, the importance of the client's own between-session work is underestimated. The client turns up a couple of weeks later for session three wondering what all the fuss was about, feeling transformed. I often find that the most rapid change occurs between sessions two and four, and that most clients use only four of their six sessions, and then choose to stop.

Counsellors may become anxious about 'pushing' their clients to deal with issues too soon, fearing that they are following their own agenda rather than that of the client. Is it going to make things worse if there is too little time to deal with an issue? What happens if Pandora's box opens on the sixth session? In my experience, this is very rare, but GPs will not be totally rigid about their six sessions. If the counsellor has established a good working relationship as a member of the primary team, the GP will be open to allowing a couple of extra sessions for a few clients perceived by the team as needing it. Hoyt (1995) warns against the guilt some counsellors may feel about not providing all things for all people. Calling it institutional countertransference, he emphasises that there could be a tendency to respond to everyone's neediness and dependency on the institution to provide the help that they want.

Feltham (1997) offers another interesting perspective against short-term therapies. He suggests that therapists may gravitate towards short-term work because of their own unresolved infantile material; that it is a form of counter-resistance. As many therapists gravitate toward the profession because of their own damaged pasts anyway, this seems irrelevant, providing the therapy works for the client and is well supervised.

Counsellors who have reservations about this method of working should not embark on it until their concerns are addressed, as often any anxieties expressed by the client about the approach are a projection of the counsellor's. Anxieties should be discussed in supervision, exploring the realities and the fantasies of working this way. Meeting another counsellor who works using TLT who will share the pros and cons of various techniques can reduce anxieties and fears. Remember that good time-limited therapy is conducted with the use of appropriate skills and with conviction. As Hoyt (1995) pointed out, short-term therapists believe that clients can make beneficial movement at once with skilful assistance.

What are the techniques of working in a time-limited way?

The first point to be made is that time-limited therapy is not long-term therapy cut short. It is a very specific way of working, that integrates the traditional person-centred (Rogers, 1961, 1980) and cognitive (Beck, 1975, 1987) approaches and incorporates the techniques used in brief therapy (de Shazer, 1985, 1988; O'Hanlon, 1990; Cade and O'Hanlon, 1993) and action (Carkuff, 1987; Egan, 1994) models. Integrative approaches are becoming more common (Corey, 1991) as therapists realise that the approach should fit the person, and not vice versa as it has often been in the past. The following sections will elaborate on how the integration works. As the different aspects of each method are discussed, I am assuming that the reader already has an understanding of each approach. It is not intended here to go into their theoretical depth. Those readers with insufficient knowledge of the approaches referred to should consult the book-list at the end of this chapter.

Humanistic underpinning

For TLT to work effectively, the basic foundation of the skill is the relationship between the counsellor and the client. Trust, and the core person-centred conditions of empathy (the ability to enter into another person's world and almost to experience it from their perspective), respect (or unconditional positive regard), and genuineness (or realness) are essential. There should be no barriers of status or power; so as a counsellor, you need to convey from the outset that the client is in charge of his or her own counselling process. Rogers (1961) believed that clients would find their own way through their therapeutic process, providing the climate provided for them in the therapy was right. So, for the duration of the client's journey, the counsellor may help read the map, and show the possible directions, but the client must be clear that she treads her own path. By your manner, therefore, you are saying to the client, 'I like you, I make no judgements about what you may say to me, I accept you as you are.'

This way of being (Rogers, 1980) provides the key underpinning for TLT. However, adopting purely a person-centred approach is a necessary but not sufficient method for working in TLT. Person-centred counselling, in truly Rogerian style, is totally non-directive. Clients may meander for a long while before reaching their desired goals. This means that, as counsellors, we may look at the map but we offer no directions. Clients have to follow their own routes, which take them where they will. To reduce the time spent, therefore, it is necessary to introduce some street signs to show the client where he is going.

Cognitive strategies

By introducing cognitive strategies into the process, the time taken to reach achievable goals can be greatly reduced. It may be noticed that Beck's cognitive therapy is recommended rather than Ellis's rational emotive behaviour therapy (REBT) (Ellis, 1967, 1971). This is because the theoretical underpinnings of Ellis and Rogers can almost be viewed as bipolar. Beck had developed his model independently of Ellis, and although he used the same directive, time-limited and structured approach to change maladaptive behaviour and irrational thought processes, he incorporated more humanistic concepts into his cognitive therapy. Beck et al. (1979) endorsed Rogerian core conditions as facilitators necessary for, but not sufficient to produce, optimum therapeutic change. Beck's challenges were kinder than Ellis's, gentler, and the concept of the power of the therapist in his or her interpretation of what is rational was greatly reduced.

Thus for TLT, on to our humanistic underpinning we overlay our understanding of the cognitive distortions that can cause so much distress in our clients. We gently challenge their ideas, point out inconsistencies, and remark on paradoxes. All of the while we are maintaining a caring demeanour, so the client can become aware of her idiosyncrasies without feeling stupid or inadequate. Challenges to verbal or non-verbal behaviour should not make the client feel defensive, but should be held up gently as a mirror to reflect back to the client.

Two other useful aspects of cognitive therapy brought into TLT are the use of teaching, and the use of homework, both of which tend not to be encouraged in traditional long-term counselling approaches. Teaching clients how people react, whether with physical or emotional processes, can enormously facilitate the work being done. Sharing with the client our knowledge of, say, the contribution of adrenalin in stress responses and panic attacks, equips the client with a greater insight into what is happening to him outside the counselling consultation room. This insight will provide them with greater control of their own situation and will reduce fear and anxiety. Similarly, teaching people about our understanding of how bereavement and loss can affect a person helps to normalise the process for them. This, again, reduces the fear and anxiety that people experience when they find themselves awash with emotion that they cannot contain. In understanding the process the client will then go along with it rather than fight against it; and in my opinion the process is then often shortened.

I can almost see some therapists throwing up their hands in horror at the suggestion of teaching clients processes that are controversial even in the literature. What I am suggesting, though, is not about teaching dogma, or whether one theory overrides another, but about teaching a client what is usual given a whole set of circumstances. We know that bereavement causes certain reactions, whether we believe it is a process or not, and it is teaching clients our understanding of what to expect that is important. It is about normalising what feels to them as abnormal reactions. Keeping knowledge and understanding of a process to ourselves increases our status and power over the client. There is no time for this in TLT. If we give this knowledge to our clients, they can use it in between-session work. As Hoyt (1995) illustrates, if we give a client a fish, she can eat a meal. But if we teach her how to fish, she can feed herself for ever.

Between-session work is very important in TLT. By having homework assignments, i.e. tasks between sessions, clients feel very involved in their own process. This also stops clients from being passive in effecting change in their lives (Dryden and Feltham, 1992). These tasks vary; for example they include: a specific activity to be conducted at home either with or without a partner, diary assignments, writing letters, using elastic bands for cognitive thought stopping, exercise regimes, affirmation or assertiveness exercises, reading books, contacting support groups, or watching or monitoring exercises in the case of scaling. (Most of these tasks will be elaborated upon in more detail throughout this book.) The counsellor must note what task has been given, because the client will be expecting you to refer to it in the following session and to check for progress. It is very rare for a client to ignore homework set; even the very depressed client will come and say: 'I tried to find days that were 2, but there just weren't any. In fact I rated them all at 1 or 0.'

This gives a necessary indication of clients' participation in their sessions, and the motivation to improve even if they cannot see through the blackness at the time. Most of the time, the homework will have been carried out, or a valid (or sometimes invalid) reason will be offered for not having done it. This, again, will help the counsellor to gauge the motivation of the client to participate in his own process. Invalid excuses should be gently challenged, not excused or allowed. Clients like to feel involved, and have on occasion asked for a homework task when I have not set one.

Throughout the use of TLT it needs to be made clear to the client that they are in charge of their own process. Being passive while waiting for the counsellor to 'make them better' is not appropriate. So, we have opened the map, and created signposts for the client's journey. What else can we do?

Brief therapy tools

The aim of solution-focused brief therapy (SFBT) is for the counsellor to encourage the client to concentrate on the solution, not the
problem *per se*. One important concept in SFBT is that people are
changing all the time (George, Iveson and Ratner, 1990). Yet when a
problem overwhelms clients, time seems to stand still as they sink
deeper and deeper underneath it. SFBT encourages clients out of
their time trap by continually referring them to the future solution, or
to skills they have used with problems in the past. In doing so,
clients are not encouraged to elaborate on their problems. Indeed
some therapists work with their clients without being really clear as
to what their clients' difficulties are. If clients do start discussing the
problem, the therapist guides them back to the solution.

I find that easy answers to the solution are often not what the
client wants or needs in the early stages of TLT. Clients need to
elaborate on their difficulties, because often the counsellor is the
only person who is willing to listen to them. Clients want to be
assured that the counsellor fully understands their perspective on an
issue, so it is important that they know it has been heard. Indeed, I
find that hearing the client's difficulty in minutiae (debriefing)
actually enhances the developmental process, allowing people to
move on much more rapidly. For TLT, then, it is essential to get the
balance right between hearing the extent of the problem, and
encouraging the client by showing your attention to detail for a
session or two, and then encouraging the client to move on and
consider alternative perspectives leading to the choice of action.

SFBT is a strategic way of working, usually conducted by a therapeutic team. The team watches the counselling session through a
video link or one-way mirror, and advises the counsellor on the
process when the counsellor leaves the client for a case discussion.
Even a single-handed counsellor using SFBT will leave the client for
a period before the end to think and assess, and then report back to
the client an overview of these deliberations. So here, again, a power
structure is created where instead of the client and counsellor
working equally as a partnership, the counsellor and the rest of the
team become the people in charge of the process.

One very useful tool of SFBT is that of scaling:

> *Counsellor:* If 0 is in the pits, and 10 is the best you could be, where are
> you now?

Clients find this a very useful exercise as it helps them to quantify
how they are feeling, and gives them an abstract concept through
which they can monitor their own progress. I find that even clients as

young as seven or eight are able to scale how they feel. It also allows clients to conceptualise short-term goals to help them progress through their therapy. For example:

'If you are at 4 now, what would life be like if you were at 5? What would you be doing differently?'

The second part of this question is very important, as clients often feel that progress depends on someone else doing something differently. Here, clients are encouraged to examine how they will change themselves.

The miracle question (Cade and O'Hanlon, 1993) is another tool that is commonly used in SFBT. This is where clients describe how their life would be if by a miracle all their problems were taken away. Clients often find this a rather esoteric line of questioning, no matter how well it is conveyed to them, as their pragmatism often gets in the way. However, an extension of the concept of the miracle question can be by using scaling for the future:

'On our scale of 0 to 10, where would you like to be?'

It is not often that clients say 10; they usually suggest that 10 would be unrealistic, so 8 or 9 would be their goal. The counsellor continues:

'So what is life like at 9?'

The client then starts to define their ultimate goal for counselling: 'If I get to this, life will be really good.' This gives the counsellor clear aims for the counselling process. Elaboration of this would-be situation should be encouraged with 'what else?' questioning. When all the differences have been outlined, the counsellor asks:

'What would you be doing differently if life was at 9?'

This moves clients on from thinking about what their ideal situation should be, to what they need to do to bring it all about. If a negative response comes back, for example:

Client: Oh, no, my husband (wife) will never change, so life will never get to 9.

then self-help needs to be reinforced:

Counsellor: Well, that may be so, but that does not mean that you must always keep responding to him (her) the way you do. What changes could occur in you?

As well as confirming the need for self-change, this encourages the client to stay in charge of his or her own process.

Affirmations are also important to clients. Clients need to be praised for the progress that they are making between sessions. This belief in success should always be conveyed with confidence and the strategies clients have used in making their progress needs to be highlighted. For example:

> *Counsellor:* Last time when we did some scaling, you said you were feeling at about 4. Where are you today?
>
> *Client:* I feel so much better today. I guess I must be about 7 or 8.
>
> *Counsellor:* 7 or 8! Wow, you really have done well, haven't you! You've moved a whole 4 points up the scale. How have you managed to do that?
>
> *Client:* Well I've talked to my friends a lot and I have talked to you.
>
> *Counsellor:* OK, well you've talked to people, but you have done the work. You have pulled yourself so far up the scale that you have doubled the score. How have you done that?
>
> *Client:* Well, I felt so overwhelmed by it all at first. That this was just happening to me and all around me. Then I got to thinking that this isn't right . . . that I'm losing myself. So I started making some rules, and I insisted that Joe stuck to them. He was surprised at my reaction at first. Then to my surprise he did stick to my rules; that made me start feeling better.
>
> *Counsellor:* So you created some boundaries for yourself, and in doing so you took control.
>
> *Client:* Yes, that's it. I felt so out of control. And now, even though the situation isn't what I would want, I feel in control again.

Here the counsellor has affirmed and praised the client's contribution to the developmental process, and reinforced that this was done without anyone's help; that it was the client's own work. This empowering of the client is the core of TLT. By teaching, highlighting and gently challenging, we are reinforcing to our clients that they can do their own work. They can improve without us. The success of the therapy is when the client says: 'No offence, but I don't need you any more. I can do the rest of this on my own now.'

Of course, not every client does report progress from session to session. Very often clients get worse before they get better. Affirmations are still important here:

> *Counsellor:* Last time we did some scaling and you said you were about 4. Where are you today?
>
> *Client:* Well I slipped right down. Sometimes I feel so bad, I don't want to get out of bed in the morning. I guess I must be right down to 2, or even 1.
>
> *Counsellor:* You are feeling really quite low. How come you're not at 0?
>
> *Client:* Well, I have to keep going for my children. So I do get up and see to them, but I feel so awful all the time.

Counsellor: So you really feel bad all the time, but you manage to keep doing the day to day things for your children's sake. That must take a great deal of effort. How do you do that?

Client: I tell myself, 'It's not their fault that you're like this. Don't spoil their life. You have got to pull yourself out of this.' And I do – well, enough to keep going for them.

Counsellor: Well that shows tremendous willpower on your part. Perhaps you are stronger than you realised.

Client: Perhaps I am.

What is important in TLT is that these tools be used only after a thorough exploration of the problem. So in our client's journey, we have opened the map, created signposts, discussed the options of the route to take – now all we need do is to help them decide which method of transport they will use.

Structuring the sessions

Egan (1994) has given counsellors a useful working model of helping which lends itself well to structuring TLT sessions. Davis and Fallowfield (1991) feel that the use of Egan's approach is important in a health care setting because of its pragmatism. Egan's method is probably the most commonly used model of counselling taught in the UK today, as one of its primary goals is to assist clients to become more effective at managing their own lives. In its most simplified version, the three-stage model has core skills that enhance the counselling process. Here, along with these core skills, are the TLT skills already mentioned:

STAGE 1: EXPLORE
- active listening by empathic reflecting or mirroring what is said
- paraphrasing what the client has said
- summarising the presenting issues and the feelings
- focusing to make issues more explicit or concrete
- highlighting non-verbal behaviour
- debriefing
- general scaling
- use of silence

STAGE 2: UNDERSTAND
- gentle cognitive challenge
- advanced empathy (reading the meaning behind the words)
- offering alternative perspectives
- teaching about process

- scaling for the future
- reframing

STAGE 3: ACT

- encouraging change
- affirmations
- homework tasks
- evaluating and monitoring action
- reviewing options (e.g. force-field analysis)

It can be seen that the method starts as one of gentle overview of the presenting problem(s), which are covered in great detail. This establishes trust and encourages the empathic stance of the counsellor. The counsellor then moves on to introducing the cognitive challenges and changes the focus of the sessions away from the problem on to coping strategies or solutions. In the list, some of Egan's proposals have not been included, for example immediacy, or the discussion between the client and counsellor about their relationship. This is very valuable in long-term therapy, as it allows any dynamic in the therapeutic process to be highlighted. Transference and countertransference issues can be acknowledged. However, with TLT, there is really no time to spend on 'how are we getting on?' Time is precious and all should be the client's time.

Structure of the contract

TLT requires a clear structure, which can facilitate the developmental process (Day and Sparacio, 1989). Clear structure not only enhances the therapeutic relationship, but fosters client's confidence that they can effect change, which is correlated with actual improvement (Garfield, 1986). As mentioned previously, a six-session contract does not imply six weeks of work. Indeed the whole process will take many months. It should start with an assessment session, where the counsellor and the client meet and make a decision whether or not to continue with the contract. (This assessment will be discussed in detail in the next section.) My assessment sessions are of 30-minute duration. The six 50-minute sessions progress with the first two or three spaced at approximately two-weekly intervals.[1] If the counsellor feels that the client is a suicidal risk, however, these can be brought closer. Frequency can be varied according to the client need, with the emphasis being on the least intrusive intervention (Hoyt, 1995). As the sessions progress, the length of time between sessions should be extended. I also find that one further 50-minute session six months after the last of the six (which has parallels with the two-plus-one approach) is very useful to review work that has been done without the counsellor. Clients often report a process of self-therapy during this time, for example:

> *Client*: When this happened to me, I imagined myself telling you all about it. Then I thought, what would you have said about this? And I could imagine your reply. You would have made me look at why I was reacting the way I was, and where I was coming from. So I did, and you know what – it worked!

These review sessions can have a profound effect as, throughout the six-month period, the client still feels connected to the therapeutic relationship. Even though this is fantasy, it feels extremely supportive for the client. Of course, not all clients want to take up the six-month one-off option, so they are not allowed to book it until close to the time. The structure of the later session is mostly explorative, with the counsellor hearing and reviewing in detail the client's progress and making use of affirmations. What needs to be reinforced is how much work they have done for themselves totally without the help of a counsellor. The review also allows the counsellor an opportunity to evaluate the work that was done (Elton Wilson, 1996).

The structure of the counselling contract is illustrated in Figure 3.1.

Hoyt (1995) emphasised that it is better to stop ahead of schedule, leaving sessions in hand, than to extend to six sessions for the sake of it. The flexibility of the contract is reinforced by allowing clients a series of time-limited courses over their life-span, to enable them to deal with specific life events as they arise. The knowledge that they can return for another course is very supporting of the client, and makes it less likely that the option will be taken up. This concept of episodes of short-term psychotherapy was described by Morrill (1978) as interrupted continuity.

Assessment

Strict separation of assessment and treatment is impossible (Barker, 1992). Anything a therapist says or does during an interview is either therapeutic, non-therapeutic or counter-therapeutic (Tomm, 1987). Good assessment is invaluable in TLT. It allows for the technicalities of the counselling process to be discussed, allows clients who have never had any kind of talking therapy before to 'get the feel of it' and to get initial anxieties out of the way, and it allows both the counsellor and the client to decide whether they want to engage on a contract and what their expectations will be. The aim of the assessment for the counsellor is to decide if this client is an appropriate candidate for TLT. As Daines, Gask and Usherwood (1997)

Referral by GP:

　　　　　　　　one week to 10 days' delay

Assessment – 30 minutes → proceed? → Yes   No → referral elsewhere → stop

　　　　　　　　two weeks' delay

Session 1 – 50 minutes → need more? → Yes   No → stop

　　　　　　　　two weeks' delay

Session 2 – 50 minutes → need more? → Yes   No → stop

　　　　　　　　three weeks' delay

Session 3 – 50 minutes → need more? → Yes   No → stop

　　　　　　　　three weeks' delay

Session 4 – 50 minutes → need more? → Yes   No → stop

　　　　　　　　four weeks' delay

Session 5 – 50 minutes → need more? → Yes   No → stop

　　　　　　　　six weeks' delay

Session 6 – 50 minutes → ready to end? → No   Yes → stop

　　　　　　　　　　　　　　　　↓

　　　　　　　　　　　　　　Referral elsewhere

　　　　　　　　six months' delay

Review –　　50 minutes　　How did it go?

Figure 3.1   *Structure of a TLT contract*

point out, however, good assessment is not just something that occurs at the initial point of referral; counsellors should be monitoring and reviewing throughout the counselling contract.

Lemma (1996) argues that good assessment is a challenge for the therapist as he has to use his psychological knowledge and skills interventions on the one hand, yet remain open to the possibility that the client may not fit into any preconceived theory. The counsellor needs to ask of himself: what is the client's real difficulty (which, of course, may not be the one the client actually presents)? What is the client asking me to do? Is it achievable? Figure 3.2 gives an example of the thinking process the counsellor is required to undertake while the client unveils her story. The counsellor's questioning leads the client along various avenues at this stage, in order to evaluate how the contract will be conducted. Remember that this is not a counselling session *per se*, so leading questions are appropriate in the assessment. However, the Rogerian way of being is extremely important, so that trust can be rapidly established.

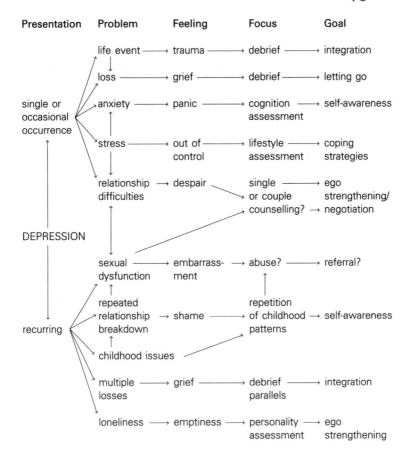

Figure 3.2 *The assessment flow for the presentation of depression*

To follow Figure 3.2 through from presentation to goal, you as the counsellor need to ask yourself the following questions:

- What is the presenting difficulty?
- How often does it occur?
- What is the underlying problem(s)?
- How is the client experiencing this?
- What will be the predominant focus of the counselling?
- What would be my goal for this counselling contract?
- Is this achievable in six sessions?
- Does this client have a psychiatric history?[2]
- Has the client tried other forms of counselling or therapy?
- Does the client have any other forms of support?

- Do I like this client?
- Should I accept this client or should I refer on to another agency?

This forms the basis of the assessment. Having sub-vocally answered the relevant questions, it is necessary to determine what the client's goals for the counselling session are. Are they realistic, given the short period of the contract? If not, then it is necessary to negotiate more achievable goals, or to discuss referral to another agency. Does the client appear to like me, and seem willing to work with me? Budd (1994) reminds us that transference exists between counsellor and client before they have even met.

It is at this stage that I tend to introduce the practicalities of the counselling contract. I remind clients of the leaflet they have received (Appendix 1) which highlights details of confidentiality, boundaries, appointment-making, etc. I then ask whether they have any questions about the process. I used to do this at the beginning of the assessment session, but I changed it to toward the end, as I found that clients were so full of the story they wanted to tell that these kinds of formalities kept getting in the way.

When it is clear what kind of process we are undertaking, I reiterate to the client the negotiated aims of the counselling contract before the client leaves. So right at the beginning of the counselling, the client is already clear about its ending. Clients often feel ambivalent about the ending of a psychotherapeutic relationship, as although they want the therapy to end, they have enjoyed its close-ness. I find that clients often count to themselves how many sessions they have had, which helps to prepare them for the ending.

It can be seen from Figure 3.2 that this is where the psychological knowledge of the human process is vital. Without it, the counsellor will not be able to follow the route from client presentation to potential goals in an assessment session. The ability to do this reduces the time needed in a counselling contract. It allows both the counsellor and the client to focus immediately on the issues at the core of the difficulty, rather than using time on peripheral issues. It is also necessary to have a clear understanding of the psychological process involved for people with mental ill-health, psycho- or sociopathic behaviour, and personality disorders. TLT is not appropriate for any of these people, and they should be referred on to the secondary mental health services. However, some short-term work could be beneficial. Chapter 13 elaborates on this.

What needs to be remembered is that you as a counsellor will not always get the assessment right. No one is infallible, and after a couple of sessions you may realise that you are taking the wrong tack. In that case, be flexible and change the route. Nothing is in tablets of stone, flexibility is the key, and there is no developmental work that is not useful or worthwhile. Not all clients' agendas are for change; they may have attended for ulterior motives (like litigation proceedings, court directives, or on the insistence of a significant other). The counsellor needs to be mindful of not being too naive in assuming that because a client attends the surgery for help, that is really what they want.

Summary

Rather than being the poor relation of long-term therapy, time-limited therapy offers a new service to the public that has never been available before. The relationship between the counsellor and the client can be as intense as that in longer therapies and the developmental work undertaken can be equally profound. Withers (1995) likens the intensity of brief therapy to a conversation with a stranger on a train, or an intense homosexual encounter in a toilet. Time-limited work is more tiring, more demanding, and sometimes more anxiety provoking for the counsellor. As such, the counsellor needs to be well trained and experienced not only in counselling skills, but also in psychological knowledge.

TLT is more active and more interventionist than traditional approaches. It becomes more selective and concentrates on key issues, requiring the client to be more concrete and focused. It can be more challenging, but it can also be more satisfying. The key words for this approach are therefore: **time**, **focus** and **self-help**.

Recommended reading

Cade, B. and O'Hanlon, W.H. (1993) *A Brief Guide to Brief Therapy*. New York: Norton.

Corey, G. (1991) *Theory and Practice of Counselling and Psychotherapy*, 4th edn. Pacific Grove, California: Brooks/Cole.

Egan, G. (1994) *The Skilled Helper: a Problem-Management Approach to Helping*, 5th edn. Belmont, California: Brooks/Cole.

Notes

1 I allow a 45–50-minute session for each client. However, I do not feel that a client needs to take all of that time. Some take only 20 or 30 minutes (especially

PART II

4

Counselling for Anxiety and Depression

Often thought of as two extremes of an emotional pole, depression and anxiety are actually inextricably linked (Montgomery, 1991). Depressed people often experience states of anxiety when going into public places; most commonly supermarket and post-office queues, pubs, cafés and restaurants, or buses or trains. Being thrown into a public arena in these situations turns people from the black of motivationless despair to acute panic and anxiety. Similarly, people who experience regular panic and anxiety states frequently become depressed as they conceptualise themselves as losing control of their lives. However, Finlay-Jones and Brown (1981) felt that although depression and anxiety may coexist, they can be separated, as depression is a response to loss whereas anxiety is a response to danger. Previously, the most common recourse was medication. In a poll conducted by MORI, 80 per cent of the population felt that counselling was a more appropriate way of helping people with depression (MORI, 1992) than drugs, yet it is still not the first choice of many GPs. This chapter reviews some of the various forms of depression and anxiety, highlights assessment criteria and offers ways of helping people with time-limited therapy.

What is anxiety?

Anxiety is a form of nervousness or fear. Fear is an appropriate response in circumstances of threat to the well-being of oneself or another. It is a physical reaction whereby the sympathetic nervous system switches on – a process called 'fight and flight'. This is the body's evolutionary response when people needed to be physically prepared to deal with threats of danger by fighting or running away. The adrenal gland pumps out extra catecholamines of adrenalin and noradrenalin, which stimulates the heart to beat faster and breathing to increase. People feel hot, sweaty and shaky and the stomach shuts down digestive processes (often experienced as the stomach 'turning over').

In people presenting with anxiety difficulties, the sympathetic system has switched on inappropriately. The 'threat' perceived is an emotional or psychological one, not a physical one. As the autonomic system kicks into its protective mechanism, people feel the various physical changes described above, and the brain interprets these as fear. This then invokes a cycle of persistence where the feelings of fear make the sympathetic system pump out more adrenalin, which increases the physical symptoms, which increases the feelings of fear. Logic goes out of the window at this time, as the mind starts racing with the pumping adrenalin. Worst-case scenarios become the main focus of attention, as people start ruminating, exaggerating and catastrophising their 'what if' problems. Small worries are blown out of all proportion, confidence is lost, and they become very insecure, clingy and dependent on their significant others. Weight may be lost as people burn off calories by constantly worrying, or alternatively, weight may pile on as they eat their way through the refrigerator desperately seeking comfort from all their concerns. Sleep disturbances occur, mostly the inability to get to sleep at night as the mind is constantly racing, and/or early morning wakening as worries flood in on the ever-present rollercoaster.

> Sharon was a bubbly 20-year-old living with her boyfriend. She worked as a clerk and was friendly and well liked by her colleagues. At an evening meal in a restaurant, her boyfriend ordered a rare steak. As she stared at him tucking into the bloody cut of meat, she felt overwhelmed with nausea, and had to rush off to the toilet to vomit. She was unable to eat her meal. Thereafter, she stopped eating in public situations, for fear of vomiting. This led to her avoiding public places, like pubs and cinemas, in case she felt nauseous. If she could not avoid a public situation, she became so anxious that a state of panic was induced. Arguments ensued with her boyfriend as she increasingly restricted their social life because of her anxieties about how she might feel. As her relationship started to falter, she became low and withdrew from her friends and work colleagues.

Panic attacks

Panic attacks are cases of acute fear, which often surge into people when they least expect it, although people can often talk themselves into panic attacks, too. They complain of being in bed asleep, or of 'not worrying about anything', when the body kicks into a full sympathetic rush. People start gasping for breath, hyperventilating, experiencing palpitations or very real chest pain; they visibly perspire, they may faint, feel nauseous or vomit. The experience is so strong that people fear that they are going to have a heart attack, stroke, or physically go mad. The fear of this happening in a public place increases the fear and perpetuates the process. So people then start withdrawing from public places; they stop going to the shops, then stop going to work, then stop meeting their friends, then stop going out at all. This is not true agoraphobia although it is often called this, but is an agoraphobic-like reaction to their anxiety. This social phobia occurs because the fear of the physical symptoms has been replaced by a fear of the experience of fear, which obviously is scary and unpleasant. As people feel more and more out of control of their lives, depression looms and perpetuates the anxiety.

Vicky attended a counselling assessment session with her husband Phillip. She had fainted on several occasions, yet the doctor had found nothing to account for that physically. Phillip insisted that it was Vicky's job in a primary school that was too much for her. It was too stressful, they (her colleagues) expected too much of her, and he demanded that the counsellor should tell her to give it up. Vicky said she enjoyed her job very much, and although it was a demanding one, it was important to her. The counsellor probed for any other stressors in her life, but there did not seem to be any. They both confirmed when asked that they had a good marriage. Vicky was asked to attend the counselling sessions on her own.

When Vicky returned for her first session, the counsellor alluded to her husband's attendance at the previous meeting. Vicky explained that Phillip would not let her go anywhere on her own, he attended all such appointments for doctors or dentists. Indeed, she was not allowed to visit her family of origin on her own, or go to the shops, or the supermarket. The only place where she could go alone was to work. It transpired that Phillip was obsessively jealous. He monitored all phone calls she made, listened to conversations she had with her friends, and would frequently turn up at home to see what she was doing or if she had been anywhere. (Phillip was self-employed, so had freedom of movement.) She even found him listening outside the kitchen window one day when she was having a female friend round for morning coffee. Vicky objected most strongly to this lack of trust, which was totally unfounded, even though he had had an affair a couple of years previously. Phillip resented her job as he could not check up on her there, and he resented the little bit of independence her salary gave her. He therefore used to leave bills out for her to pay when her salary was due, which in effect would use up all her money. By the end of the session, Vicky realised that although she loved Phillip, she did not like him, and did not like what he had turned her into; weak and dependent with no sense of herself as an individual. Any thoughts of her acting as an independent person brought up a surge of fear and panic.

Phobias

A phobic reaction can be considered as an extreme form of a panic attack in response to a specific stimulus, like a spider, snake or an enclosed space such as a lift. It causes tremendous fear with physical responses similar to those mentioned in the last section. Phobias are generally considered to be conditioned responses in which people have learned, by association, to respond to the stimulus in a negative way. Lives are restricted in order to avoid the feared objects, and then the more they are avoided, the more they are feared. People with phobias are aware that their fears are irrational, but that does not help them control the conditioned response. Many strange phobias can be developed by people in certain circumstances. Although we may have some empathy with people who develop fear of spiders, snakes or birds, some people develop phobic reactions to something as benign as colours, string or dust. In our stressful society, social phobias – particularly agoraphobia (fear of open spaces), claustrophobia (fear of confined spaces), emetophobia (fear of vomiting) and monophobia (fear of being alone) – seem to be the most common. Research shows that the prevalence of social phobia (fear of social situations) is high and is underdiagnosed by GPs. Social phobia can lead to depression, alcoholism or suicidal behaviour (Weller et al., 1996).

Depression

Depression is common: 20 per cent of the population will suffer an episode of depression at least once in their life. A chronic state of mild depression affects 3 per cent of the population at any time. Depression can take various forms, and can affect people in different ways. Most people feel a sense of helplessness and hopelessness, with no motivation or ability to help themselves. They slide into a pit of despair, often described as a 'black tunnel'. There are no feelings of joy and no sexual libido. Everything is an effort. There is a feeling of alienation, of feeling cut off and out of place; isolated. People may experience bouts of anger, becoming verbally or even physically aggressive. The more angry and tense a person becomes, the less sleep they will have, increasing the vicious circle of tiredness and irritability (Crisp, 1986). Or they may just crash into a lifeless state with no desire or energy to maintain their standards of hygiene. There is an overpowering feeling of malaise and fatigue, as time seems to stand still. Insomnia is common, particularly early morning wakening, as are disturbances of the digestive and menstrual systems. Diurnal variations of mood occur, most commonly feeling worse in the mornings. Memory loss is often distressing.

Depression has been categorised by the medical profession (as they have a tendency to do) into two forms: endogenous depression and reactive depression. Endogenous depression is said to be within the person: that they have a family history or a genetic predisposition to be so. Paykel (1979) found that for 11 per cent of his sample, there was no external precipitant, suggesting that the majority of depressive cases are reactive. Storr (1983) alternatively argues that the word 'endogenous' should be forbidden in psychiatry, as it is used to conceal doctors' ignorance of an external cause. Gotlieb and Hammen (1992) argue that there is no convincing evidence to support this dual classification.

Reactive depression is a response to circumstances or events that provide the catalyst for the feeling state (Beck, 1983; Oatley and Bolton, 1985). Brown and Harris (1978) felt that two kinds of circumstances provoke depression: an acute event such as a bereavement or loss, or major chronic difficulty, like unemployment, lasting more than two years.

I have never come across a truly endogenous depression; there has always been a reason for it somewhere if you dig deep enough. If there are no obvious life events, stressors or losses, childhood issues usually provide the key. Jacobson, Fasman and DiMascio (1975) and Beck, Sethi and Tuthill (1963) found empirical evidence to support an association between childhood experiences and adult depression. It is important to try to ascertain where the depression comes from, as this knowledge gives the client the choice to continue to be depressed about an issue, or to move on from it. Depression is mostly psychological, partly physical with an interplay with socio-environmental influences (I expect a medical doctor would reverse this balance). I believe that in many cases depression serves a purpose for the individual, and it helps if the client can discover what that purpose is. Crisp (1995) agrees.[1] He reasons that depression is a very mature emotion, given the state of our society, and he adds that depression may be essential for personal growth, making people sadder but wiser.

> Victor was a retired regimental sergeant major. He was very punctilious and precise and you could see your face in his polished shoes. When he attended the assessment session, he shifted uncomfortably in his chair.
>
> *Client*: I am not sure what I am doing here really. I suffer with depression. I have done for the last 10 years. Usually when I get depressed, I come to the doctors', she gives me a course of medication, and after a few months I'm fine again.
> *Counsellor*: Is there something different this time?

Client: Well, yes. The medication hasn't worked this time. It's very frustrating, I don't want to be feeling like this.

Counsellor: How are you feeling, Victor?

Client: Awful! I really am very low. And I'm on a very short fuse. My wife and I are arguing all the time.

Counsellor: So you're very low and irritable. What do you feel is the reason for your depression?

Client: It's endogenous. The doctor told me that when I first started getting it 10 years ago. She asked me if I had any thing to be depressed about. I told her no; I'm happily married, I have two grown-up sons, our house is our own, and we have no money worries. She told me then that it was endogenous depression, and it was just something I would have to live with. Usually the medication works fine, so I don't know why she sent me to you. I just need something a bit stronger, that's all.

Counsellor: You said that you and your wife were arguing a lot lately. What is it that you argue about?

[*Victor then proceeded to rage about the difficulties he experienced with his wife and her behaviour. Towards the end of the session, after a great deal of anger and frustration had spewed out:*]

Counsellor: You seem to be very different, you and your wife, and these difficulties that you describe have been infuriating you for a number of years. Has anything different occurred in your relationship recently?

Client: No . . . well, not between us. My youngest son left home last month, so it is just us now.

There are some people you would expect to feel depressed, for example the long-term unemployed, people experiencing marital difficulties, or people within two years of a bereavement. We also know from the Brown and Harris (1978) studies that women with three children under the age of five are at high risk of depression. But a woman with just one child may feel similarly low and isolated, especially if she had an interesting or challenging career before she had her child, and more especially if she has little social support in the extended family or network of friends. Being a housewife and mother for some women is a fulfilling career; for others it is pure drudgery. A woman alone in a house all day with a young child lacks intellectual stimulation and peer group company. For this reason single parents are especially at risk. Working mothers may not escape depression, however, as they take on two full-time roles and often feel guilty or cheated that they are not at home with their babies.

Other people at risk of depression are those who find themselves in a situation over which they have no control and cannot escape.

Jonathan was 47 years old when he was made redundant from the company for which he had worked since leaving college. He managed to obtain a temporary job for two months after his redundancy, but had not worked for the following two and a half years. He used up all his redundancy pay when his unemployment benefit ran out to help pay for the mortgage and support his two teenage daughters through university. When first unemployed, he attended the job centre daily, and over the years wrote hundreds of job applications, obtaining very few interviews. Most of the rejections were based on his age. Now he rarely attends the job centre, and cannot produce the motivation to open the newspaper for employment advertisements. His wife managed to get herself a part-time job to help make ends meet, but that made him feel worse about himself. As he sank into his depression, he rarely got up before noon, and sat watching the television all the day and evening until the early hours, as he found it difficult to sleep.

Post-natal depression

At a time of giving birth, many women are in a state of euphoria. It can therefore come as blow if some time after the child is born, the woman slumps into a depressive state. Most women experience a short period of the blues a few days after the birth as the hormones readjust. But post-natal depression (PND) can leave women feeling confused, guilty and afraid. They may feel too ashamed to admit how they feel, struggling on with baby routines. Often they wonder if they really love their babies, and then are consumed with feelings of guilt and shame at what a 'bad' mother they must be. They find it difficult to tell others of their feelings as they are so frequently told how happy they *must* be to have such a wonderful child. Common symptoms presented are similar to ordinary depression. These include irritability, worse moods at the end of the day, frequent crying, loneliness, fatigue, loss of libido and ability to show affection (Nieland, 1993). Puerperal psychosis, which affects one or two in a thousand women (Murray and Stein, 1989), is a more extreme problem, and requires referral to the secondary health care team as the baby may be at risk.

The birth of a child is a very sensitive time in a family system, and changes the dynamics of the interactions of its members. Some fathers feel pushed out by the attention mother and baby receive, or jealous of the closeness of mother and child; especially at the breast, which had heretofore been their domain. The mother may sense the difference in the feelings in their partnership, and become nervous and insecure in the tiredness that a newborn inevitably produces. Arguments then ensue, or sometimes even worse: a dreaded silence that is pregnant with anger and tension. Depression for both husband and wife may be just round the corner, but it is usually only the wife's depression that is picked up by an astute health visitor.

Sometimes it is not picked up at all if the gap between the birth and the onset of depression is greater than four or five months.

There are some predictors of post-natal depression. As already mentioned, one is the birth of the third child when the eldest has not reached five. Or it may be some form of birth trauma, for example a complicated birth, premature birth, or the baby being whisked off into intensive care for medical intervention. Medical services are wonderful at dealing with these kinds of crises. But months on, the mother crashes into despondency in a delayed trauma response. She had to 'cope' at the time, but the enormity of the situation creeps in at a much later stage, especially if the mother had no way of expressing how she was feeling at the time. Other hypotheses as to the cause of PND are offered in the literature, such as the influence of dopamine (a neurotransmitter in the brain), but once again that is viewing the situation from purely a biochemical base, and I do not feel that people are purely functioning (or malfunctioning) organisms.

> Jennifer was pleasantly surprised when she found that she was pregnant, and her husband Richard was equally excited at the birth of their first child. Jennifer worked full time throughout her pregnancy until the week before Samuel was born some three weeks early. Once at home with the child, Jennifer found herself increasingly remembering aspects of her own childhood, which was not a happy time. She had had an emotionally and physically abusive father, and was still very afraid of him. She found herself reliving the fear of her childhood, and sank into what was considered by others as an unaccountable depression. She tried to 'protect' Samuel from Richard by never letting him be alone with or handle his son. Richard was extremely hurt by Jennifer's behaviour, and interpreted it as her wanting to keep Samuel all to herself; i.e., he was no longer needed or necessary. As arguments ensued, Jennifer shared with Richard some of the difficulties she experienced as a child, and they realised that she needed some form of therapy to help her deal with her feelings.

Manic depression

Manic depression is bipolar in that the client swings from very high periods of mania, down to very low depressive phases. The client, and the client's family, becomes very distressed as the moods swing without warning. The mania phase is particularly difficult, as the client takes risks and behaves in ways that would not be considered characteristic, becoming disinhibited, perhaps with grandiose ideas with delusions or hallucinations. A pressure to keep talking accompanies a decreased need for sleep.

Fromm-Reichman (1949) suggests that manic-depressives often come from large families with many children, in which several father-figures assume responsibility. This inhibits meaningful parental relationships and leads to depressive episodes in adulthood. However, the cause of manic depression is not really known: it is generally considered as endogenous rather than reactive, and does not tend to respond well to talking therapies. Treatment is most commonly by medication using lithium, which is a salt naturally occurring in food and water, so blood levels need to be regularly checked. This medication tends to take the high and low peaks off the mood swings and to hold the person at a level mood. Some clients find this chemical level distressing, however, as the normal swings of mood that individuals have from day to day are not experienced. Overdosage of lithium can be toxic, causing damage to the kidneys and nervous system.

Manic-depressives are considered to be very creative people when they are in their mania phase (for example Van Gogh, Schumann, Byron and Winston Churchill), and another disadvantage of the medication is that it removes, or reduces, this creativity.

> Susan asked her GP if she could see the practice counsellor. She had been taking lithium for 10 years and would very much like to stop taking it. She used to experience periods of mania before the medication, when she would work continuously without stopping for days at a time. She never seemed to feel tired, and made executive decisions that were totally unrealistic, which presented difficulties for the company for which she worked. She made continuous sexual demands on her husband, sometimes in inappropriate places. Feeling he could never satisfy her demands, he left her. Then, as the reality of her behaviour would sink in, she would slip into a dark depression, spending days in bed with the curtains drawn, refusing to answer the door or the phone. Years later, however, she felt she could no longer continue with her medication as it was. She said, 'You don't feel high, you don't feel low. You don't feel good, you don't feel bad. You don't feel.'

Learned helplessness

Learned helplessness is a very severe form of depression in which clients lose the ability to spontaneously develop coping strategies to deal with the situations in which they find themselves. This lack of ability to develop such responses, and the increasing dependence on others, is a conditioned response which occurs as people feel out of control of their lives. As with ordinary depression, they experience feelings of hopelessness, helplessness, lack of joy, loss of libido and loss of appetite (once again, either not eating or eating anything and everything). They have a very negative cognitive set that intrudes on any coping strategy that they might think of themselves or that might be offered to them from other people. It is usually a very slow continual progression downhill for these people, so often the closest to them (partners, parents or close friends) are the last to notice the change until the burden feels really heavy. Research has shown that such people also have depletion in noradrenalin, but whether the problem causes the depletion, or the depletion causes the problem is anyone's guess. Seligman (1975) has suggested that the loss of ability to cope comes from learning that one is out of control: that is, they have learned to be helpless. Other researchers have suggested that negative cognitive attributions (Abramson, Seligman and Teasdale, 1978), lack of self-efficacy (Bandura, Reese and Adams, 1982), or the disruption of the roles by which they define their worth (Oatley and Bolton, 1985) also make significant contributions to their helpless state.

People with this form of depression do not respond well to time-limited therapy. By the very nature of their condition, they are unable to develop autonomous, spontaneous coping strategies to help them regain control of their lives. They need repeated, consistent cognitive-behavioural interventions together with the insight that long-term therapy can offer. More importantly, they may have been in their depressed state for so long that living without their depression is too scary to contemplate (here, again, is the notion of the purpose of depression).

> Brian was one of the GP's 'heartsink' patients whom he referred (tongue in cheek) to the practice counsellor to get him off his back for a few weeks. Brian was in his early 40s, and had been suffering with agitated depression since he had a 'nervous breakdown' some 10 years previously, when he stopped working. Brian had huge swings of mood from free-floating anxiety to deep, suicidal despair. He was extremely thin, and his eyes protruded from his skeletal face, darting in anxious fear. He had an extremely patient wife who worked full-time to support them both, and then after work prepared and cooked the evening meal, and did all the household chores. Brian sometimes drove her to the supermarket if he was not feeling too anxious, but rarely waited for her, leaving her to struggle home on the bus with all the week's groceries.
>
> Brian started to talk to the counsellor about his difficult childhood and the death of his father when he was 15 years old. Over a number of sessions, Brian started to improve. He recognised that he had an eating disorder, and started on a diet recommended by the practice dietician. As he began putting on weight, he became physically stronger, and started undertaking regular exercise recommended by the counsellor.
>
> The change in his physical and emotional appearance was so apparent that the GP suggested that he would soon be well enough to return to

work. The enormity of what was happening then hit Brian. If the doctor no longer signed his sick notes and indicated he was fit for work, he would no longer receive the invalidity benefit which had paid his mortgage over the last 10 years. He would not be entitled to receive unemployment benefit, as he had not made any contributions. His wife did not earn enough to pay the mortgage. He had been 'off on the sick' for the last 10 years; what employer would consider employing him now? And anyway, the responsibility of working and paying his own mortgage was too scary to contemplate. He did not know how to do it any more. Brian stopped eating and exercising and crashed back into a deep depression. In that position, he felt safe.

The suicidal client

In the UK, 4,000 people commit suicide each year with 100,000 hospital admissions for attempted suicide. Of those who attempt suicide and are unsuccessful (parasuicides), 15,000 will make a further attempt within one year. One thousand of these will be successful within one year, and another 3,000 will be successful within five years (Scotchman, 1996). These are conservative estimates:[2] there are many more people who choose a form of death in which the outcome is more ambiguous, like walking into the path of a car, or having a driving accident. It is the second most frequent cause of death, after road traffic accidents, for young male adults.

If the person is depressed, then he is 25 times more likely to attempt suicide. Depression is linked to adolescent suicidal girls, and there is a link between conduct disorders and suicidal boys. Most suicides occur within three months following the beginning of improvement from a depressive episode, as that is when the individual has the energy to put her morbid thoughts and feelings into action. Many are ambivalent about living or dying, gambling with death by leaving it to chance as to whether others will save them. Studies of hundreds of suicide notes indicate that although suicidal people were extremely unhappy, they were not necessarily mentally ill.

Research has shown that 85 per cent of people who intend to commit suicide tell someone within one month before doing so, with a gestation period, or time lag, between the warning and the act (Barraclough et al., 1974; Gunnell and Frankel, 1994). Yet a myth still exists that if a person tells someone else, then it cannot be a serious attempt; more a 'cry for help'. Women are three times more likely to try to commit suicide than men, but men are more likely to be successful because they use more violent forms of ending their lives, like guns, knives or ropes.

Suicidal intent takes different forms. There are those who slide into a deep depression, where life seems to offer nothing; there seems no point to being alive. To these individuals, it takes a great deal of strength and willpower not to die. The critical point for these clients, i.e. when they are most at risk, as already mentioned, is when their depression starts to improve. For others, there is no depressive illness, but a self-loathing that is so strong, maybe because of some past traumatic incident or guilt over a past misdemeanour, that the desire to self-destruct takes precedence over all else. Others may be grieving for a loved one and the desire to die is part of the searching process; to be together again. Or an individual may be going to die anyway of some form of terminal illness, and wants to precipitate the death to remove pain and preserve dignity. As Lemma (1996) suggests, a coherently worked out suicide plan can give these clients a sense of inner peace.

Clients who are bereaved by suicide have deeper grief responses as they experience a triple loss of rejection, disillusionment and self-doubt (Middleton and Williams, 1995). These mourners also tend to have suicidal tendencies themselves (van Dongen, 1988). Guilt is high on their agenda. People bereaved by suicide feel guilty over it, and some feel blamed by others for the death. Mourners often demonstrate a preoccupation with the death scene, yet are shrouded in a veil of silence as people do not wish to talk about it. Being unable to unload their feelings can hinder the grieving process, causing intense and painful reactions (Cain and Fast, 1972).

Counsellors who feel their clients are at risk from self-harm should check the medication that the client is receiving from the GP, as the client is most likely to overdose on this medication. If the client is taking SSRIs (specific serotinin reuptake inhibitors), or the newer antidepressants like lofepramine, then self-harm is unlikely to occur by this means. If the client is taking tricyclics, it will be necessary to discuss your fears with the GP so that he can consider prescription quantities.

> Marion had taken two overdoses in her recent past before seeing the counsellor. The first time was when she found that her husband of some 22 years was having an affair, and the second time when he told her that he was going to leave her for the other woman.
>
> *Client*: There is no point in talking to you, as I am quite clear. If Arthur leaves me, I will have nothing left to live for. My children have grown up and don't need me. They'll soon get over it – me not being there. But I will never get over not having Arthur. We've been together since I was 14. I don't know what life is like without him. I don't want to know. If he leaves me I will do it again, and this time he won't be coming back to find me. This time it will work. I've told him. I said,

'you leave me and I'll kill myself'. He doesn't know what to do at the moment. He's very angry, but I don't care. It's about time he started thinking of me instead of himself and this other woman.

Counsellor: It sounds like you're very angry, Marion, and that you want to punish Arthur in some way.

Client: No, I'm not angry any more. I was when I first found out. But now I'm too tired to be angry. I'm so drained, I don't really feel anything at all. I love Arthur so much, I couldn't possibly go on living without him, that's all. I've made him my life, and if he isn't there, I can't be either.

Arthur left Marion three days later.

The client on medication

For a counsellor working in a medical setting, the issue of medication is inevitably going to be raised with various clients. Some GPs will choose not to prescribe psychotropic drugs with a counsellor in post; others send the patient to the counsellor because prescribing has failed. Others prescribe automatically even though the person is to see the counsellor.

Many counsellors refuse to see clients who are on medication, the argument being that there is no point trying to get clients to express their feelings if those emotions are locked in a chemical strait-jacket. This may be true for clients on benzodiazepines, but not for those on antidepressants. However, if one agrees with the premise that anxiety and depression have both psychological and physical aspects, both psychotherapy and medication have a place in a holistic overview of what is happening. Research shows that some people who have very severe depression respond well to psychological interventions, but not so well as they do with a combination of drugs and therapy (Perry, 1990).

When psychotropic drugs first hit the market in the 1960s and 1970s, there is no doubt there was a lot of over-prescribing. It took years to realise the full extent of addiction to prescribed drugs (Johnstone, 1989). What needs to be remembered is that individuals with long-term addiction to psychotropic drugs, particularly benzodiazepines, can present with symptoms similar to those presenting with anxiety and depression, e.g. headaches, palpitations, lack of concentration, amnesia, low self-esteem, bowel and stomach complaints (Armstrong, 1996). So current medication must be checked out. More recently, SSRIs have become flavour of the month, and these, too, have probably been over-prescribed (Breggin, 1991), considering counselling is now so widely available. But there is a place for medication in some cases. Sometimes clients become so depressed that they slide too deeply into an unmotivated blackness to want to work with a counsellor. Sometimes people become so anxious that they become a danger to themselves or to others. Sometimes people cannot function on a day-to-day level without pharmacological aid. Sometimes medication will keep that person alive. Sometimes medication is useful. Having said all that, the pharmaceutical representative of a company selling a well-known brand of SSRIs visited me. She had noticed, and had her suspicions confirmed by the local pharmacist, that the prescribing of this drug had rapidly reduced in our area. Was I against its prescription? I affirmed, as I have already described, that sometimes I feel medication is useful, but when patients have access to TLT, it is not so often required.

Although it is OK to discuss medication with a client, e.g. length of time it takes to work, side-effects, etc., it is not OK for the counsellor to advise the client to be on a certain medication, or off altogether. That is the GP's domain, and the counsellor should not be tempted to cross this boundary.

Assessment

In the short space of time available for assessment, the counsellor needs to decide who to include and who to exclude in a counselling contract. Assessment requires the counsellor to ask appropriate questions to form a hypothesis or formulation as to how the counselling contract may move the person forward in order to remove the client's presenting distress. (Chapter 3 gives an example of a flowchart used in assessing a client with depression.) The counsellor needs to ask either of herself or of the client:

- What symptoms is the client presenting with?
- Would these suggest that the client is anxious or depressed, or a combination of the two?
- Is the client on medication? If so, what?
- What influence may this medication have on the client's thinking, feeling and behaviour?
- If the client is anxious:
  - are there obvious causes for the anxiety?
  - are there times when the anxiety is more pronounced than others?
  - does the client experience difficulties in a cyclical pattern? PMT?
  - is there something over which the client has lost control, e.g. a traumatic incident?
  - are the client's anxieties realistic or are they exaggerated and catastrophised?
  - can the client link his emotional difficulties with his physical experience of anxiety?

- If the client is depressed:
  - are there obvious medical causes for the depression, e.g. recent heart attack, hyperthyroidism, hypertension, breast cancer, chronic pain?
  - is the client on medication which may produce depression, e.g. steroids?
  - does the client only experience depression in the winter months? Seasonal Affective Disorder?
  - is the client suicidal?
  - has the client made any suicide attempts in the past? (They are 27 times more likely to do so in the future if they have – Hawton and Fagg, 1988)
  - were the client's previous suicide attempts foiled, or did she seek intervention after the act?
  - was a note left in a previous suicide attempt?
- Is this the first or an occasional incidence or is this a problem that keeps occurring?
  If this is a single occurrence:
  - is the client responding to some form of loss?
  - is the client under physical/emotional stress at work or at home?
  - is the client experiencing relationship difficulty?
  If this is a repeated occurrence:
  - is the client repeating behaviours rather than remembering past issues?
  - does the client have unresolved childhood issues?
  - has this client been abused in some way?

As the assessment unfolds, it becomes clear to the counsellor whether or not the client should be accepted for time-limited therapy or referred on to a more appropriate agency. In the scenarios already described in this chapter, Sharon, Vicky, Victor, Jonathan, Jennifer and Marion would all be candidates for TLT. Susan and Brian would not. Deeply entrenched learned helplessness such as Brian's has taken years to establish, and therefore needs considerable de-conditioning. It would be difficult to know who to refer him on to, however, as people like Brian have been through the system for so many years: he would already have seen relevant secondary mental health professionals when he had his first breakdown. Referral would therefore be through the private or voluntary sector, but again, because of the nature of his condition, he would be reluctant to take it up. TLT may also be inappropiate for people with long-term benzodiazepine addiction, as they commonly are unreliable attendees, are uncooperative, and frequently become stuck in the therapeutic process (Armstrong, 1996; Hammersley, 1993; Hammersley and Beeley, 1992). Marion would be accepted for TLT, but because of her suicidal ideation she would also be referred to the secondary mental health team. They would provide home visiting and out-of-hours back-up that the counsellor cannot provide. Susan, the woman with manic depression, would require referral back to the secondary mental health team without the introducion of TLT.

TLT procedures

Explore why the client feels so hopeless or so anxious. What is going on in their lives? What are the stressors that they are currently experiencing? Listen to the feelings that are being expressed, and hear the feelings that are not being expressed. Offer them back to the client tentatively. Remember, depression may be unspoken anger which may be more acceptable to the client than the expression of that anger. Depression and anxiety often have a purpose. They can be considered as forms of regression (Hughes, 1993): for example retreating to one's bed in a 'I can't do anything, you'll have to look after me' mode is retreating into a child state. Similarly, anxiety and social phobia are regressive as they require the client always to be accompanied by a significant other, just like a child. If the person does not feel safe, a tantrum (manifested as a panic attack) ensues.

The depressed and anxious client has numerous stories of how many people have told them to 'pull themselves together'; that there are people 'out there' with real problems, and they should think themselves lucky. It is important, therefore, that the counsellor allows the client to experience the pain by acknowledging and validating it. The client may test the counsellor, by asking if the counsellor feels the client could 'snap out of it'. A non-committal reply is appropriate here: 'It is not as easy as that, is it?' acknowledges the client's difficulties.

Explore transgenerational issues with clients. What is their relationship with parents? What was their childhood like? Did their parents exhibit any of the problems the client is currently experiencing? Also explore losses: not just bereavements, but also marriage breakdowns, children leaving home, redundancy or retirement, hysterectomy, etc. Has the grieving been conducted appropriately and effectively, or is there still some unfinished business?

In this early stage of the TLT process, the client must be given lots of space to think and feel, and to assimilate his thoughts. The counsellor should not fill gaps of silence, unless they are creating tension, as this intrudes on the client's process.

If you suspect a client is suicidal, ask her outright. If this is confirmed, allow her to explore these feelings without feeling judged. Accept what the client is saying and do not try to argue, persuade or cajole. Encourage the client to talk about the suicidal ideation in detail. Remember, you will not be encouraging the client to act in this way; in fact it may have the reverse effect because someone is listening. First, clients should be encouraged to talk in depth about methods of self-harm: when, where, how? Explore their fantasy of death: what does suicide mean to them? What is it like to be dead? What will you be seeing, hearing, feeling? What will it be like for those left behind? As the client talks of the suicidal ideas, make a mental assessment of the risk that this client may indeed hurt herself. Find out:

- Has she ever tried before?
  If so, what stopped her?
- What has helped in the past?
  Can it help this time?
- Does she have the means and the opportunity?
  Has she told anyone else?
  What support does she have?
  Who will help her talk or be with her?
- Are there obvious signs of neglect of personal appearance or hygiene?
- Is the person disengaging from significant others, withdrawing or becoming isolated?
- Is there a preoccupation with death and related themes?
- What time of year is it? April and Christmas are the 'at risk periods' for suicide.

Make an assessment of the risk of real harm (see Eldrid, 1988 or Hawton and Catalan, 1987). If you feel the client is a high suicide risk:

- Ask for permission to talk to the GP or the secondary mental health team to get the person out-of-hours help and support.
- Do not promise to keep suicidal plans secret, especially if you do not get permission to enlist outside help.
- Try to obtain a 'keep-safe' agreement until the next time you see the client, e.g. 'Will you be able to support yourself until the next time we meet?'
- Write the phone numbers of the Samaritans, and any other numbers of support people on a piece of paper for the client to place by her phone. Do not give your number unless you are willing to be contacted 24 hours a day.
- Annotate the medical notes 'at risk' so that the doctors will be aware when prescribing or answering distress calls.
- Express your feelings of care and concern to the client.

The counsellor has to remember, however, that it is not her responsibility to stop a client from committing suicide no matter what. The ultimate responsibility of whether a person lives or dies is that person's.

Understand: As the client overviews her life situation and expresses the feelings that have been held back, a dawning of understanding occurs for both client and the counsellor. The reasons for the client's feelings start to show through the fog of emotion, and start to become clear.

The relationship between the counsellor and client will be established now, with the client engaged in the therapeutic process. The space that the counsellor gave to the client leads to feelings of trust and empowerment, so it becomes a safe environment in which the counsellor can gently challenge the client's negative automatic thoughts. Negative cognitive set is a feature of anxiety and depression, which is why it perpetuates itself. The counsellor needs to ask the client to look in more detail at her thinking processes, and to challenge what may be catastrophised or exaggerated. Words like 'ought', 'should' or 'must' need to be focused upon, and the logic of these 'mustabatory' thought processes examined. For example, a client experiencing panic attacks should be challenged as to the feared outcome:

Counsellor: What is it, when you experience these feelings, that you fear is going to happen to you?

Client: My heart beats so fast I feel it is almost coming out of my chest. I'm sweating and I find it hard to breathe. It feels like I'm going to have a heart attack – I even get pains down my arms.

Counsellor: How often does this occur?

Client: It used to be just now and then, but now it happens every day at least once. Sometimes more.

Counsellor: Have you ever had the heart attack you fear?

Client: No . . . it just feels like I will. I get scared.

Counsellor: Yes, it is a very scary sensation. What was the worst thing that happened to you when this occurred?

Client: I went into town, and it happened in a shop. I had to leave my shopping and get out fast. I had to get out into the fresh air. I thought people might notice me.

Counsellor: So, the worst thing that happened to you was that you had to leave the shop without the shopping that you wanted. You didn't have a heart attack and you didn't become ill?

Client: No . . . I just felt bad.

Counsellor: So really you are not scared of having a heart attack because this has happened to you loads of times, yet it has never made you ill. What you really fear are the feelings that you *think* feel like a heart attack. You really fear the feelings of fear.

Client: Yes, that's right. It feels so awful, that I start thinking to myself 'are the feelings going to happen today?' I dread it. And then, as I'm thinking about it, it seems to happen.

Counsellor: So you almost talk yourself into one?

Client: Why, yes, I suppose I do. But I can't stop thinking about them.

The above scenario not only challenges the catastrophising of the client, but helps him or her to reframe what is happening; that this is not the sudden onset of a serious illness, but the misinterpretation of a physical happening. Once the client reframes the experience of panic attacks, they usually start to lessen quite drastically. At this point it may be appropriate to explain (or teach) about surges of adrenalin, so the client can fully understand what is happening to his or her body. Deep diaphragmatic breathing exercises should be described and demonstrated to help bring in the parasympathetic responses that reduce feelings of anxiety (covered in more detail in Chapter 5).

Scaling for the future is virtually impossible for a client in the black pit of despair. There is no future for such a client; indeed, they do not want a future. Or the best future they can think of is death so that there will be no need to feel like this any more. Scaling should therefore always be kept close to the client's present state of awareness, and questions only asked of one point on either side of the client's present feeling state. For example:

Counsellor: Where are you on the scale today?
Client: I'm still at rock bottom, at 0.
Counsellor: What would life be like if you were less than 0?
Client: If I was less than 0? Oh, I'd want to die. To kill myself. I don't feel that bad, thank God!
Counsellor: You wouldn't want to harm yourself?
Client: I have thought about it once or twice. But it is not something I have seriously considered.
Counsellor: So you don't feel as bad as you could do then?
Client: No, I suppose not. Not as bad as that.
Counsellor: What would life be like if you were at 1?

Here the counsellor has had the opportunity to explore any suicidal ideation within scaling for the future, and has enabled the client to reframe how bad the feeling state actually was.

Actions: If I had the ability to prescribe, one prophylactic I would insist upon would be exercise. Exercise can help dysthymic disorders considerably, as it produces the body's natural antidepressants, endorphins. Exercise also releases stress and tension, increases energy and alertness levels and reduces fluid retention. People often complain that they feel too tired to exercise. I counter that they are too tired because they have taken *no* exercise. People also complain that they are so busy they cannot fit exercise into their life. My counter to this is that our lives should be structured around our exercise programme, rather than fitting exercise into our lives.

For people who are severely depressed, recommend lots of rest and recuperation for the body to recharge. Walking is about the only exercise that a depressed person can muster the energy for, so set a regime of a daily 15-minute walk, increasing in speed and duration to a daily 45 minutes of brisk walking which is cardiovascular (sufficiently fast enough to feel the heart speed up). People with dogs have a perfect excuse, but it must be reinforced that the walking needs to be brisk, not an amble. Depressives will argue against this, of course, because of their negative cognitive set, saying that they are too tired or too unmotivated to leave the house. Gentle insistence on the benefits will help here. Exercise becomes its own best advocate, as people really do feel better for it. Also recommend lots of relaxation, soaks in the bath, and trying not to do too much.

For those experiencing acute anxiety, greater exercise is needed to use up the excess adrenalin that is being created. Once again, regular cardiovascular exercise of walking, jogging, swimming, cycling, etc., will use up the adrenalin that is interpreted as free-floating anxiety. The exercise will make people feel calmer, which in turn will stop the intrusive thoughts. As already suggested, teach breathing techniques for dealing with panic attacks and anxiety states. For those who are not type A personality (see Chapter 5), relaxation tapes may also be beneficial as they dissipate adrenalin and thus have a calming effect.

Homework tasks, particularly for the developing social phobic, should focus on going to places which have hitherto been avoided. Tasks such as going to the supermarket, local pub or cinema should be tried between sessions. When evaluating homework, focus on the successes, and not on the failures. For example:

> *Counsellor:* How have you got on with going out?
>
> *Client:* I haven't done at all well, really. I tried ever so hard to get on a bus with my friend but I just couldn't do it. The bus pulled up, and I saw all the people on it looking at me, and I thought 'Suppose I panic when I am on there and I can't get off? They will all be looking at me.' So I froze, and just let the bus pass by as if I were waiting for another one. My friend was good, she didn't try to push me. She just said we would try again another day. I feel so disappointed. I feel I'm never going to get back to normal.
>
> *Counsellor:* What other things did you try?
>
> *Client:* Oh, I went to the supermarket and did the shopping with my mother. That was OK. The worst bit was at the end when you come to the check-out and have to pay. That's the bit where you are at the point of no return. You can walk around the shop all right because you know that at any time you can leave your trolley and walk out. But at the check-out you have to see it through. Anyway I did that. I was frightened that my hand would shake when I signed the slip, so I turned my back to the assistant while I did it, and Mum looked away, so that was all right. And my husband took me to the pictures last week. I sat on an aisle seat in case I had to get out, but the film was so funny, I

didn't realise where the time went. But I wonder if I am ever going to get better you know, it is taking so long.

Counsellor: But you have made tremendous progress since I last saw you! How long is it since you have done the shopping at the supermarket?

Client: Well, it must be getting on for four months now. And I can't remember the last time I went to the pictures.

Counsellor: So can't you see how well you have done – how much you have moved on? When I first met you, you were hardly going out at all. Now you can go to the supermarket and the cinema. That really is very good progress.

Client: Yes, I guess it is really. I hadn't thought about it like that, but now you come to mention it, I am doing a lot more on my own lately. I even went to the local shops on my own yesterday, and I haven't been out on my own since all this started.

Here the counsellor, in evaluating the homework tasks, has changed the negative set into a positive one, making it more likely that in between future sessions the client will continue to try tasks that had previously failed. Recommending reading for the client to obtain greater understanding is another useful homework task. Suggestions are at the end of this chapter.

Sleep disturbances are common with depression and anxiety. Check out what the bedtime rituals are for those who cannot get to sleep. Alcohol should not be taken to assist sleep, as this is a maladaptive strategy. Nor should the person eat late at night. Physical and mental activity should start to be reduced mid-evening with a winding-down process of a short walk or warm bath to relax. A warm milky or chocolate drink before sleeping will also help (not tea or coffee because of the caffeine). For those who do sleep but experience early morning wakening, suggest that it is better to get up rather than to lie in bed with all the thoughts rushing through the head. Pottering around for half an hour or so, making and drinking a warm drink, and maybe reading for a short while (or doing the ironing – that's boring enough and it's useful!) before returning to bed will allow the system to reset into going-to-bed mode, and sleep will be more likely. Some clients fall into a habit of staying up very late at night when they sleep badly, hoping that they will become so tired that they will sleep no matter what. This is another maladaptive strategy as it not only makes the person overtired, but disturbs the normal sleep cycle as well. So this should be discouraged, and sensible bedtime hours (especially for the depressed, who need to sleep a lot) should be reinforced.

For the client exhibiting phobic responses, the homework tasks need to centre on the feared object, so that the fear can to be slowly desensitised. The client should start practising relaxation tasks at home on a regular basis. Once such techniques are mastered, the feared object can be brought into the client's awareness in a non-threatening way. For example, if the client is experiencing arachnophobia (fear of spiders), desensitisation would start with looking at photos of spiders while the client is in a relaxed state, both within the session and at home, enlisting the help of a family member. When this becomes easy, the client is introduced to tiny, real spiders enclosed in a glass container. The goal in TLT is not to get the client to kiss and cuddle a tarantula, but to have sufficient control to be able to cope with household spiders without experiencing intense fear. Deeply entrenched phobias, however, would probably need more than the six sessions provided in TLT, and it may be more appropriate to refer to the local psychology department for longer term cognitive-behavioural therapy. There are also some very good self-help groups around the country, like Triumph Over Phobia, which helps people with their phobic and obsessional symptoms.

To counsel people experiencing anxiety and depression within six sessions requires good counselling skills and physiological knowledge. This knowledge can be conveyed to the clients, who often feel out of control of their own bodies. Thus some information about the autonomic nervous system can have a calming effect. Watch out for little traps that may encourage you to think the client is better or worse than they really are. For example, remember that diurnal variations affect how clients present themselves to you. They may present as near suicidal if their appointment is early morning, but by late afternoon things may not seem half as bad. Encourage clients to take control of how they feel by exercising and doing homework tasks. Reinforce successes and affirm how well the client is doing. This will empower the client by making him feel less hopeless and helpless and therefore less anxious and depressed.

Recommended reading

Jeffers, S. (1987) *Feel the Fear and Do It Anyway*. London: Arrow.

Marks, I. (1978) *Living with Fear*. New York: McGraw-Hill.

Peale, N.V. (1953) *The Power of Positive Thinking*. London: Simon & Schuster.

Rowe, D. (1983) *Depression: The Way Out of Your Prison*. London: Routledge & Kegan Paul.

Notes

1 Personal communication.

2 S. Scotchman, personal communication, 1996.

5

Counselling People under Stress

Stress, according to Freud, is the price we pay for being civilised. Leading financial institutions believe that lost hours from stress victims cost about 3 per cent of wages, which for a typical City bank would cost about £15 million a year (Cooper, Cooper and Eaker, 1988). Drink-related absenteeism, a typical maladaptive strategy for coping with stress, costs approximately £700 million per year (Tyler, 1993). Research shows that 40 million working days are lost each year through stress-related illness, costing approximately £4 billion (Cooper, 1990). Stress has become the twentieth-century plague.

More and more people are presenting to their GPs with common (and not so common) symptoms of stress. Increasingly people are succumbing to recognised stress-related illnesses. Some of these illnesses are life-threatening, e.g. coronary heart disease, stroke, thrombosis, hypertension, ulcerative colitis and asthma. Others are life-damaging, e.g. irritable bowel syndrome, ulcers, eczema and psoriasis. Depression and anxiety are other ways the body manifests stress. This chapter reviews the difficulties individuals experience as a result of stress. It highlights stress management techniques that can be recommended to the client, and it describes how time-limited therapy can be linked with stress management tuition.

The psychology of stress

The word 'stress' is actually a misnomer, as stress is actually another word for arousal. Stress is the physical response when the sympathetic part of the autonomic nervous system switches on to produce the 'fight and flight' response. In this response, the heart beats faster and breathing increases and becomes shallower. The stomach stops its digestive processes to allow the energy produced by catecholamine production (adrenalin, noradrenalin and cortisol) to go to the muscles in preparation for any threat. Pupils dilate, making vision more alert. Hair becomes prickly and stands on end. Perspiration is produced. The desire to evacuate one's bladder or bowel is strong as the sphincters relax.

This arousal, or stress, is appropriate and adaptive in situations of physical threat where the person is under some form of personal danger. Thus stress, *per se*, is not bad. We need a certain amount of stress to get out of bed in the morning. And it has to be said that some people perform their best on a deadline-driven 'adrenalin buzz'. Stress becomes maladaptive, however, under conditions of emotional or intellectual threat, called stressors. The body produces the same kind of physical response to stressors, which may be an event, a person, or even a thought, that is considered by the person to be threatening. The stressor event may be a happening that occurs in one's own life, or is vicariously experienced in someone else's life. The stressor person maybe someone that one finds threatening or intimidating, like a boss, a mother-in-law or a violent partner. The stressor thought may be a belief: for example if you believe the person you love is having an affair with someone else. Whether that thought is fact or fantasy, it can produce the physical symptoms of arousal. When there is an overload of stressors in a person's life, this produces an overload of arousal reactions, or stress, leading to breakdown or 'strain'. So what people are really talking about when they say they are stressed is actually strain. Stress and adaptability go together. Stress (or strain) is what occurs when adaptability breaks down; when the adaptive mechanisms are pushed beyond their limits.

There are many common symptoms that people under stress somatise. Although stress is a cognitive, or interpretative, reaction to stressors, the physical symptoms experienced are very real and often very distressing. Here the mind/body link is at its weakest; people feel totally out of control of what is happening to their bodies, which of course exacerbates the stress.

Presenting symptoms are:

- inability to concentrate
- loss of memory
- confusion
- constant fatigue
- carelessness/clumsiness
- bowel complaints
- early morning wakening
- loss of libido
- loss of appetite
- preoccupation with aches and pains
- frequently wanting to cry
- mood disorder: irritability, depression or anxiety
- listlessness
- waves of panic, sweating, trembling
- feelings of isolation
- preoccupation with work or home

- feeling overwhelmed
- despair

I find it is useful to examine where the stressors are in a client's life, as this aids the choice of appropriate management strategies and helps the client to understand what is happening. Stressors can be usefully categorised into life events, chronic stressors, daily hassles and personality factors. Understanding these categories, and being able to explain the processes to the client, helps in a time-limited environment.

Life events

We all experience events as we move through our life development. Such events, even when they are positive, like getting married or having a child, can be extremely stressful. Some events are of our choice, like moving house, taking examinations or changing jobs. Others are thrust upon us, like bereavement or redundancy. These, of course, are harder to accept because they make us feel so out of control. Even events like Christmas and family holidays, which are supposed to be happy times, actually cause people an incredible amount of stress.

Holmes and Rahe (1967), understanding the link between life events and stress-related illness, developed a social readjustment scale for people to check through. The score from 43 life events experienced by the person over a two-year period would indicate whether physical illness is likely to occur in the near future: the greater the magnitude of the score of the life events, the greater the probability of disease occurrence. This is a very well known and interesting inventory that provides people with an indicator of how many stressors they have had in their lives. The only problem with this schedule is that lives (and people) are not as simple as that. It is not the life event *per se* that is stressful, but how the individual *perceives* that event that counts. For example, scoring the highest on their list is death of a spouse. Yes, losing a partner can be an earth-shattering blow and grief is very stressful. But not everyone grieves for their dead partner in the same way. Some people may be relieved that the person has died, either because she was terminally ill or in considerable pain or because the relationship was violent or abusive. One person said to me, 'Thank goodness I got rid of the old bugger! That saved me the hassle of a divorce.' She was clearly not stressed or grieving. Personally, I would have put death of a child in a higher position than death of a spouse. I would also have included the death of a pet, which upsets people greatly. I have heard a trainee counsellor say in supervision, 'Well, it's only a dog, I'm not sure what all the fuss is about.' But if the client has had the dog from a puppy, rearing it with the children for 15 years, it has become a part of the family and a part of their life, and they experience real grief reaction.

A similar situation can be found in divorce, the second highest scoring event on Holmes and Rahe's list. Here again, not everyone finds divorce monumentally upsetting. Yes, some people are shattered, feel a failure, and squabbles over property and children exacerbate an already difficult situation. But for others it was the *marriage* that was stressful and the divorce is a very adaptive coping strategy for dealing with the original problem. Some people throw divorce parties, having bunting all around their house, with friends sending them 'happy divorce day' cards. These people are enjoying their divorce and are therefore not finding it stressful.

Life events are a health hazard, and major life events like retirement, bereavement and job change put people physically at risk. As noradrenalin levels soar, blood pressure rises and the blood thickens. Those with already furred-up arteries from poor diet and lack of exercise are placing themselves at risk of coronary thrombosis, coronary spasm, fatal arrhythmias and strokes. People with such events need an unloading device to help reduce the pressure – a bit like the safety valve on a pressure cooker! That is where counselling is beneficial.

> George was the manager of a company with a workforce of 50. He was totally absorbed in the business, working many hours longer than required, and not taking due holiday. He felt it was preferable to be at work, where he could nip any problems in the bud, which might have become much more difficult if he were not there. George did not suffer fools gladly and was renowned for his short fuse. He was overweight from eating rich food and a large consumption of alcohol, particularly from business lunches. When George was at home, he did very little as he was overcome by fatigue. He had little time for his wife and considered her complaints ungrateful, given the lifestyle she had because he worked so hard. One morning, George went to work, to be greeted by a redundancy notice. Ten days later, George had a heart attack.

Chronic stressors

Life events may be chronic stressors. These are the kind of stressors that stay with the person over a long period, and basically sap the stamina over time. Examples of chronic stressors are unemployment, poverty, being a single parent, caring for a sick relative or a

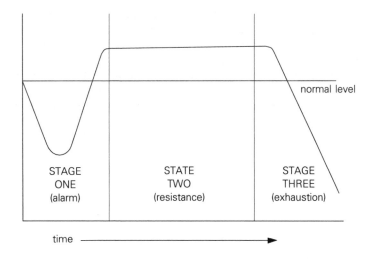

normal level

STAGE
ONE
(alarm)

STATE
TWO
(resistance)

STAGE
THREE
(exhaustion)

time

Figure 5.1 *The General Adaptation Syndrome (after Seyle, 1956)*

handicapped child. Whatever else goes on in the individual's life, the chronic stressor always seems to be there in the background. Environmental stressors, like war, weather and pollution are also chronic stressors.

Seyle (1956) demonstrated how people respond to such stressors, which he called the general adaptation syndrome.[1] When the life event first occurs, the body's adrenalin levels shoot up in order to deal with the situation (see Figure 5.1). They then plateau at a level that is considerably higher than is normal for that individual, to provide sufficient arousal to cope with the ongoing stressor. This change in the homeostatic balance of endocrine hormones, however, is very bad for the system. It can be analogous to battery acid: it is fine in the right place, but too much leads to a corrosive overflow. Eventually, exhaustion takes place, and the body 'burns out'. The distance in time between stage two and stage three for each individual varies according to how much stress resilience the person learned as a child (Rutter, 1985), what coping strategies are employed to deal with the stress (Lazarus, 1966), and how much social support the person has (Brown and Harris, 1978). Thus we could be talking of months or years difference, but eventually exhaustion will occur. This may take the form of a physical illness, most commonly with chronic stressors bowel, stomach or chest complaints. Alternatively the mind seems to shut down, as if coping with anything, even making simple decisions like what to have for tea, is too much. This used to be called a 'nervous breakdown', but 'burnout' is the more modern expression. Burnout is when an individual works too hard for too long in a high-pressure environment (Kelly, 1992). The person collapses into a complete state of physical and mental fatigue, which takes many months to repair. Interestingly, people with ME, or chronic fatigue syndrome, had similar extremely stressful and busy lives immediately prior to their initial viral infection which precipitated the illness (see Chapter 12).

> Tina was in her forties and had three children. Her eldest child had cerebral palsy and needed 24-hour care. Her other two children, a boy and a girl, were in their late teens. Tina's daughter had always helped her mum with her elder brother, but at 17 she decided that she had had enough and went to live with her boyfriend in another town. Tina felt bereft, and missed her daughter's help badly. Tina's husband was a builder employing five men. He worked long hours six days a week and was rarely home to help. When he was home on a Sunday, he concentrated mostly on work issues, and did not feel it was his role to be involved in domestic arrangements, especially as his wife coped so well with all that. He also relied on Tina to keep the company books and pay the wages as she was good with money, and he could not afford to pay someone to do it. When she told him she was struggling to cope, he shrugged and pointed out that there really was no alternative. When Tina's other son started to play up in a typical adolescent fashion, Tina found herself wandering around the house all day in tears, incapable of doing anything.

Daily hassles

We all have daily hassles, don't we? We all experience frustrations when things go wrong, or we forget things, make a mistake, or someone else lets us down in some way. You know the kind of day: you wake up with a start and realise that the alarm did not go off and you are already half an hour late for work. You rush downstairs in a panic while you are still dressing and find that the dog has done a whoopsie on the carpet (because you have stepped in it!). Without any breakfast, you rush out the door, and as it slams shut you remember you have left your house keys inside. Resolving to deal with it later, you leap into your car and with a squeal of rubber start to pull away. But the wobble on one side of the car tells you that you have a flat tyre. Pulling the car to a halt, you rest your head on the steering wheel clenched with white knuckles, and you notice that you have only been up 20 minutes and already the day has been fraught with disasters. When arousal levels are already high, it all becomes too much to cope with.

These continual hassles have a way of getting on top of us. Delongis, Folkman and Lazarus (1988) found that an increase in daily hassles was associated with decline in health and mood. As the autonomic nervous system goes into threat-preparation mode, cortisol levels increase, the immune system lowers, and allows a way in for colds and viral infections. Thus two or three days following a 'bad day' puts an individual at risk of coughs, colds, sore throats, etc. Kanner et al. (1981) devised a 'Hassles and Uplifts' scale to assess the daily and cumulative impact of everyday demands. Among the hassles they include are personal worries about weight, health and appearance, family worries about food prices, domestic bills and property investments, and community worries like vandalism, theft and violent crime. These are offset by uplifts that give a sense of well-being, like good friendships or going out for a meal.

Of course, going to work gives us our greatest hassle, as well as (for some) our greatest adrenalin buzz. The following are the most common work-related hassles:

- time pressures – working to unreasonable deadlines
- work overload – too much work for one person to manage within the time
- work underload – insufficient work to do
- role ambiguity – not being sure what your job, or someone else's job, is
- commuting – traffic chaos, late buses, cancelled trains
- personality clashes – worse if it is the boss
- constant telephone interruptions

These are the kinds of frustrations that people start becoming preoccupied with. The ruminating becomes obsessive, interfering with daily activity as concentration drops and memory becomes unreliable. The person wakes early in the morning with all the memories of what was going on yesterday swirling around in the head, and then thoughts rush to planning what to do today to try and cope with it all. Thus insufficient sleep leads to constant fatigue and to worry about not sleeping, which in turn makes the person less likely to sleep well. As fatigue increases, motivation to exercise (if any was done at all) diminishes. Fatigue also interferes with the appetite, so eating properly ceases to be a priority. Junk food is snatched to fit in with a busy day, and lunch is often eaten at the desk in between phone calls. Long working days without breaks lead to a reduction in performance because of low sugar levels and insufficient time out. The pressure to work harder is increased, and it all becomes a vicious downward spiral.

Bullying is a problem that many people have to face, not only at school, but at work as well. Bullying starts off as a daily hassle, but over a long period moves into being a chronic stressor. The symptoms of being bullied include absenteeism, under-performance, and a reduction in self-esteem. People lose the ability to make decisions or take initiatives. If a line manager or senior officer is the bully, the victim feels powerless and trapped, and starts to exhibit the classic symptoms of stress. Research (Adams, 1992) shows that bullies may be male or female, and that bullying happens to men and women equally. Sexual harassment – mostly for women but it does happen to men – produces similar feelings of despair. There seems to be a stereotypical bullying situation. A company, already suffering from corporate anorexia, overloads the more senior staff following redundancies of junior staff. The senior staff start to buckle at the knees from the pressure. Irritated at his seeming inability to cope, the manager reasons that he could replace this (now expensive in terms of salary) senior member of staff with a cheap alternative. Redundancy for senior staff is expensive, but if this man resigned from his own volition. . . .

Terkel (1975) felt that work was about violence, to the body as well as to the spirit. 'It is about ulcers as well as accidents, about shouting matches as well as fistfights, about nervous breakdowns as well as kicking the dog around. It is above all (or beneath all) about daily humiliations.' People who cannot accept that work is stressful, who adopt a stiff-upper-lip approach, pretending they do not feel as bad as they do, are most likely to somatise their problems and develop physical illnesses.

Bill was a successful and well-known research chemist working for an American company in the UK. On reaching his fiftieth birthday, he still managed to publish his findings and keep ahead of his field. His American parent company appointed a new line manager over Bill, a man just half Bill's age and planning to go places. The new boss wanted to make sweeping changes, and set Bill tasks which Bill considered demeaning, as they were research projects that he had already undertaken and published some 20 years earlier. Bill's protests at the waste of company time and money fell on deaf ears. The research department now was a place of atmosphere and tension, as other older researchers were similarly under-mined. Increasingly these people left, leaving Bill as the oldest person in the department. All the work that Bill produced, even on minor tasks, was challenged for its accuracy and returned for amendments, even when Bill knew it was in fact correct. His salary was reduced in real terms because it was performance-related, and he was now no longer allowed to undertake the kind of work to which he was accustomed. He felt he could not leave the company, as it was the only one of its kind in the locality, and he could not move at present because that would interfere with his children's education. He felt trapped and demoralised, but could not risk having time off work as that would be used against him. He therefore took high doses of antidepressant drugs to get him through his day, but these interfered with his performance and led to his making mistakes, which again were used against him. Bill had changed from a confident, successful and outgoing man, to a broken, nervous and ill man due to his boss's subtle bullying tactics.

Personality factors

Of course there are hundreds of different personality combinations, but there are three types most commonly linked with stress research. These are called, excitingly: type A, type B and type C. In any stress management programme it is extremely important to consider the personality of the individual concerned, otherwise you are in danger of increasing the stress rather than reducing it.

Type A personality (Rosenman, Swan and Carmelli, 1988) was recognised by researchers back in the 1960s as a significant contributing factor in people with coronary heart disease. A classic type A person would be ambitious, competitive, aggressive, focused and time oriented. Twenty-four hours in a day were not really enough; 26 would be preferable. So they try to cram 26 hours worth of work into their day. They are often perfectionists and become irritated with others who cannot work as quickly and efficiently. as they do themselves. They are poor delegators, as they prefer to do something themselves rather than watch someone else do it slowly or wrongly. A vignette of a classic type A would be as follows: You are late for an appointment (as you commonly are because you leave everything until the last minute so as not to waste time). You are driving to your destination, exceeding the speed limit as is common. You drive through a set of traffic lights just as they have turned red. Into your path pulls a little old lady driving a Morris Minor, who is enjoying her afternoon drive to the shops. Her average speed is 20 m.p.h., but she tends to slow down as she passes the hat shop so that she can view the latest arrivals. If you are a classic type A personality, your knuckles will be white on your steering wheel, your jaw will be clenched, protruding through the steering wheel, and your teeth will be grinding as you voice profanities about geriatric drivers being banned from the road. You will be driving with your front bumper inches away from her back bumper as you try to intimidate her off the road. You will be setting yourself up for your own state of stress.

Type A personality is learned behaviour: babies are not born with such drive and ambition. But from childhood parents, teachers and later employers reinforce this personality characteristic. People want students and workers who give their all to their work, who are always industrious, who are focused, who have ambition and charisma. For employers, it is the most cost-effective personality characteristic, because such employees will work many more hours than they are required or salaried to do. The armed forces positively select for type As in their recruitment, as they are most likely to have the drive and the 'killer instinct' and these characteristics are consistently reinforced in their training.

Of course, not all type As are classic. But you can view these personality factors as on a continuum to the archetypal: people may possess many of the characteristics of a type A, but not all of them. A good proportion of the characteristics, though, means that the person is at risk. Type A individuals, by their personal drive, aggression and competitiveness, set themselves up for life-threatening illness caused by stress. Rosenman et al. (1964) found that there were four indicators for people who developed coronary heart disease (CHD) and drew up a coronary risk profile. They found that 85 per cent of individuals develop CHD in their thirties and forties if they have:

- a parental history of CHD
- elevated diastolic blood pressure
- high cholesterol and triglyceride levels
- the presence of type A behaviour

Research shows that people exhibiting type A behaviour have elevated adrenalin and noradrenalin secretion, and excessive noradrenalin levels when they are angry (Chesney and Rosenman, 1985). As already suggested, such levels are dangerous. Thus type A people are a risk to themselves.

Type B personality is the opposite of type A. These people are so laid back they are (metaphorically) almost comatose. They procrastinate: they will not do anything today if they can leave it until tomorrow. They are unambitious, and rarely complete tasks they set themselves. They have a very Greek, philosophical approach to life: relax, no problem, don't worry! These people, research shows, are the people most unlikely to develop coronary heart disease (they are too tired to have a heart attack!). The only time they are going to be at risk from stress-related illnesses is if they have a type A person as their significant other; e.g. a parent or a spouse. Under those conditions, the type A person will give the type B person a lot of hassle about what he is not doing, and that will create a lot of nervous tension. Basically, type A and type B people are incompatible rather than complementary, so such relationships rarely work in the long term.

Type C personalities tend to be carers who may be professional carers or caring for a sick mother or handicapped child at home.

Type Cs are nervous and anxious, constantly fussing and worrying about their charges. They generate a lot of adrenalin as they make their caring role into a chronic stressor. They tend always to put the cared-for person first, ignoring their own needs. They rarely take time out from their caring, feeling guilty if they do. Type C individuals, psychoneuroimmunological research has shown, have low immune systems mostly from the high levels of cortisol and are therefore more likely to develop cancer-related disorders (Society of Behavioural Medicine, 1987).

Rosemary had worked as an insurance clerk for 15 years. She was a supervisor for her section, and was proud of their performance compared to other sections in the department. Her boss held her in high regard, and would trust her with work that needed to be completed efficiently and accurately. Rosemary always rose to meet the challenge of the day, and would often work through her lunch break, not leaving in the evening until her desk was cleared. Very often her boss would give her work to do that other people had not finished, but she never complained. She was proud that he always considered her. 'Give it to Rosemary,' he would say; 'she'll do it.' Rosemary was married with two children in their early teens. After her work, she would rush home and prepare the evening meal for the family. The children would be at home after school, waiting for her to come home and feed them. Even her husband, who very often would be home from work before her, would be reading the paper waiting for his meal. Rosemary would rush through her evening meal so that she could wash up and clear away. She then had time to do the other household chores before she fell into bed at ten o'clock. Her life always ran smoothly providing there were no unforeseen happenings. If anything unexpected occurred, it threw her completely into disarray. One morning, she woke in the early hours with diarrhoea and flatulence. She had never had time off sick before and did not want to start now, but the complaint left her feeling drained and in so much pain that she decided to stay at home and not eat until the problem had passed. But it stayed. Three weeks later, after various tests, her GP diagnosed irritable bowel syndrome and told her she would have to learn to live with it.

Irritable bowel syndrome (IBS) is a common stress-related problem and it is thought that 8–22 per cent of the population suffer from the various symptoms, although less than a third of sufferers consult their GP (Spiller, 1994). IBS sufferers who consult their GP tend also to be anxious and prone to depression (see also Chapter 12). Research evidence suggests that stressful life-styles or life events precede IBS. During high levels of arousal, digestion stops and may not recommence until the end of the day or night-time. Thus all food eaten during this time is trapped in the stomach, with associated corrosive effects on the stomach and gut.

Assessment

Because some of the symptoms of stress are so classic, they are relatively easy to identify. The kinds of questions that need to be asked are:

- Is this person exhibiting signs of stress?
    Are there physical symptoms of body aches, headaches, stomach and bowel complaints?
    Are there psychological problems of confusion, memory loss, lack of concentration?
    Are there emotional problems of mood disorder, outbursts of anger or crying?
    Are there behavioural problems of sleep disorder, increased drinking or smoking?
    Are there relationship problems of arguments, withdrawal, or loss of libido?
- Is this client a type A?
    Is there a sharp aggressive style of speech?
    Is the person easily bored, only pretending to listen?
    Does this person feel guilty when relaxing?
    Does this person try to do too many things at once?
    Is this person time orientated?
    Is this person materialistic?
- Is this person a type C?
    Does this person continually worry?
    Does this person overlook his/her own needs for someone else's?
    Does this person ever get any time-out from the caring role?
- Is this person on medication?[2]

The majority of stress cases do very well with TLT; indeed it is often the presenting problem that requires the least input from the counsellor, so only two or three sessions may be necessary. A person with a very severe case of burnout, however, takes many months to recover. Such people are off work for well over six months, so sessions need to be spaced out well. In the scenarios mentioned in this chapter, all of the clients George, Tina, Bill, and Rosemary did well with fewer than six sessions. George never worked again as he was incapacitated by his heart attack and later surgery, but he adapted well with a new lifestyle. Bill could not tackle his bullying boss head on, but he learned a new power in accepting his lot, and not giving his boss what his boss really wanted – Bill's resignation. Tina's son went into respite care whilst she recouped, and Rosemary learned to say no.

TLT procedures

Denial is a big problem with stress. It is the kind of thing that happens to others, not to you. It is also something that others do not respond well to. If someone has time off work with a broken leg, that is well accepted, but tell someone that you have stress and you see the blank look and suspicion of malingering appear. So people find it difficult to admit that they are under strain from stress in the first place. Insisting that they are stressed is unhelpful. It is better to allow the client to get used to the idea during the assessment and first session. It is more likely to be accepted if the GP has said they are stressed than if the counsellor says so.

Explore the stressors being presented. What is going on in your client's life that is making them somatise the physical symptoms that they have just described? Listen to the stressors that are being acknowledged and hear the stressors that are not being expressed. Most commonly, clients will present with just one set of looming stressors, like trouble at work. Open questions will soon reveal that there is very often stress at home in the relationship or family as well. It is this multiple stress context that very often makes people feel they are cracking at the seams.

> *Client*: So you see, I really can't cope with the amount of work they are giving me to do within the time, and my complaints simply fall on deaf ears. It is so frustrating! Why won't they listen to me when I tell them I can't do it all!?
>
> *Counsellor*: So, you feel overwhelmed by the volume of work you have to do, and the deadlines they expect you to do it by, and the frustrating part that makes you so angry is that your boss is not interested in whether you can cope or not, he just wants the work done. We can come back to the work situation in a minute, but I'd just like to check out – are there any other stressors in your life at the moment?
>
> *Client*: No, not really. . . . My parents are elderly, and I'm the only child, so it's quite a responsibility having to see to them all the time. Not that I begrudge them the time, it's just that the older they get the more demanding they become in wanting me to do jobs around their house. But it's not really what you would call stress, it's just a hassle that interferes with my weekends, that's all.
>
> *Counsellor*: What about at home? How is your relationship with your wife and daughters?
>
> *Client*: Well, now you come to mention it, it isn't really that good at home. My wife and eldest daughter are constantly rowing. It's only the usual teenage stuff, and I have to say that I think my wife is much too strict on Beth. It's almost as if my wife resents the lifestyle and freedom that Beth has, so she imposes unnecessary restrictions and household chores to keep her at home. There wouldn't be half the rows if she would only accept that a 17-year-old needs to spread her wings a bit.

Of course, when I stick up for Beth when I feel my wife is being particularly unreasonable, she turns on me then and accuses me of taking sides and being unsupportive. Then, she doesn't speak to me for days after to punish me. In all honesty, I do feel I could walk out sometimes just to get some peace and quiet. I could cope with my job better if home wasn't like a war zone. But wherever I go, whether it is to work, to my parents or home, I just get pressure! Pressure! Pressure! My only safe haven is the pub.

Exploring maladaptive coping strategies is also useful. How does the client cope with the stressors? The most common maladaptive strategies, which can do more harm than good, are excess of alcohol, tobacco, drugs, caffeine or food. Similarly, clients who bury themselves in their work, throw tantrums, withdraw and avoid situations, indulge by staying up late or impulse buying, or are totally passive, hoping it will get better and waiting for change, are all using damaging methods of coping with stressful lives. It is important not to be critical about these strategies, but just to highlight them and ask how they help. The client will not need to be told they are maladaptive (others have probably already said so frequently!). It is also unhelpful to give up any of these that may be addictive at this time, as that is also stressful. So if a client volunteers to give up smoking or drinking, acknowledge that it would be a very beneficial thing to do at a later time, but right now, on the premise of 'a little of what you fancy does you good', aim for reduction rather than cessation.

When the denial barrier is broken, and all the stressors thoroughly explored, it is time to move clients into **understanding** what is happening to their bodies. At this stage, the process is less one of counselling and more one of guiding and teaching. Clients are interested in knowing what is happening to them and why they are responding the way they are. Research has shown that clients wish to learn about the physiological aspects of their stress (Gregson and Looker, 1996), which helps them learn about the relevance of management strategies. So explaining the physiological process is valuable. I always recommend a stress book at an early stage, as this reinforces all the information that the counsellor provides. Somehow, it is more believable when it is seen in black and white. The one I recommend at the end of this chapter, *The Joy of Stress*, is particularly good because it covers type A personality well, and uses humour (a very good stress-management strategy). I also point out that if they get *The Joy of Sex* by mistake, that is OK as sex is also a good stress-management strategy.

Although the stressors are the client's predominant agenda, I suggest that any coping strategies are placed on the back-burner for the time being while we concentrate on the physical fitness aspect.

This gives the client a little space from the problem and a focus to work on. So the homework from the first session is to make any adjustments necessary to diet and exercise. Diet is important: besides the issue of being over- or underweight, when the person is buckling at the knees from the pressure of stress, a good, nutritious diet is essential. Convenience and junk food snatched on the run increases internal stress as a high fat intake added to high arousal leads to excessively high blood fat levels (Gregson and Looker, 1996). Instead, fresh fruit and vegetables in quantity, complex carbohydrates (pasta, potatoes, rice and wholemeal bread) with white meat and fish become high priority, eaten at regular intervals. For those already very physically low, vitamin supplements help. The client should make a meal of their meal – slow down, savour and enjoy what they are eating, making plenty of time to do so, and do nothing else simultaneously.

Dehydration is common for people who have not the time to think about topping up their fluid intake. Dehydration thickens the blood and wrinkles the skin. Early symptoms are fatigue, then headaches, then thirst. Coffee and tea, both of which are diuretic, should be reduced to only a couple of cups a day, supplemented by lots of water and fruit or herb teas. Coffee and tea contain caffeine that stimulates the production of adrenalin and noradrenalin, activating a stress response. Such drinks should therefore be kept to a minimum.

I talked of the importance of exercise in the last chapter. It is even more essential when the client is pumping out all this excess adrenalin because of the stressors. Type A clients especially tend to be on the go all the time, and need to exercise as their best way of relaxing. Do not suggest to a type A client to try a relaxation tape, as these people hate it and would find it stressful! Discuss various forms of cardiovascular exercise, and explore with the client the preferred method. Also explore alternative therapeutic stressors which can relax, like gardening, DIY, or whatever the client enjoys as a pastime. If you have a stressed type B client, she will love relaxation tapes, meditation or yoga. I always keep a stock of relaxation tapes for clients to borrow to try for themselves. I tend to find that the physical symptoms of stress are so scary to the client that they conduct their homework very well. They read the book, and soon find the diet and exercise making a great difference to the way they feel. As they feel stronger physically, the stressors are put more in perspective, and clients often start invoking changes, most commonly by telling people what is happening to them and how they feel.

With improved physical fitness, clients are ready for **action** on their prevailing stressors. If the major stressor is one at work, which it most commonly is (particularly for teachers and those working in banking or insurance), spending time talking about time-management skills is useful. In particular: drawing up daily agendas, setting specific and realistic goals for the day, prioritising, eliminating time wasters, blocking out interruptions, delegating, making advance preparations, and learning to say no. Taking time out, both in terms of days off and holidays, and taking appropriate lunch breaks by getting away from the working environment for 20 minutes, can make enormous difference both to how a person feels and to the quality of their work performance. It also helps if the client can start to develop some cognitive resilience, by being open to change, striving for realistic goals, developing a philosophy of how she wants to live (e.g. like working to live rather than living to work), and being active in seeking solutions to problems rather than focusing on failure.

Changing type A behaviour is another important aspect to discuss. You cannot change a type A personality into a type B, nor should you want to. But, as Cooper (1989) points out, if they can survive their first heart attack, they stand a good chance of avoiding a second one if they work at it. A reformed type A is called a healthy charismatic, because he has kept all the drive and charisma, and dumped the aggressive, competitive, perfectionist, time-orientated traits. Homework tasks that involve self-monitoring, slowing-down exercises, avoiding competitive situations, and increasing time limits for jobs all aid the individual's self-awareness. *The Joy of Stress* suggests some more facetious tasks for changing type A behaviour, like attending a meeting without speaking, driving behind learner drivers without overtaking, standing in shop queues without becoming impatient, and watching television documentaries without switching to see what is on the other side. Type A individuals are dynamic, so they will be very entertaining as they recount their challenge to change themselves:

> *Client*: Well, I read that book you said to get.
> *Counsellor*: Good. Did you recognise yourself?
> *Client*: Recognise myself? The book was written about me! As I read I said to myself, 'Oh my God, this is me!' Even that bit about eating, shaving and reading all at the same time. I do that! In the mornings before work, I use my electric razor, so I can shave while I grab a bit of toast, and skim through the morning newspaper. I even take work papers with me to the loo so I don't waste any time! So I thought that I would have one day of watching myself to see if I did many type A things. They were just stacking up! On the way to work I ran through a red light, blasted my horn at someone driving too slow, and had an argument with a woman who parked in the place where I usually park. At work, I shouted at my secretary because she had a spelling mistake in a letter,

snatched a report off a colleague because he was too slow to finish it, and went home an hour and a half later than I could have done because I had that extra report to finish. At lunch, four of us meet up and walk to the next building to the staff canteen. I found that I walked in front of them to speed them up. I had finished eating my lunch 10 minutes before the others, then I found myself constantly looking at my watch because I wanted to get back, and kept trying to end the conversations of the others so they would get on with their lunch so we could get back to work. I just didn't realise – they must think I'm a right pain! After work I went for a game of squash with an old friend, but he beat me – so I spent the rest of the evening fuming and hardly spoke to my wife.

Counselling people who are under stress requires good counselling skills, substantial physiological knowledge, and good teaching skills. Of course, a thorough knowledge of stress-management techniques is essential, otherwise the counsellor is just paying lip service to the helping role. Helping in this way is very rewarding, because people change their life-styles very quickly, and as a consequence have more enriched lives, even if that means living with chronic stressors.

Recommended reading

Hanson, P. (1987) *The Joy of Stress*. London: Pan.

Notes

1 Although still highly influential, Seyle's model has been usurped by more modern and sophisticated theories of stress (Henry, 1986). However, it is still a very simple model that can be quickly explained to clients, and enhances their understanding.

2 A beta-blocker like propranolol is the most common stress prophylactic as it inhibits the adrenalin and noradrenalin receptor sites, which stops the heart rate from increasing so much (Durel et al., 1985).

6

Counselling People with Post Traumatic Stress Disorder

When people are involved in, or witness, a trauma of some sort, they experience a severe form of arousal reaction. This experience of trauma varies according to the individual's resilience and coping abilities, and it is the individual's perception of the event that is important rather than the counsellor's assessment of the severity of the trauma. The Disasters Working Party found that after such an event, 40–70 per cent of people experienced chronic distress in the first month, 24–40 per cent after one year, and 15–20 per cent for longer than two years (Home Office, 1991). Such events may be experienced either personally by being involved in an event or vicariously through witnessing one. They usually involve threat and/or damage to life and limb, although people can experience PTSD from minor road traffic accidents. What counts for the individual is that the event is outside usual experience and that the individual perceives it as threatening.

In trauma situations, the brain has a wonderful way of detaching the individual from the event that helps to prevent adrenalin levels rocketing. People often describe feeling detached from themselves (a form of splitting): that they are watching themselves in the event rather than participating in it. Everything seems to slow down into slow motion, where minutes seem like hours, and it is like watching a movie.[1] When the event is over, the client may go into the numbness of shock, which removes him rather from the intensity of emotion, although he may be feeling an arousal reaction of shakiness, perspiration, and a sick feeling in the stomach.

Later, however, the brain will be trying to make sense of what has happened during the traumatic incident. The memory base is analogous to a filing cabinet, with different memories filed under various headings. But a traumatic incident is outside usual experience, so the memory does not know where to file the event. It therefore keeps replaying it, like a videotape, over and over again in the mind's eye in the form of daytime flashbacks or in dreams. This not only interferes with normal functioning, it also makes the person nervous and agitated with an acute startle response. Noises seem louder, lights brighter and smells stronger. The replay of events then starts to preoccupy the person, who ruminates on the event and the constant vivid images. Individuals may feel acute relief at still being alive after the event, but also acute guilt if others have died. Feelings of anger and resentment bubble up against significant others who were not there and do not know what it was like. Expressions of sympathy and support are bitterly rejected as the individual withdraws within herself. In turn the partner or spouse may feel spurned and rejected and the relationship may be put under threat.

> Josh was a junior officer in the Air Training Corps. After a weekend exercise, he was taking a couple of cadets home through a rural district. The landscape was low and flat, the road was deserted, and as it was very dark with no street lighting, he had the car's headlights on full beam. There was no other traffic in this lonely area. The cadets were still in high spirits, laughing and joking in the seats behind him. Then Josh became aware of a log lying in the middle of the road. As he slowed down, planning to drive around the log, he saw in his lights that it wasn't a log, but a person lying face down. He brought his car to an immediate halt and rushed out to the recumbent person. To his horror, he realised that it was one of his own cadets who had left him only some 10 minutes previously with three or four others. His stomach turned as he looked at the staring eyes and thought the young man dead. He gingerly felt for a pulse and could not feel one. Rushing back to his own car for a torch, and firing orders to the others to get help, he searched around for the other passengers. A few yards away, off the road, he found the car upside down, its wheels still spinning, with the three other young men lying injured near it. All his years of training in discipline and first aid came into immediate effect, and he tended to each one in turn with admirable calm and tenacity. When the emergency services arrived some 10 minutes later and took over, they praised his actions and reassured him that he had done all the right things. Josh, however, could not stop shaking.
>
> Two months after the accident Josh went to his doctor. He had received a commendation for his actions on that night, but he was still finding it difficult to cope with. His personality had changed: he had become short-tempered and irascible; he had also lost his confidence. He was experiencing constant flashbacks of the log lying in the road and the vacant staring eyes, even though this young man, as did all the others, survived the accident.

There are many events that can lead a person to experience PTSD, and it is not possible to cover them all. However, I have found that the most common presentations in General Practice are experiences of rape, road traffic accidents, and violent assault.

Rape

Rape is a personal violation that produces a deep trauma response in a woman. It is a crime of power and violence, rather than a basic sexual offence, in which the persecutor wants to exert his power and dominance over his victim and wants to humiliate her. The woman will feel violated, humiliated, ashamed and dirty. There will also be additional fears of pregnancy and sexually transmitted diseases (STDs) which prolong the offence. In a study by Rothbaum et al. (1992), 94 per cent of their sample of rape victims were experiencing distress symptomatic of PTSD within days of the event and 47 per cent were still suffering 3–4 months later. Although the police are now very aware of the trauma to women who have been raped, and do their best to conduct their investigations in a sensitive manner, the courts are not so protective. Many women have been re-traumatised through criminal proceedings with prolonged interrogations in the witness-box by the persecutor's counsel, or by the persecutor himself if he conducts his own defence. The woman has to relive the event, discuss her previous sexual history in detail, and counter challenges that she encouraged or consented to the offence. The humiliation is repeated. To the woman, it feels like being raped all over again. Many women who have been raped by someone they knew have also been continually hassled by their attacker and/or his family in between making the complaint to the police and the case coming to court.

Not all women will take their trauma to the police, for the above reasons. But they will take their distress to their (usually female) GP. The GP and the practice nurse will help with any problems of pregnancy or STDs, but are less able to deal with the psychological damage, as pharmacology is insufficient to help in such cases.

Road traffic accidents (RTAs)

RTAs seem to be the most common presentation of PTSD in General Practice. Even in the most minor accident where no one was hurt, and only minor damage has been done to the vehicles, people can later experience anxiety and panic, usually because they are preoccupied with what might have happened. Travel anxiety after an RTA is extremely common even in the most confident and competent of drivers (Mayou, Bryant and Duthie, 1993). Following an accident the client may be afraid of driving even a short distance. Similarly, as a passenger she may be nervous, hyper-vigilant, and will be pressing her foot to the floor to find the imaginary brake pedal. This can be extremely exasperating for the driver, as his passenger becomes a source of irritation and distraction, thus increasing the risk of another accident.

Solicitors increasingly send clients to counselling when considering litigation for trauma following an RTA. This means that some clients may be attending counselling for the wrong reasons – for financial reward rather than psychological help. It may also mean that some clients may not be ready to engage in a psychotherapeutic intervention (Kolber and Kolber, 1995) which can impede the counselling process. However, the counsellor may find this prevents the trauma from becoming a disorder, so it is still beneficial for the client. The counsellor will be asked by the solicitor to submit a progress report for a reasonable fee. The counsellor should always ensure that he has the client's written permission before doing so.

Violent assaults

Victims of violent crime, e.g. muggings, common assault and marital violence, are all at risk of PTSD. These people find that they not only 'relive' the event in their mind's eye – either in the form of flashbacks or recurring dreams – but that they also 'refeel' the blows that they received. This sensation produces the fear response described in the section on panic attacks in Chapter 4. Thus panic attacks in these people are common. The physiological response under the original conditions of threat was an appropriate one. It becomes dysfunctional, however, at the *memory* of such a threat. However, as with other fear situations, the client knows that the fear is irrational, but gets trapped into a self-perpetuating cycle from which he feels he cannot escape. This produces avoidance behaviour, as already discussed, which in turn increases the feelings of fear.

> Jason was a 22-year-old security guard working for a shopping mall. One night after he had taken his girlfriend home after a night out, he drove to a nearby bank that had a servicetill to withdraw some money. He could not find a parking place outside the bank, but managed to find offstreet parking around the block. He withdrew his cash from the bank and started to walk the couple of streets back to the car. He felt a sensation that he was being followed, and turned several times to check, but he could see no one. He was used to being in dark, quiet places as he regularly had to work nights, and he was a big lad who felt confident he could handle himself in times of difficulty, so he scolded himself for his jumpiness, yet quickened his pace. With some relief, he reached his car and placed the key in the lock. At that instant, two men jumped him from behind. One held a knife to his throat and demanded his wallet. The other

was trying to wrench his car keys from his hand. Jason saw red and lashed out at one of his attackers, kicking him in the groin. As the attacker lurched forward, his head butted Jason's, jerking his neck on to the knife. Jason felt a searing pain in his throat and fell to the floor with a gasp. His attackers kicked him over and over to get him out of the way, rifled his pockets, jumped into his car and drove away. Jason's neck was bleeding profusely, and he had a feeling that his life was ebbing away as the blood pumped out. A witness to the incident, who had been too afraid to intervene when the attackers were there, now came running up to help Jason. He wound his sweater around Jason's neck, pressing on the wound. He called for an ambulance on his mobile phone. Jason remembered very little after this as he slipped in and out of consciousness. He had 43 stitches in his neck, which now has a very visible and ugly scar. He was unable to work as a security guard again, as he could not face working the night shift. He could not even walk down his own street at night without getting into a panic attack. He and his girlfriend split up because of his moodiness and the rows they started to have. He did not care about her anyway – how could she possibly understand how he feels? How could anyone?

Assessment

One can distinguish between two forms of PTSD: acute and chronic. If the problem is acute, the client has been experiencing symptoms for one to six months. Such episodes can be dealt with effectively with TLT. People with chronic PTSD have been experiencing their symptoms for longer than six months. Their problems will be much more entrenched and they are likely to be experiencing more consequential difficulties. Such cases may need to be referred to a specialist in Critical Incident Debriefing. Questions to ask to establish diagnosis are:

- Has this person experienced some form of trauma?
    Does this person have flashbacks or nightmares of the event?
    Is there an increased sensitivity of the senses?
    Is the person hyper-vigilant?
    Is the person irritable and angry?
    Is the person experiencing some form of sleep disturbance?
    Are there certain parts of the event that the person cannot remember (psychogenic amnesia)?
    Is this person withdrawing from significant others?
- Has the person experienced these symptoms for more than one month?

Friedman (1988) points out that drug therapy alone is necessary but not sufficient to remove the symptoms of PTSD. Medication produces sufficient symptom relief to enable the counselling to be more effective, especially in the short term. The dual role between GP and counsellor working together are especially pertinent in these cases.

TLT procedures

The symptoms of PTSD are notoriously difficult to treat (Muss, 1991). In TLT, the whole approach changes from the usual open style to a more focused method. The exploration of the traumatic event needs to be covered in minutiae (debriefing). Start to **explore** with the facts before the event – what the client was doing, feeling, what the weather was like, details of the environmental context – leading to the awareness that something bad was about to happen. Then go through the event, embellishing the facts with sensory impressions (smells, sights, tastes) and emotions. If the client speeds up to get through the story, slow her down by asking questions about small details. Normalise reactions and feelings by emphasising the normality of such reactions to abnormal circumstances.

This debriefing helps the client to **understand** what has happened to him, to get a 'cognitive grip' (Parkinson, 1995) on the event. During each following session, check to see if there has been a reduction in the symptomatic reactions. If the client continues to 'see' parts of the event either in flashbacks or dreams, debrief those aspects again, as the brain is still trying to make sense of it all. When the client gets to the stage where symptoms are reducing, it is useful to move her on to looking at any damage in relationships that the problem may have produced. It may also be useful to the client, if she wishes, for her partner or spouse to attend the last couple of sessions for a frank exchange of views and feelings. **Actions** will be based on homework tasks that reduce avoidance behaviour.

In the case of rape, the trauma may be presented to the counsellor either immediately after the event, after a period of time when the client realises she is having difficulty coming to terms with it, or throughout the court proceedings (which may be a couple of years after the event). Counsellors may be reticent to debrief a client who has recently been raped because they know that she has been through it repeatedly with the police. A balance needs to be found between helping a client tell her story, and risking re-traumatising her. This is especially so if the counsellor is male, and he needs to consider very carefully the gender influences on his client. However, the police will have debriefed the facts of the event. The counsellor should debrief the feelings by concentrating on the sensory experiences of the client – 'what did you hear, see, smell?' as well as 'what did you feel, what were you thinking?'

Clients also need to talk about their current relationships that are most likely to be adversely affected by the rape. Husbands, partners or boyfriends may respond negatively not only to the offence, but also to the victim. They may feel that their territory has been invaded, and may even blame her for being in a certain place at a certain time. She will be blaming herself, too. Their sexual relationship will also suffer, as often the woman will want (understandably) to withdraw from sex. Her partner, however, may not understand, as he was not the perpetrator, and her withdrawal may leave him feeling hurt, rejected and even more powerless. The woman's feelings of shame and humiliation may increase because she knows she is pushing him away, and does not really want to, yet she cannot stop herself. If the relationship is not a strong one, it may subsequently falter.

The counselling focus will be multifaceted. The trauma and any PTSD, plus her feelings for herself and others (especially over a court case), and her feelings about her sexuality will need individual counselling. The woman's relationship and any sexual difficulties will need couple counselling. Within the time-limited concept, therefore, it is preferable to consider these as two separate (i.e. individual and couple) six-session contracts. This will help keep the focuses separate, and allow adequate time for dealing with the various issues.

For clients involved in RTAs, the focus of the sessions will be to debrief the accident, and then move on to desensitise the travel anxiety. Homework should firstly encourage the client to ride in a car passenger seat, commencing with short journeys. The client should be encouraged to engage in some other activity like reading or doing a crossword, rather than concentrating on the road, which would increase the state of anxiety. When this is mastered, the client should be encouraged to drive short journeys, then longer journeys, and finally past the scene of the accident.

In cases of violent assault, the focus will be on recapturing the confidence and trust of the person in the rest of society. Fear and distrust of fellow human beings is a common thread running through such cases, as well as fear and distrust of similar people or similar situations.

Counselling for PTSD in General Practice is probably more common than people realise, and the skill of debriefing can help a person bring normality back into their lives again.

Recommended reading

Parkinson, F. (1993) *Post-Trauma Stress*. London: Sheldon Press.

Note

1 This is also common at times of bereavement.

7

Counselling for Bereavement, Loss and Death

A common patient presentation at the GP surgery is someone who is suffering from the distress of bereavement. This may be in the early stages of loss, particularly if the mourner is unable to sleep. It may also be at a later stage, weeks or even months after. The person will say to the doctor, 'I should be over this by now, so why do I feel so bad?' This chapter looks at the difficulties people experience with loss, and offers suggestions as to how the counsellor can help within a time-limited framework.

The psychology of grieving

Grief is readily identifiable if the death is a relatively recent one, but it is sometimes missed if there has been a considerable time span between the death and presentation to the doctor. Other forms of loss can produce a similar kind of psychological process as bereavement, and sometimes this is missed, too. Such losses may be: loss of a partner through separation or divorce, loss of a faithful monogamous relationship through the adultery of the loved one, loss of a baby following miscarriage, stillbirth or termination of pregnancy, loss of an internal organ e.g. hysterectomy, loss of a job following redundancy, or loss of a home following mortgage repossession. A loss process may also occur when someone receives a poor prognosis for a significant other who has become terminally ill. This is called anticipatory grief, and often the bereaved person is quite accepting when death does occur because most of the grieving has been undertaken beforehand (Parkes, 1973).

I have suggested that grieving for bereavement or loss is a process. By this I mean that the emotional reaction has a beginning, a middle and an end. But that is the biggest generalisation one can make about how an individual will grieve. Each bereavement is unique, and each person will respond in an individualistic way. Some people have proposed that mourners go through a series of stages in the bereavement process, and have used an adaptation of Kübler-Ross's (1970) stages of people who are dying. Other than the obvious consequential difference, it does seem that people are more complex than this concept of progressing through a simple series of stages would imply. Others have suggested that bereavement is a series of phases (Bowlby-West, 1983; Parkes, 1972) or a series of tasks that need to be undertaken (Worden, 1991). All these views have merit, and the counsellor will be able to relate some aspects of each theory to each individual, but rarely will one find an individual that fits totally into a theoretical mould. Having said that, there are some common features to the process that the counsellor will be able to identify:

- shock/disbelief/numbness
- grief reactions – crying, anger, guilt, loneliness
- emotional exhaustion/ depression
- acceptance/letting go

People are commonly shocked and numb when someone they love dies, particularly if the death is unexpected and sudden. The person is numbed into a sense of disbelief, not wishing the news to be true: 'I'll wake up in a minute and find it was all a bad dream.' Some people describe themselves at this stage as separating from themselves, as if they are watching everything from a distance rather than participating in the events. This reaction was discussed in the last chapter in response to trauma. This psychological splitting is very functional, as it gives people the space to make the necessary arrangements for funerals, registration, etc. It allows them to be carried through the first few days, almost on automatic pilot. Very often, reality breaks through at the funeral. As the mourner stares at the coffin and realises who is inside, grief takes over.

Grieving is a cocktail of emotions that surge into a person's psyche, seemingly without rhyme or reason. One can be in company having ordinary conversations one minute and be in floods of tears the next. People obviously feel sadness and distress, but they may also experience bouts of anger, guilt, anxiety, loneliness and isolation. The mourner may search for their loved one by visiting the graveside, crematorium, or even by staying at home amongst all the clothes and personal belongings. Or the person may become listless, restless and unable to settle, unable to sleep or eat, losing interest in everyday things.

> No one ever told me that grief felt so like fear. I am not afraid, but the sensation is like being afraid. The same fluttering in the stomach, the same restlessness, the yawning. I keep swallowing. (Lewis, 1973: 7)

Individuals may feel they have seen, heard or smelt the dead person. They may feel reluctant to share this initially, fearing being disbelieved. It can be a relief to be informed that this is, in fact, a common occurrence.

Understandably, the person becomes very tired and emotionally drained after weeks and months of emotional turmoil, and this can lead them to feel very low and even depressed. This is a common time for a person to go to their GP, but the link between the depression and the bereavement is not always made. The prescription of antidepressants may be an outcome of such a visit, which does change the way the person feels. Unfortunately, all it does is delay the grieving process, which then goes on hold until the medication is stopped. Grieving is painful, and in order to get to the end of the grieving process, people do need to experience the pain.

Very often, people describe their mourning as a long dark tunnel. The light at the end of this tunnel is the acceptance. Not that the dead person is no longer important and the mourner has 'got over it', but the person can now be remembered with love and affection and without fresh pain. The mourner has adjusted to living without the dead person and can move on to considering a new form of life. How long the process lasts, from start to finish, is as long as a piece of string, but a good rule of thumb is between one and two years (Worden, 1991). The first year is always the worst, as the mourner has to cope with birthdays, Christmas, etc., and thinking, 'This time last year we were doing this.' The first anniversary of the death is often a dreaded event, but can be a benchmark for improvement thereafter. Of course, the extent of the grief is a direct function of the quality and intensity of the relationship lost; the greater the love, the greater the distress, the longer the grieving process. However, there are existential determinants, too. No matter how deeply we may love our parents, there is a sub-vocal expectation that we will outlive them. In that sense we have a preconscious expectation that one day they will die. Similarly, as a couple move into their later years, there becomes another preconscious expectation that, one day, one of them is going to die and leave the other behind. They may even discuss this overtly and make plans. Such anticipated deaths are easier to deal with than the sudden death of a partner in early years, or the death of a child, which produces enormous existential anxiety because it is out of the order of things. Some people seem to assume that if the client is an older adult, they are more used to losses, and therefore not affected so badly. This is a fallacy, and as Twining (1996) points out, the loss of a child is still devastating even if you are 85 and your child was 60.

Angela was a motherly woman whose family was everything to her. Her three children were now all grown up and had children of their own, and

Angela enjoyed being a grandmother. Recently, her own mother had died, and she was finding the death really difficult to cope with. She kept crying all the time and had been unable to return to work for over two months. Her husband was now becoming impatient with her, insisting that she start to 'pull herself together'. The counsellor debriefed the death of Angela's mother, and then asked her if she had experienced any similar feelings before. About 25 years previously, Angela had a fourth child who had died suddenly when she was seven years old. Angela, of course, was devastated. The doctors had told her husband at the time that the best thing he could do was to take her home and get her pregnant again. Another baby would take her mind off her loss. Angela became pregnant straight away, and then would not allow herself to cry for her lost daughter in case her unhappiness damaged the new child. As Angela recounted the experience, and the counsellor encouraged her to talk about it in detail, Angela realised that her present grief was not for her mother so much as for her dead child for whom she had never finished grieving.

There are gender differences in grieving. Culturally men are not expected to express long and painful episodes of emotion. They may cry less, and throw themselves into activities in order to bury the pain.

Blocks to grief

The counsellor will also be referred clients who have been unable to grieve, or are grieving dysfunctionally. Here are some of the reasons why people, consciously or subconsciously, block their grief:

- inability to say goodbye
- harsh words spoken before death
- no body to bury
- being the strong one
- death in violent circumstances
- unfinished business
- not being allowed to grieve (especially children)

Where the death has occurred in violent circumstances, or where a child or young person has disappeared without trace, these are both forms of unfinished business. Grieving will not be considered appropriate until the body is found; there will always be the lingering hope that the person is alive somewhere. If the body is found, grieving will still be put on hold until the perpetrator of the crime has been caught and sentenced. Then the business will be closed and the grieving can begin.

Being 'the strong one' is a common trap that people can fall into – especially English people with their 'stiff upper lip' cultural expectation. One member of the family sees others distressed and decides to keep strong so as not to exacerbate the grief of the others. It is rationalised on the basis that someone has to keep together emotionally otherwise the whole family will go to pieces. So the grief is denied. This is linked to the English cultural desire to sweep death under the carpet. The dead person is whisked away to a chapel of rest, rather than being kept at home, where people are encouraged to visit and say goodbye. Sometimes very little is said at the church service, or the whole celebration may even be dispensed with, with a short, 10-minute crematorium service and with people immediately dispersing. Fortunately, the Celts still feel the need for wakes, and such events allow people to grieve collectively and openly. Other cultures similarly show open, public grieving which encourages the mourning process. Counsellors need to be mindful of the differing cultural and ethnic backgrounds of their clients (Scher et al., 1987), and must understand the differing rituals of death and bereavement. If the counsellor is unsure, it is best to acknowledge this to the client and ask for an explanation, rather than making possibly incorrect assumptions.

Bereaved children

Children can have a bad time when a family member dies. To protect the child from the distress (Bowlby, 1980), particularly if it is a parent or sibling who dies, the child may be sent away to live with another relative while the grieving parent has time to recover. This feels to the child like a double loss: being abandoned by the dead person and the remaining parent. The child is then brought back into the family situation and is expected to carry on living without the dead person as if he or she was never there. The child has also been denied the right to say his own farewells. As Brown (1966) reasons, it is not so much the shock of the bereavement that affects the children, as what happens afterward.

Children who are allowed to grieve present a variety of symptoms similar to those of grieving adults. They may also manifest further behavioural symptoms such as delinquency, stealing, depression, truancy, or a regressive phase at school (Black and Urbanowicz, 1985; Brown, 1966). Childhood grief can have long-lasting effects. Research has shown that adults bereaved of a parent in childhood are more likely to develop psychiatric problems later in life (Brown,

1961; Brown and Harris, 1971), and are more likely to attempt suicide (Birtchnell, 1970; Dorpat, Ripley and Jackson, 1965). Even older children can be traumatised by the death of a parent.

Ron was a 39-year-old managing director of a small company which was doing well. Happily married with two children, he was astonished to find that he was suddenly overcome with bouts of crying. He had no control over these tears, which were totally unpredictable and proving to be embarrassing.

Counsellor: Have you experienced any losses recently?
Client: Losses? No, I have had a fairly uneventful life. The only loss I have ever had was my father who died years ago when I was 16.
Counsellor: When did these bouts of crying actually start?
Client: About two months ago. I remember I took the kids to Wembley to the Freddie Mercury memorial concert. I remember being really overcome at the concert, and really sobbing, but we all put that down to the emotion of the moment. It was a very moving concert. But it seemed that that evening opened the floodgates, and I've been so emotional ever since.
Counsellor: Who did you think about when you were at the concert?
Client: Why . . . my father. I was thinking about my father!

The client then related that when he was 16 he won a scholarship to study for six months in America. Shortly after he had arrived in the States, his father had a sudden heart attack and died. Ron wanted to fly back, but his mother would not let him, reinforcing that his father would have wanted him to stay and finish his studies. He did stay, but when he arrived home six months later, his dad was dead and buried, and everyone had got on with their lives. No one wanted to talk to him of his dad's death, yet Ron had not started his grieving. When he went to the cemetery, it did not seem real. He just could not believe his dad was in there. He realised, in retrospect, that the only time he had cried for his father was when he first heard the news.

Pathological grief

Dysfunctional grieving can take three forms (Bowlby-West, 1983):

1 somatisation into physical symptoms that may include anxiety states, skin eruptions, palpitations, fainting, nightmares, fatigue, gynaecological, urological or intestinal symptoms;
2 identification with physical symptoms of the dead person. Bowlby (1980) describes two children who developed symptoms similar to those of a dead sibling at the time when they reached the same age at which the sibling died;

3   hysterical conversion. In dysfunctional families, adults may develop symptoms similar to those of the dead person, or may replace the dead person with another who has similar physical symptoms. For example, a man whose wife dies of breast cancer may find himself falling in love with a woman who was also having treatment at the oncology unit. Such replacements will abort any grief process temporarily, but may later produce psychosomatic symptoms to cover up the inner distress. This would eventually interfere with the replacement relationship.

Norma was a bright 20-year old with a promising singing career. Her GP referred her to the counsellor as she was experiencing extreme panic attacks and had a need to constantly clear her throat. A feeling of being stifled, or choked, and an inability to breathe precipitated the panic attacks. Norma was under a great deal of stress with her family of origin and this was causing a strain on her relationship with her fiancé. It was felt that because of these problems and the pressures of public appearances, that she was somatising her stress. However, it transpired that her maternal grandmother, who was also a singer, had lived with her parents for the last five years of her grandmother's life. Norma was 10 years old at the time, loved her grandmother very much, and wanted to be like her when she grew up. The grandmother died slowly and painfully with throat cancer, and Norma had vivid recollections of seeing her grandmother gasping for breath as she passed her bedroom door. As Norma's career followed a similar path to her grandmother's, she had subconsciously identified with her illness.

Losing a baby

The incidence of miscarriage, or spontaneous abortion, is high (18.2 per cent: OPCS, 1994), so it is a regular presentation at the GP surgery. After the loss sometimes medical procedures are required in the form of surgical dilation and curettage (D & C). Medical staff deal very well with the medical procedures. What they do not deal with so well is the woman's psychological state. She is often given platitudes to ease her distress; most commonly, 'Well, you're young and healthy dear, go home and try again.' But that is not how a woman feels she wants it to be. She needs time to think about the baby she has lost, and to grieve over it. Women also find it distressing that (spontaneous and surgical) aborted foetuses are sluiced away, so some more forward-thinking hospitals are now arranging communal burial sites and chapel services. When a baby dies *in utero*, women should be given the option of seeing and holding their child. Medical staff do not always give this option, on the grounds that 'it didn't look very nice', so it is whisked away before the woman has a chance to protest. Yet I have found that women who were given the opportunity to see and hold their dead child look beyond the visible deformities and just see their beautiful baby.

Losing a baby through birth trauma (stillbirth) or sudden infant death syndrome (SIDS/cot death) is more traumatising. Giving birth to a dead baby, or finding your baby, whom you have grown to love, dead for no apparent reason, can invoke PTSD (as in the last chapter). As well as the immediate distress of the loss of the child, the mother will continually replay the event in her mind, desperately searching for the answers to the questions: why? was I to blame? why me? Guilt is uppermost: I must have done something really wrong, or I must be a bad person for this to happen to me. Many women experience 'hearing' babies crying in the night and get up out of bed to tend to them. This interrupted sleep adds to their distress.

With cot death, another intervening factor which increases the guilt is the involvement of the police. Although the police are more sensitive to this issue than they used to be, they still have to investigate the sudden death as a potential crime until the post-mortem report is received, which may be a day or two later. This means that the parents have to be interviewed, and the 'scene' of the death is cordoned off and investigated. All this serves to increase the feelings of guilt and blame that the mother is apportioning to herself. Similarly, parents often feel appalled that a post-mortem is required; it is bad enough losing their baby without its body having to be cut up.

Hospitals have now become much more attuned to the trauma of parents who lose a baby. They provide clothing and a cot, and take Polaroid photographs of the child dressed and lying in the cot. They will take hand- and footprints of the dead child, and snips of hair for the parents to keep. The hospital chaplain will arrange a funeral service, which can be conducted at the hospital chapel if the parents wish. All of these arrangements are very rewarding for parents who are still trying to come to terms with the trauma of what has happened to them. The mementoes are very important later on in the grieving process, as the time that the parents spent with the child is so short, they very often begin to wonder if it was at all real. The photos provide confirmation, comfort and a means of sharing the grief with the rest of the family.

Some women choose to terminate their pregnancies because they feel, for whatever reason, that it is not appropriate for them to have a child at that time in their lives. Or they may have been advised to have the termination following scans or amniocentesis tests that predict abnormalities. This is called by the medical profession a 'therapeutic termination', although I feel that this is a contradiction in terms. In my experience, I have found that even women who genuinely did not want to have their baby experienced a sense of loss over it. This is consistent with interviews conducted for the Rawlinson Commission (1994). The reaction does not have to be immediate. The initial response may indeed be one of relief. But later, reality breaks through. It may be years later (Hayton, 1995) when the woman chooses to have a child. A planned pregnancy brings up issues of one's own childhood and lost children. The woman may start wondering what the child would have been like now, what it would be doing, etc., and this can invoke a grieving process. This is less likely to occur if the grieving was completed at the time of the termination. The conflict for the woman is that she feels she should not feel loss, or guilt, or any other feeling because she chose to have the termination. The counsellor can help just by validating and normalising these feelings.

For women who have a termination on the basis of the child's abnormalities, or risk of abnormalities, the feelings are mostly the guilt of 'what ifs?' What if the child had not had an abnormality? What if the tests were wrong? What if the abnormality had been so mild that it could hardly have been detected? What if I have murdered my child unnecessarily? This is especially poignant for women who have already had children, as they have a greater awareness of what they are missing. The termination is also traumatic *per se*, as it will be an induced birth of a dead child. As with stillborn babies, it helps grieving parents if they can hold and say goodbye to their child (no matter what it looks like) and have the appropriate mementoes. Termination leaves a great gaping hole in women's lives, and they want to fill it with another baby, especially when the time is reached when others who were pregnant at the same time as them are now parading around with their new babies. Friedman et al. (1963) warn against couples who seek to replace a child before the grieving is completed. Their study shows that such couples are in danger of having a distorted and pathogenic relationship with their new baby.

> Julie had spent seven years trying to get pregnant. The third IVF (*in vitro* fertilisation) programme had finally succeeded. She had an easy pregnancy and went into labour a week before full term. Suddenly her placenta abrupted (ante-partum haemorrhage), and the medical staff had to fight to save the life of both Julie and her baby. The baby suffered a cerebral bleed during the birth process, which severely damaged his brain. After three days, his life support systems were switched off and he died in Julie's arms. Julie's grief was confinable for six weeks, then she crashed into suicidal despair. Her feelings of loss were not only for her dead baby, but also for her lost fertility. As she was nearly 40, she realised that her chances of having another baby were becoming more remote.

Facing death

Sometimes clients are referred to the counsellor because they have a terminal illness. In my experience, clients facing their own death are often more worried about their nearest and dearest than about their own demise. Of course, there are times when they will feel angry or scared, feeling it's unfair, and grieving for lost opportunities. It is important that the counsellor can make the space for the client to express all these without the counsellor feeling overwhelmed by the inevitability of the situation. But the client also has a lot to do in this period, depending on how well they feel, and whether illness has incapacitated them in any way. There may be places to be visited for the first or last time. There may be visits to distant friends or relatives to say farewells. They may wish to write letters, make a will, or conduct last-minute business. Or they may wish to discuss their own funeral arrangements and their future wishes for their children and partner. This is clearly a lot to do when the person is already feeling weak physically and vulnerable mentally. Even those with a really strong religious faith and perhaps no fear of death may find their beliefs wobble under the strain of it all.

Kübler-Ross (1970) has outlined five stages that people go through before death. These are denial, anger, bargaining, depression and acceptance. But, as with bereavement, I feel that each death is unique with some common threads woven in between. One such thread, if the person lives long enough, is a period of disengagement from their loved ones when death is imminent. Loved ones may feel rejected by this, but really it is a time when all the tasks are done and the person can have the peace and quiet to take stock of what is happening and have some inward reflections. Once again, this may be a time when the dying person wishes to close unfinished business although sometimes they choose not to, and this of course is their right. But most commonly it is a time when the person wants company but peace. They want to feel a loving presence, but they do not want their peace to be invaded.

It may be that the counsellor is seeing a couple, one of whom is facing death. The role of the counsellor is to help the couple come to terms with what is about to happen and help them experience their anticipatory grief. When the one partner dies, the focus of the counsellor moves on to the bereavement issues of the remaining partner. Trust and bonding will already have been set up between this client and the counsellor, and the client will feel comforted that the counsellor knew their dead loved one. It is important to remember, however, that the counsellor will also experience a sense of loss at the absence of the other partner, and this needs to be shared in supervision as well as in the sessions with the remaining partner.

Assessment

If clients tell you that they are finding it difficult to get over someone's death, then of course the assessment is done for you. It is more obscure, however, if the client presents with depression or other symptoms but does not relate it to a loss, as in Ron's case previously described. If a client has an unexplained depression, it should be part of the counsellor's open questioning to ascertain if they have experienced any losses. If the client admits to the loss, but denies a connection to present feelings, it is still worth pursuing for a while to determine the situation. It will soon become clear by the way the client responds whether this issue has been resolved or not. Appropriate questions may therefore be:

• Have you had any losses in the past?
• How close were you to that person?
• Did you have the opportunity to say goodbye?
• Was there any unfinished business?
• What do you miss?
• What don't you miss? (Check out for idealisation of the person: this may suggest a dysfunctional reaction.)

Also in the assessment watch for losses that the client does not interpret as such, like loss of job or relationship, what is missing in your life lately?

All the clients discussed in this chapter were helped with TLT, although Norma also received three additional cognitive-behavioural therapy sessions as her identification with her grandmother was so deeply entrenched.

TLT procedures: helping the bereaved

Having said that a bereavement process is anywhere between one and two years, why am I including bereavement counselling in therapy that lasts for fewer than six sessions? Firstly, we know that bereavement counselling helps reduce the risk of psychiatric and psychosomatic disorders (Parkes, 1980). Secondly, we know that bereavement is strongly associated with increased risk of morbidity and mortality (Stroebe and Stroebe, 1987), and thirdly those who do have counselling benefit a great deal from the counsellor just normalising the feelings and giving permission to grieve. It is unnecessary for the counsellor to be with the client throughout the bereavement process, so long as the counsellor can be available at critical times. Such times may be: a month after the death when the help of friends and relatives has started to dwindle, anniversaries, birthdays, and some time around Christmas. Even though the gaps between these sessions may be longer than for other presenting problems, the client still feels contained and held by the counsellor, knowing that they can go over the same ground as they have done in the past without fear of rejection or boredom. One important point: always refer to the facts of death. Do not use euphemisms like 'passed over', 'gone to sleep' or 'gone to Jesus'. And always refer to the dead person by name.

When the counsellor realises that a loss is involved in the client's presenting issue, the counsellor should **explore** the client's loss. Once again attention to detail is crucial. Some clients will want to rush through the telling of the story, as if its awfulness will go away if you stop speaking about it. Open questions as to the details of the sequence of the events are therefore vital to the debriefing process:

* What was the person like?
* How close was your relationship?
* Did you know it was likely to happen?
* What was the weather like on that day?
* What would you have done on that day if this had not happened?
* When did you first realise that something bad was going to happen?
* What was your feeling then?
* Were you with the person when he died?
* What did that feel like?
* Did you visit the person after the death?
* How did he seem to you?
* Are you glad you went?/Do you regret not going?
* Did you have to make the funeral arrangements?
* How did that feel for you?
* How did the funeral go?
* Who has been most helpful in supporting you?

These questions should not be fired at the client in rapid succession, but should slowly and gently take the client through the story, allowing plenty of spaces for crying and silence for remembering. Non-verbal communication, like handing a box of tissues, gives the client permission to keep on crying. This form of debriefing aids the person to conceptualise what has happened, and to start filing the appropriate, less traumatic parts away in the memory bank. It also allows the counsellor to explore whether there has been any form of unfinished business to resolve.

In addition, it is necessary to find out if the presenting loss is the only loss that the client has experienced, or whether there have been others that may be compounding the present one. Our memory is mood linked, and present distress reminds us of times we have felt like that before. As with Angela's case, the presenting bereavement may not be the one that is causing the difficulties.

When counselling women who have lost babies, the line of questioning should follow a similar debriefing format, tracing the story through the pregnancy and birth and/or loss of the child. Once again, attention to minutiae helps the client to move away from the trauma of the situation. Ask the client what the child's name was going to be, and always refer to the child by that name, rather than 'your baby'. Ask, also, if the client is willing to show you the photos of her baby. This is not at all ghoulish as the photos look like pictures of pretty sleeping babies. Clients respond favourably to this request, as very few people want to see the photos, which feels to the mother like a rejection of her baby.

Newly bereaved clients, who may still be in shock or denial, may need to keep going over and over the events in their minds. The counselling session provides the opportunity for them to do so.

Sonia had just arrived home from picking up her children from school, when she saw the police car outside her house. They had called to tell her that her husband, Dave, had been killed in a climbing accident that afternoon. Sonia could not believe it. Dave was an experienced climber and instructor, and the climb he was taking the students up that day was a relatively simple one. She thought the police must have made a mistake and had got the wrong man. How could it be? He had done this climb hundreds of times before, both with and without students. It just did not make sense. After identifying Dave's body, Sonia demanded to be taken to the place where the fall occurred. She wanted to see the place where he lost his grip, the tree that he bounced against, and the ledge where his body crashed to a stop. She interrogated the people who were with him on the climb, and the paramedics who tried to revive him. How long did they try? She questioned the pathologist who conducted the post-mortem, the mortuary attendants, the ambulance drivers and the police. At the funeral, with a captive audience, she was still questioning. Other people were becoming extremely uncomfortable in having to relate their stories over and over again. But until all the facts were clear in her head, until she could make any sense of it, she could not allow herself to grieve.

Exploration forms the major part of bereavement counselling, allowing the client to express feelings that others may find uncomfortable. As the emotions do pop up all over the place, without apparent control, the client may express fears of cracking up or madness. The client therefore needs to **understand** that this is usual. It is important for the counsellor to normalise these feelings. Not by sharing a theoretical overview, but by reinforcing how awful it is, how painful it is, and how other people given similar circumstances respond in similar ways. The counsellor will see the expression of relief break over the client's face when he realises that other people also feel that bad when they are grieving. It is just that no one talks about it.

Clients can also understand the importance of saying goodbye, and resolving unfinished business. I find that the Gestalt technique of the empty chair is an ideal way of helping a client through these issues. This was the technique used with Ron, mentioned earlier, whose father had died when he was a young lad:

> *Client*: I see now, that I should have flown back to be at my father's funeral. I did not have the chance to say goodbye to him or to support my mother with her grief. I resented it all being over with when I got home. I just felt excluded from everything.
>
> *Counsellor*: You couldn't say goodbye to your father then, but you could try to now. Would you like to try?
>
> *Client*: Y. . .yes, I think so.
>
> *Counsellor*: Don't look so nervous Ron, just relax and look at that chair over there. Take your time, and in your mind's eye, I would like you to imagine that your father is sat in the chair, just as you remembered him when you left him when you were 16. Take your time, staying relaxed, and when you have a clear picture of your father, you can speak to him. [*Ron paused for a few minutes, staring at the chair, then he started talking. He told his father how much he had missed him, and how guilty he had felt at not returning for the funeral. He went on to tell his father what occupation his studies had led him to, and that he was now married with two children. He was disappointed, he added, that his father and his children would never know each other. At this Ron started weeping inconsolably. After some five minutes, Ron calmed again, and looked at the counsellor.*]
>
> *Counsellor*: Ron, I would like you to go and sit in that chair, your father's chair, and reply to yourself as if you were your father. Take your time, relax, and imagine yourself in the empty chair.

Ron was soon replying to himself. He was telling his son how proud he was of his achievements, and how proud he was of his grandchildren. The counsellor noted that the voice tone and pitch were different from Ron's during this conversation. Ron swapped places two more times. On his own initiative the conversation was brought to a close after they expressed their love and said their farewells.

Before this form of technique is approached, a strong bond of trust must be established between the counsellor and the client. If the client expresses reluctance, however, the technique should never be pressed.

Another way of dealing with unfinished business is to give the client a homework task of writing a letter to the dead person, or writing poetry, once again expressing all the things that were left unsaid or undone. This can be a very cathartic process for clients, and they may wish to read the letters to the counsellor or they may wish to keep them private. It also helps if they can go to the place where they feel closest to the dead person, which may be the cemetery, a favourite place – back garden, wherever – and re-read the letter as a way of delivering it. Some women have found it valuable to write a letter to their dead baby, expressing all the shattered hopes and dreams that they had for the little life. Some have shown this letter to other members of the family, who may have become a little impatient with the client's grief, as the only means to get them to understand how they truly felt.

The goal of this stage of the counselling process is for the client to understand that any unfinished business needs to be closed.

Miriam could not understand why she could not get over the death of her mother some nine months before. Miriam was one of three children whom the mother used to play off, one against the other. Miriam had an unhappy childhood, always feeling the scapegoat of the family, and always being the one that 'got the good hiding'. As an adult, Miriam's relationship with her mother was ambivalent. Sometimes Miriam would be in favour, other times the other two siblings would be set against her. At the time of her mother's death, Miriam and her mother had not spoken for six months. Miriam actually preferred this state of affairs because at least she was left alone. But her mother sent for her, and as she knew her mother was soon to die, Miriam went. She arrived at the hospital minutes before her mother died. Her mother did not say anything, she only smiled at her and then died. Miriam had interpreted this smile as a reconciliation. The blow was soon to come, however, when the will was read. Instructions had been left that the will was to be read publicly immediately after the funeral at a gathering at the family home. However, a (probably well-planned) crisis in the solicitor's family meant that the will was not read until two days later at a small family gathering. The will attacked Miriam without mercy for being a wayward and ungrateful child who abused and neglected her poor lonely old mother. Miriam was totally disinherited, all worldly goods being left to her brother and sister. Miriam was mortified, not so much at being disinherited, although she could not believe how avaricious her siblings had become. But what she could not get over was that this attack was planned to be public. She also realised that the smile that her mother had given her at the end was not one of reconciliation, but one of satisfaction that Miriam had actually turned up, allowing her plan to succeed. Miriam could not let go of the viciousness of her mother's plan; her mind churning it over and over, night after night without sleep. The counsellor knew that this business needed to be closed.

Counsellor: Miriam, what do you feel your mother wanted to do to you by this? What do you feel she hoped to achieve?

Client: She wanted to destroy me! She wanted to get to me even from beyond the grave!
Counsellor: She was successful in that, wasn't she?
Client: Yes, she succeeded all right. How will I ever be the same again? How can I ever live with the shame?
Counsellor: So mother has won then? You have let her win?
[*Miriam looked up sharply and took a deep breath.*]
Client: No, she has not won, because I will not let her win!.

Miriam did not have a sleepless night about her mother thereafter.

Most of the **action** that the client needs to do will relate to the sorts of tasks that Worden (1991) proposed. These will be tasks like clearing out the belongings of the dead person, learning the skills of the jobs that the dead person used to do, or just going out and meeting others rather than becoming trapped in lonely isolation. Some clients may start to panic and may want to make life-changing decisions. Although we cannot advise our clients, we can warn against the advisability of this. For example, moving house within a year of bereavement (unless the client is forced to by circumstances of the death) may lead to an unwise choice and thus an expensive mistake. Similarly, entering into another committed relationship within two years of losing a loving partner is really a psychological replacement, and, as already has been discussed, does not promise well for the long-term prospects of that new relationship.

Helping the terminally ill

There are two ways the counsellor in General Practice may be required to help those who are dying: either by helping the ill person to come to terms with facing his own death, or by helping the prime caregiver (usually the spouse or the adult child) to cope with the death of the one she loves. In the former, the role of the counsellor will be predominantly to support the client through the process as he nears death. The procedures will be explorative in allowing the client to understand what is happening to him and to determine what he wants to do, if anything, in the time he has left. In the latter case, the role of the counsellor is all of those previously mentioned, plus an advisory role for those clients who have not faced death before and therefore do not understand process and procedures. Such clients will continually ask the counsellor for advice in certain situations, and I feel it is important under these circumstances to provide information. The following case highlights my point:

Peter first attended the counsellor presenting with stress at work. He also had a chronic stressor of his wife's, Alison's, breast cancer which had been treated two years previously, but had clearly traumatised him. At his second session, he had received the news that Alison's cancer had returned and the prognosis was poor. The counselling focus therefore changed from stress management strategies to helping him come to terms with his wife's illness and the probability that she was going to die. Peter and Alison had a young son, James, who, along with his wife's illness, became the focus of Peter's sessions. As the cancer became more aggressive, the focus of the counselling changed to: how can I give my wife a good life for the time that she has left, and how can I prepare myself for being a single parent?

The counsellor and GP spoke regularly of the progress of both Alison and Peter, so the counsellor was well informed of how soon the death was going to be. The GP shared with the counsellor his disappointment that Peter felt he could not let Alison die at home, because he felt he would be unable to cope. The counsellor realised that as death was to be within days, the focus of the next session had to be changed again to: how can I give my wife a good death, and how can I prepare my son for his mother's death? The counsellor asked Peter, if the shoe was on the other foot, where would he like to be when he died? What would he want? Peter realised that Alison should stay at home and that he would be able to cope with everything because of all the back-up support he was receiving from the primary health care team.

Peter's mother-in-law came to stay in the weeks leading up to her daughter's death, and this gave Peter support and help, but also presented him with a dilemma. Peter had been asking the counsellor about how to prepare his son, and the counsellor had advised honesty and openness, and recommended books that he could read with his son about dying and death. Mother-in-law disagreed. She wanted the child to be protected from the death, and for all details to be kept from him. Peter asked the counsellor: what should he do? Would he be damaging his son by allowing him to see his mother die? The counsellor pointed out that children deal with death much better than adults do, provided that they are involved and informed. Peter went home and told his son that his mummy was going to die. They talked about it, and cried together, but James dealt with the news very well. Alison died two days later in the night. Peter, would not allow Alison's body to be taken away until James had woken in the morning and had seen his mother dead. James explored his mother's face in great detail, opening her eyes and her mouth, checking for reactions. Then he kissed her and said goodbye.

When the funeral was over, Peter's mother-in-law prepared to go home. She admitted to Peter that she had not agreed with the way he had dealt with James over Alison's death. Children were not involved in such aspects of death in her day. However, she admitted that now she felt differently. James had handled the situation very well.

They all had different kinds of grief. James had lost a mother, Peter had lost a wife, his mother-in-law had lost a child; but they had all grieved together as a family.

Time-limited therapy for clients with a terminal illness may sound paradoxically harsh. If the client's time is limited anyway, why place a limit on the number of sessions for therapy? In my experience, GPs usually lift the restriction on the number of sessions in these cases on compassionate grounds. However, I find that the number of sessions taken up by the client rarely exceeds six anyway. Why? Often because the client has too many other things to do in addition to being physically weak and emotionally vulnerable. But, of course, most of it depends on the length of time between the news and the death. In some cases it will only be weeks, in other cases months or even a couple of years. Sometimes the time estimated is wrong: for example someone who is told they have only three months may in fact last a couple of years. It is unlikely that the person will want therapy for this length of time.

Receiving a diagnosis of terminal illness constitutes a life (or death) crisis which makes people re-evaluate their values and goals and creates feelings of anxiety and depression (Lair, 1996). Much of the counsellor's approach in the early stages of TLT will depend on whether there was already a relationship between the client and the counsellor before the client knew she was going to die, or whether the counsellor was involved in informing the client of this news.

Breaking bad news

Sometimes, the GP will ask the counsellor to help tell a client some bad news about his, or someone else's, terminal condition. GPs are used to telling patients bad news, but that of course does not mean they do it well. A doctor's goal is to cure, so an inability to do so can produce a sense of frustration or feelings of failure. So, it may be because of the GP's own sense of inadequacy or sense of failure that the news may be told quickly and abruptly, with no real time for the person to absorb the awfulness of what has just been said. For GPs to involve the counsellor in this is not a cowardly way out, but a means of using the special relationship built up between the counsellor and the client. If a GP asks me for help in this area, I invite the GP into the counselling session at an early stage. I give the client five minutes or so to settle and tell me any burning issues. I then tell the client that the GP would like to come and discuss the current situation in the session, if they are agreeable. When permission is given, the GP can then deliver the news and answer any medical questions that the client may wish to ask. The GP then leaves, giving the client the time and opportunity to explore the news just received in more depth with the counsellor. This is a much less brutal way of hearing and conceptualising the unwelcome message.

Some simple rules for the counsellor in this situation:

1   Never be tempted to discuss medical situations outside your own realm of factual knowledge.
2   Always be truthful. If the client is in denial over, say, the length of the prognosis, it does not help the client for the counsellor to collude with that denial. If the doctor has said the patient has 'weeks' to live, and the client is interpreting this as 'months' then it is important to reinforce the real time scale.
3   Always prepare the client for the receipt of bad news: 'Dr Jones would like to come and talk to you in about five minutes as he has some bad news from your wife's latest tests. He has already spoken to her about this, and she has asked him to tell you the results. Do you feel able and willing to see him for this, or would you prefer to discuss it another time?'
4   If it is known in advance that the bad news is to be given at a particular session, make arrangements in advance. Arrange for the client to be accompanied home from the surgery, and ensure that the person is not left alone for a considerable period immediately after hearing the news. This will prevent any impulsive suicidal behaviour.
5   Make sure that the client has an appointment to return for counselling within a week of hearing the news.

We have already discussed Kübler-Ross's concept of stages of dying, and denial is an important aspect of the death process. As mentioned in relation to grieving, denial has its usefulness, and is a natural part of the process. When a counsellor is exploring the forthcoming death of the client, it is not for the counsellor to try and force the client out of his denial (Lair, 1996). This denial may come and go, so people talk about dying in one session, then make plans for returning to work in the next. At the same time, the counsellor must not collude with the denial. It is necessary, therefore, before seeing the client, to check with the GP on the progression of the illness and on the prognosis, which may be continually changing.

Research has shown that people who are dying have special needs for an appropriate death (Weisman, 1972) and tend to have common agendas that they wish to pursue. These are: having control, hearing painful truths, reviewing the past, maintaining a sense of humour, ensuring the presence of significant others, making physical expressions of caring, and talking about spiritual issues (Smith and Maher, 1993). Whereas some of these issues would come up naturally anyway, the counsellor needs to be mindful that it is the client's own agenda that has to be followed in the sessions, not the one that the counsellor may feel more appropriate, based on her own belief system. So, if the client wants to plot revenge against a family member rather than making his peace, or if she wants to plan her own funeral and wake rather than considering any spiritual aspects of her death, then that must be the agenda that is followed. Working through life-long emotional or psychological problems should be avoided, with the focus on psychological comfort and helping the person achieve a sense of peacefulness (Lair, 1996).

It may be that some of the last sessions conducted with the client will be domiciliary. These may be very much harder to conduct than sessions in the consulting room, as the set-up of the room may not allow for confidentiality. There may be carers around who feel resentful of the intrusion into their domain, feeling out of control and full of anticipatory grief. And other family members or friends may try to obtain 'counselling on the hoof' by unloading all their sorrows in an informal way as you arrive or leave. Boundaries are very hard to enforce, but being drawn into long quasi-counselling conversations is a mistake.

The counsellor should always take the death of a client to supervision, for the counsellor to explore his own loss issues.

Counselling for bereavement and loss, and counselling people facing death, in time-limited therapy offers clients a valuable means of feeling supported and held through the critical period of their grief. It is important to stress that not all bereaved clients will either want or need counselling. There will also be clients for whom six sessions will be nowhere near enough. Referral to Cruse Bereavement Care will provide the long-term help and support that a few clients may need. Cruse provides any bereaved person with either individual or group counselling by trained counsellors. They also provide advice and information on practical problems and social contact.

Recommended reading

For adults:
Lewis, C.S. (1973) *A Grief Observed*. London: Faber & Faber.
Surviving Bereavement (Church of Scotland video)
Tatelbaum, J. (1981) *The Courage to Grieve: Creative Living, Recovery, and Growth Through Grief*. London: Heinemann.
For children:
Perkins, G. and Morris, L. (1991) *Remembering Mum*. London: A. & C. Black.
Stickney, D. (1984) *Waterbugs and Dragonflies*. Dublin: Mowbray.

8

Counselling Individuals or Couples with Relationship Difficulties

People often visit their GP when they are having difficulties with their relationships. Although it is not a medical problem, people experience a lot of physical symptoms as a result of their problems at home. These may include insomnia, headaches, depression or anxiety. Medication will attenuate the physical symptoms, but they will persist whilst the relationship difficulty remains. GPs frequently find themselves responding to requests for advice from patients as to what should be done in certain marital situations. It is therefore with immense relief that some GPs happily direct their patients to the counsellor down the corridor, rather than advise on a situation when they are unqualified to do so. This chapter will examine some of the more common relationship scenarios of adultery, sexuality dysfunction, marital violence and infertility. The discussions will be considered to be appropriate whether the relationship is heterosexual or homosexual, although there is a section that looks at the issues more specific to homosexual relationships towards the end of this chapter.

A client may attend the surgery and start talking about a poor lifestyle and poor self-worth, and the counsellor realises that it is the person's partner who is causing much of this unhappiness for one reason or another. This then presents the counsellor with a dilemma, because the chances are that as the counselling work progresses, it will disrupt the family system so much that it may cause the end of the relationship. Although it is the client's responsibility as to whether he chooses to stay in a relationship or not, there are people who are in such a state of denial of their own behaviour that they blame the counsellor for the end of the marriage. It is for this reason that therapists have been sideswiped as marriage wreckers (Fay Weldon's book, *Affliction*, being a case in point).

> Monica was an extremely attractive and well-contained woman in her early forties. She was married with two sons and worked part-time with her husband in their business. She had been suffering acute panic attacks for some time, which were interfering with her work and social life. As she talked to the counsellor, it became increasingly obvious that the main catalyst for the panic attacks was her husband Julian's inability to control his temper. When things went wrong at work, he would fly into a fury, of

which she would get the brunt. She admitted that she was indeed afraid of him when he was like that although he never got physical with her at work. At home he would push or shove her around, but then take himself off and sleep on the couch for two or three days without speaking to her. A reluctant truce would eventually be made, and everything would be all right for a week or two, when the pattern would start again. She also found him continually critical and totally manipulative. As Monica talked about the difficulties that she had experienced in her relationship over the years, she came to the conclusion that not only did she no longer love her husband, but that she did not like him very much either. She decided to ask for a divorce. Hell had no fury like Julian's wrath over the next few months as Monica slowly but decidedly separated herself both physically and financially from him. One day, Julian stalked into the GP's surgery, and even though the GP was in the middle of a consultation with another patient, Julian started to bawl the GP out. 'It's all your fault!' he screamed. 'You and that damned counsellor of yours! Do you know she is a marriage wrecker? Well, if you didn't, you do now! My marriage was fine until my wife started seeing her! Now my wife will have nothing to do with me. That woman has poisoned my wife against me! I have a good mind to sue the both of you!'

The psychology of relationships

It helps when dealing with relationship issues to have an under-standing of the psychology of how relationships work, and what is happening when they start breaking down. We know that people are attracted to others who are similar to themselves in terms of values, belief systems, and levels of attractiveness (Marks and Miller, 1987; Stroebe et al., 1971). Paradoxically, we also know that some rela-tionships survive through complementarity: that opposites attract and complement each other like pepper and salt. However, research shows that these kinds of relationships tend to be in the minority. Falling in love is virtually impossible to research objectively, but there has been some evidence on how people behave in given situations. Stereotypically it is thought that women want romance from their relationship. This is true on one level, but women are also the pragmatic half of the relationship. Men tend to be the pure romantics when they fall in love, whereas women think of more practical issues like 'Will he be able to look after me? Will he be a good father to my children?' before they allow themselves to fall in love. This pragmatism stays with the woman throughout the relationship and if it is going to end, she is more likely to end it. Of course, these are all generalisations, and it is more likely to be the unusual case that is taken to the doctor for help.

The pioneering work of Gottman (Gottman and Levenson, 1988; Levenson and Gottman, 1985) has led to a much better understanding of relationships that are faltering. In particular, gender differences in communication interfere when a couple do not communicate well: she wants to talk about feelings and he wants to solve problems. Gottman is able to predict with some accuracy those relationships that are likely to succeed by monitoring their communication patterns and physiological processes. He has also identified various communicative styles between couples that will predict that the relationship will end. In particular, a form of emotional withdrawal occurs in one partner, whereby nothing the other partner says or does has any effect thereafter. Thus the person has emotionally separated from the partner before physically doing so. Research has shown that communication is just one of ten common presenting difficulties in marital relationships. The others are money, intimacy, work and leisure, parenting, household chores, extended family, religion or culture, friends, and substance abuse (Markman et al., 1978).

Adult developmental transitions

To understand relationship difficulties, the counsellor needs to understand adult developmental transitions. As adults progress through their lives, they move through certain phases. This normal developmental progress from young adult to elderly person involves a transition every 10 or 15 years (Levinson, 1978). These transitions bring with them a certain amount of existential anxiety, making people question where they are in life and where they are going. They will be asking of themselves 'What do I like in my life, where do I want to go, and what do I want to change?' The focus of the questions will predominantly be on home, relationships and careers.

A young woman may, in her early adult transition into marriage, be looking for someone who will make a suitable long-term partner, who will provide a home away from her parents, and provide a family. For an Edwardian or Victorian, the life-long commitment was for an average period of seven years, as the average life-span for an adult was 42 years. This period of commitment was within one adult developmental transition so it was unnecessary for a couple to go through a reappraisal process. There were as many second marriages then as there are today, only then the second marriage followed widowhood rather than divorce. Now people are living into their nineties, the life-long commitment takes on new meaning. People no longer feel that when they marry it will be for life. With the divorce rate being one in three, and one in two for second marriages, the trend we are now seeing is serial monogamy. What people are committing themselves to now, therefore, is a long-term monogamous relationship for however long it may last.

The next transition is likely to come after the arrival of two or three children. The trend is still for the average 2.4 children per family, but there is a growing number of couples who choose to have no children at all and devote their lives to their careers. This is particularly the case now as women are no longer socially prohibited from entering challenging careers, and childless women are no longer isolated and considered selfish. For those who do choose to have families, however, larger homes need to be considered, and greater income is needed to provide for them all; thus the careers of both the father and the mother will need to be considered. It is now less common for women to stay at home to look after their children and do nothing else. Most find some sort of part-time work to supplement the family income if they do not return to a full-time career. Nicolson (1990) found that in relation to men's behaviour in the role of father there are contradictions between the expectations of women and the promises of men prior to having the children in comparison with after the children have arrived. This inevitably causes conflict and strain within the relationship, as the women feel let down.

The next transition will be when people reach middle forties, and the children are more independent. An evaluation process occurs where the person examines particularly his relationship and the career that he is in. The demands of young children are not so great, although the financial demands of looming university places may be a consideration. He will be evaluating his life, halfway through, and considering the remaining half. 'When the children have left home, is this the woman I want to be alone with and go into retirement with?' It is a common time for people to start having extra-marital affairs as they find through their evaluation that their relationship is unsatisfactory; hence the coining of the term 'mid-life crisis'. However, it is not a crisis for the person who is readjusting, it is only a crisis for the person who may be discarded in the process.

As people prepare for their retirement, another transition takes place. New roles have to be adopted as people adjust to the label 'old age pensioner'. In our society, this is a less valued position than it would be in, say, Chinese culture, so questions about identity and self-worth are invariably asked. Relationships need to be evaluated yet again. No longer can she escape from him by going to work. Instead, they are thrown together under the same roof for 24 hours each day. The relationship needs to be a good one to survive, as poor relationships put a physical strain on the individual. This is one of the reasons that post-retirement has a high mortality rate. Housing also has to be reviewed in the light of changing needs and fewer demands.

The final transition comes when people reach 75–80. Those who have lost a spouse through death may consider remarrying, even if they are living in sheltered or residential accommodation. Death may become a looming prospect, with plans made for funerals and property, or it may be dismissed for fear of facing the inevitable.

These adult transitions seem relatively straightforward. However, with our new form of serial monogamy, new relationships may be formed with people in a separate transition from one's own.[1] And, of course, new relationships are not just formed with individuals, but with the family package they come with, which may mean children from one or even more previous relationships. Step-parenting presents a whole new agenda when dealing with family difficulties and will be addressed in Chapter 11.

> Judi fell in love with Brian when she was 18 years old. He was 30 at the time, and he was married with two children. The relationship for Judi was exciting, very sexual, and the secrecy of their meetings added a spice that she had not experienced before. After six months of a clandestine affair, Brian's wife found out and asked him to leave the marital home. With nowhere else to go, he moved into Judi's flat. He made it clear, however, that following the hurt he had recently experienced, he could not consider marrying again, nor would he consider having more children. Fearing she might lose him, Judi readily agreed to his terms, and they lived a relatively uneventful life for the next 11 years. When Judi came to the counsellor, it was just before her thirtieth birthday. She felt resentful of Brian, who she felt had cheated her out of the normal things that girls have, like a fancy wedding and children. He still emphatically refused to marry her or consider children. Judi's biological urge to reproduce was taking over and she started to become obsessive about other people's babies. She also found Brian, who was now 41, dull, staid and boring. They rowed incessantly.

Sexuality difficulties

Many relationships flounder when couples start experiencing difficulties within their sexual relationship. The most common complaint presented at surgery seems to be one partner's loss of sexual desire. Either partner may attend with the complaint, but most commonly it is the partner with the loss of desire, sometimes at the other partner's insistence. As I have mentioned in other chapters, loss of libido is a common symptom of psychological distress, and it is also a common side-effect of psychotropic medication. But this loss of desire may also be due to environmental factors. If the client is a young woman with small children, she may feel so tired all the time that sex is the last thing she wants when she crawls off into bed. Similarly, if the client is a middle-aged man with a stressful managerial job, he may feel he cannot cope with the pressure of performing in a sexual role as well.

But loss of desire may also be a symptom of a relationship difficulty. The couple may be growing apart, and their sexual needs may be changing. There are no rules of thumb for frequency of sexual intercourse in happy couples. Some may be blissfully happy with daily intercourse, others weekly, others may be annually. It only becomes a problem when there is a discrepancy between the couple as to how often each feels sex *should* occur.

Another important factor to ascertain is whether the lack of sex is purely due to loss of libido, or whether there is an element of manipulation going on in the relationship. Although sex is instinctual, it is capable of being switched on and off (Street and Smith, 1988). Withdrawing sex is a common weapon to use, particularly for a woman who feels disgruntled about another aspect of the relationship. For example, if she is unhappy about how often he goes out to the pub with his friends, she may feel that withdrawing sex when he has been out will encourage him to stay at home with her. Or there may be a discrepancy in sexual repertoire which makes one of the partners wish to withdraw from sex. For example, she may wish to involve other couples as part of their foreplay, or he may wish to have anal sex. If the couple are unable to discuss what they like and what they do not like about sex, secret resentments build up and desire is lost. Couples develop a number of methods to provide distance in their relationship when intimacy is under threat. The man working long hours or going to the pub limits the amount of time when intimacy can be expected, or the woman may encourage a fretting child to come into the parents' bed in order to keep her husband at bay. Triangulation is a common method used by both genders; if the focus remains on the child or children, there is no time for each other and the fear of intimacy or the threat of rejection that that may bring.

Probably the next most common sexuality problem is erectile dysfunction. This may be either failure of erection during intercourse, or inability to obtain an erection in the first place. Here the GP and the counsellor need to work in unison, as the dysfunction may have either a physical or a psychological causation. A common prophylactic, whether the cause is physical or psychological, is the injection of papaverine, a powerful smooth muscle relaxant, into the erectile tissues of the penis. A man injects himself, or he is injected by his partner, which produces an erection within 10 minutes, allowing intercourse to take place. The advantage of this is that even if the erectile failure is psychological, all fears of inadequacy and failure are removed. The disadvantages, however, are that all spontaneity of lovemaking is removed as the man has to stop to inject. He may also find it extremely embarrassing to have to do so if he is not within a long-term and trusted relationship. Plus the erection may not go down for up to four hours (priapism), which some men find distressing and painful.

Other common sexuality dysfunctions for the male are: premature (before penetration), retarded (no emission) or retrograde (semen flowing into the bladder) ejaculation. There are also men who have an inability to get in touch with their feelings and who therefore treat sexual activity as a mechanical rather than an affective process. Cole (1988), a specialist in psychosexual therapy, suggests that such men are more likely to be accountants, solicitors and electrical engineers! For the woman, common dysfunctions are: anorgasmia (inability to achieve orgasm), vaginismus (muscle spasms in the vagina) and dyspareunia (painful sex). These women may be referred to the counsellor, but it is more likely that the GP will refer them to a psychosexual therapist.

Infertility

When a young couple marry, a common goal is that they will eventually have children, and it often does not occur to them at this stage that there might be difficulties in conception. However, as the months pass and no baby arrives, pressure builds up within the relationship. They will both be asking of themselves: whose fault is it? will I be blamed? There will also be feelings of inadequacy at not being able to do what others can do so easily. Then, as they start undergoing medical tests and procedures, a great intrusion occurs into a hitherto private aspect of their relationship. Some feel much embarrassment at the questions being asked, or at having to provide specimens in bottles. Making love ceases to be a spontaneous activity, but becomes mechanical and must be done to order when the time in the woman's cycle is right rather than when they feel like it. Women respond to the disappointment of infertility significantly more than men, and take longer to come to terms with it (Brand, 1989). Often the women become obsessed by their childlessness, envying and resenting their friends who can produce babies one after the other. IVF programmes are scarce on the NHS, and the number of times a couple can try a programme are limited. Paying privately can cost thousands of pounds. So a woman is likely to feel desperation as she sees her chances of childbirth slipping away.

Most common presentations to the counsellor in this situation are when the couple reach the end of the treatment programme and have to decide between adoption, fostering or childlessness. Also, when a child conceived with difficulty is lost due to ectopic positioning, miscarriage or post-partum haemorrhage. Here the grief experienced is greater because of the greater emotional investment in the pregnancy together with the fear that another conception may not occur.

Adultery

There is very little research into the dynamics of extra-marital (or partnership) affairs (Kell, 1992), yet I find that it is the most common cause of relationship breakdown that I see in General Practice. It may be presented in one of two ways: either the person who is having the affair comes for help in deciding which person he should stay with, or the person who is left out (and considers herself to be the victim in the scenario) comes for help with the grief.

It is rare for a person involved in an extra-marital relationship to attend the surgery with a request for help with making a decision. It is more likely that he will come under the guise of increasing stress and inability to cope. Then, on exploration of the stressors, it emerges that the individual is leading a double life trying to keep two relationships going at once. When you consider how much emotional investment it takes to keep one relationship afloat, it is hardly surprising that these people are crumbling under the strain of stress!

> Roger was a company director who had embarked on an affair with his secretary, who gave him the love and attention that he had not received from his wife for years. As the counsellor helped him to explore his preference, he became quite clear that he loved his secretary Louise, and wanted to be with her. He therefore planned in his first counselling session how to tell his wife, and discussed arrangements for moving out. He went home and told his wife Sarah. However, he was shocked by her response. Instead of haranguing him and insisting that he left immediately as he had expected, she took partial responsibility for the affair. She was deeply hurt, but reinforced her love and commitment to him, and offered him as much time and space as he wanted to sort himself out. Roger's old feelings of love and respect for Sarah resurfaced. At his next counselling session he realised that he could not leave Sarah after all their years

together, and he did not want to hurt their teenage children. In his second session, therefore, he made plans to end his relationship with Louise. He went home, had a loving reunion with Sarah and ended his affair with Louise. At his third counselling session he was distraught. He could not bear to see Louise so upset. She was hardly speaking to him. He felt guilty for hurting her so much and he realised how much he loved her. He would have to leave Sarah, and go and live on his own somewhere, and restart his relationship with Louise, hopefully to marry her one day. He left the session, made up with Louise and made plans to leave Sarah. However, by the fourth session, he had changed his mind again. He had worked hard to have a nice home. He had good friends and good relationships with his family of origin. As he made public his intentions, these people whom he cared about started to turn against him. The prospect of living alone in a small flat after his luxurious five-bedroom home also seemed grim. The only person who had not turned against him was Sarah, who, despite losing a considerable amount of weight through worry, steadfastly supported him and continued to reinforce her love. He realised he could not leave her. He ended his relationship with Louise, this time for good. Sarah and Roger later went to Relate for help with their marriage difficulties.

Marital violence

Women usually present to their GP with fears about the damage of bruises and broken bones.[2] They will reluctantly admit that their partner has inflicted the damage, and often feel embarrassment and shame. The violence is commonly alcohol related, when gentle and caring husbands turn abusive and aggressive through drink. The husband may stagger home from the pub late at night to be greeted by a disapproving and argumentative wife. Feeling guilt and outrage at the criticism, he lashes out at her. Children may be watching in fear and anxiety at the doorway as they see Dad hitting or kicking Mum. Or they may rush and hide under the bedcovers, crying and wishing it would all stop. The whole family is damaged in these abusive households.

Jealousy and insecurity are other catalysts of violence. Para-doxically, the man loves the woman so much, he cannot contain his feelings. He fears losing her, so he questions and cross-questions her about where she has been and what she has been doing. He knows she looks good, so he blames her for every sideways glance she may get from another man. He bullies her into making herself look less attractive, so he can feel sure of keeping her. The violence starts. She has changed both physically and emotionally through the constant fear and oppression. He resents her change, no longer feels so attracted to her, and has no respect for her. The violence escalates.

This power and control over another human being is addictive. Although he no longer feels the same about her, she will only leave when *he* feels that he wants her to go. If she tries to leave, she will get even worse from him. Her fear of leaving him becomes even greater than her fear of staying. She is humiliated, demoralised and trapped.

But some women do not want to leave violent husbands:

Sylvia was originally married to a workaholic. Her husband gave her a good living, but she never saw him as he worked seven days a week at his business. He did not like her to work, so she spent most of her time on her own waiting for the children to come home. She was very lonely, so when the children were older, she left her husband and children and went to live in a little flat. She found herself a job, and it was there that she met George. George was a gentle giant of a man who was very caring and considerate. He took her shopping at weekends, they spent their lunch breaks together, and they spent their evenings together. Within two months, Sylvia had moved into George's home. She so enjoyed the attention she got from him that she took no notice when George became even more possessive with her. He would not let her go anywhere on her own. If they were out at a pub, he would even walk with her to the toilet lest she speak to anyone on the way. One day the postman called with a letter that needed a signature. The postman chatted in a friendly way while Sylvia signed for the mail. No sooner had she closed the door than George was rushing at her, his face scarlet and twisted with rage. He grabbed her by the hair on the back of her head, lifted her off her feet, and slammed her face into the corner of the wall. He demanded that she admit that she was having an affair with the postman. As Sylvia cried that the man was a stranger, George pulled her face away and then slammed it back into the wall. As her nose splattered blood over the wall, Sylvia lost consciousness. When she woke up, she was lying in a heap on the floor, and George was kicking her side, screaming that she should wake up and admit the truth. This then became the pattern of Sylvia's relationship with George, where he would suddenly snap and fly into an uncontrollable rage. Lies were told to neighbours and friends to account for the bruises and bites on Sylvia's body. Sylvia eventually went to her GP with a swelling on her skull. She was referred for an X-ray and she was referred to the counsellor. 'Don't ask me to leave George,' she said, 'because I won't. Ninety percent of the time, George is a lovely man and we get on very well. It's just the rest of the time, when he is in one of his rages, that I don't know what to do. I know he is going to do me some serious damage one day, but he can't stop himself. And I can't stop him either. But I can't leave him. I love him too much.'

Co-dependency

Some couples are enmeshed in co-dependent relationships. They cannot live with one another, yet cannot live without each other either. He is dominant so he needs her weakness. She is organisational so she needs his chaos. It never ceases to amaze me how emotionally damaged and dependent people manage to find one another and pair up. Here is another example, as discussed earlier, of how people are able to identify within one another their similarities in psychological need. Two common types that pair together are those who are obsessed with love (the love addict) and those who are obsessed with sex (the sex addict). Let us assume that the love addict is the woman and the sex addict is the man in a relationship. When they first meet, their relationship will be a passionate sexual one full of intense positive emotion, as both try to fill their own needs. However, as she falls deeply in love, she will be making demands on the man for the relationship to move forward; she wants marriage and babies. He will find that scary, will find her pushy, and will start to back off. The more he backs off, the more she clings. This produces intense negative emotion, so he will get mad because he is in control, not her, so he ends the relationship. She will be distraught, as her greatest fear is abandonment, so she will beg and plead for him to return. The more she pleads, the more he will stay away. Suddenly, she stops pleading. She has let him go. He cannot handle this either, as he is in control, not her. His greatest fear is also abandonment. He will look for her, convincing himself it is just to check that she is all right. At his return she is convinced he must have loved her after all. They have a passionate sexual reunion, and the cycle starts again. For such couples, their lives are one constant cycle of positive and negative intensity, which is addictive. However, just as the abuse in a violent relationship escalates, so does the negative intensity in a co-dependent relationship, with potentially disastrous results.

Divorce

Do not make assumptions about how an individual is feeling through separation and divorce. For some, it is an adaptive coping strategy for dealing with an unhappy or abusive marriage. The feeling in this situation is likely to be one of relief, and the focus will be on personal healing. However, if the client's wife has left for another man, the feelings are more likely to be of betrayal and abandonment. If the divorce is not of his choosing, he may grieve for the lost relationship and experience a similar process as in bereavement. New skills have to be learned, as the single person takes on the roles that used to be fulfilled by two people. Single parenting will also produce its own pressures for people struggling to cope with working hours and day-care for children, or struggling to make ends meet on a single salary. Access visits and maintenance payments for the absent parent can create arguments and resentment, and the children are trapped in the middle, mourning for their lost family and may act out this unhappiness behaviourally. The person's social life changes too, as friends take sides with one partner or another. Social invitations are usually centred around couples, and unattached people are considered threatening and socially unequal. A new circle of friends is therefore required at a time when a person really needs her old good friends. Loneliness is common, and anxiety and fear about being in a situation where new relationships can be formed. Hence a new wave of singles clubs, dating agencies, and lonely-hearts columns in newspapers and magazines has provided access to many people alone in middle age.

Homosexual relationships

Much of what has already been discussed applies in both hetero-sexual and homosexual relationships. Even the distress of child-lessness is an issue that some gay couples may have difficulty in coming to terms with. There are, of course, additional pressures on gay couples that heterosexual couples do not experience. For example, despite our enlightened society, there is still a considerable amount of prejudice against couples of the same sex. 'Coming out' is a big decision, and may involve making a choice between one's chosen partner and one's family of origin. There is also the fear and stigma over the HIV virus and AIDS. Some people are ignorant and anxious, and regard homosexuality and disease as synonymous. Interestingly, this prejudice is more common against male homo-sexuals than female homosexuals.

Another pressure on the gay couple comes from gay society itself. Surreptitious meeting places have encouraged a sexual openness that is not so commonly found in heterosexual society. Many gay men have multiple sexual relationships with different men in the same week, or even the same day. Many also have loving, long-term partnerships that they would not want to betray. But when infidelity is common, mixing with peers who encourage it can put a monogamous relationship under threat. I have met many men who do both: they enjoy the security of a long-term relationship either with a same-sex partner or in marriage with a woman, but they also periodically enjoy the sexual promiscuity of the gay scene. Unfortunately, research has shown that risk exposure in these sexually active situations is still consistently high (Sherr, Strong and Goldmeier, 1990) despite all the health education campaigns promoting condom use.

Assessment

Some clients attend the counselling session admitting that their stress/anxiety/depression is due to difficulties within their relationship, as did Judi (mentioned earlier). Other clients have difficulty in saying or admitting this because they feel ashamed or disloyal, as did Monica. Sometimes clients present with depression or anxiety without relating the real reason for their symptoms to their relationship. Vicky, discussed in Chapter 4, was experiencing panic attacks but did not realise that it was her husband's behaviour which was causing her to respond in that way. Some people are in total denial that there is a problem in their relationship, as was Victor also discussed in Chapter 4. It is very difficult therefore to provide a rule of thumb in these cases, so a process of elimination at the assessment session will enable the counsellor to determine which focus to take. In order to be non-threatening, the questions should move from the general overview to the more specific:

- What does the family at home consist of?
- What are the domestic arrangements in respect of work and house/childcare?
- What social support does the family have in the extended family network?
- How are things at home?
- How do you feel about your relationship?
- What are your feelings for your husband/wife?
- Do you have a good sexual relationship?

I always ask about the client's sexual relationship, even if there is another obvious reason for the relationship difficulty. This is because discrepancies in sexual satisfaction can exacerbate problems and cause unspoken words to fester. Other relationship problems can also contaminate hitherto good sexual compatibility.

Some clients are not sure that their relationship is under threat, but something is making them uneasy and unwell:

> Elizabeth had been married for seven years, and she and her husband Andrew had two young children. Elizabeth was becoming increasingly anxious and nervous, and this was provoking rows between her and Andrew. Andrew had been staying out late in the evening, which was unusual, and he had been spending a lot of money. When Elizabeth challenged him, he blamed her saying it was her nagging that made him want to stay away. She became convinced he was having an affair, and would frantically search his pockets and continually question him as to his whereabouts. He accused her of being a 'headcase', 'paranoid', and a 'nutter', and demanded that she go to the doctor to 'get her head sorted out'. The doctor prescribed antidepressants, and referred her to a CPN

who, in a one-off session, diagnosed her as an obsessive depressive with paranoid delusions. By the time she got to the counsellor, she had lost all belief in her own sanity. However, the counsellor helped her to dismiss her husband's assertions and to focus on her belief in herself to increase her self-esteem.

Meanwhile, between sessions two and three, the GP received a phone call from Elizabeth's mother-in-law. She was very distressed at what was happening to Elizabeth, of whom she was very fond. She wanted the GP to know that her son Andrew was indeed having an affair, and had bragged to his parents that now that Elizabeth was on antidepressants, he could have custody of the children should they split up as he could prove her mental illness. The parents were horrified, but felt unable to challenge their son – hence the phone call to the GP. The GP conveyed this information to the counsellor, but they both felt trapped by their confidentiality ethic. The GP therefore started reducing Elizabeth's medication while the counsellor carried on encouraging Elizabeth to believe in herself. Fate fell into her hands after a few weeks, however, when, after a row, Elizabeth grabbed Andrew's car keys and ran out before he had time to protest. She drove for a few miles in distress, but then had to stop with a puncture. Feeling everything was against her, she opened the car boot – only to find credit card receipts for meals, jewellery and ladies' lingerie, using his mother's address. Although it confirmed the worst for her relationship, Elizabeth was triumphant. It confirmed that she was not going mad after all.

When an individual admits to a relationship difficulty, it is then appropriate to consider couple counselling. Enquiries need to be made to ascertain if this is a viable prospect.

- Does your wife know that you have come to a counsellor?
- How does she feel about it?
- Would she be willing to come too?
- How do you feel about her coming along with you?
- Would you like to go and discuss it with her and let me know next time if it is something that you both would like?

It is preferable to work with the couple in relationship difficulties, because it takes two to tango, and there will always be problems on both sides. However, if the partner is unwilling, working with the individual is the second-best option.

TLT procedures

I feel it is important, when starting on a couple counselling contract, to see both partners alone for at least one or two sessions before seeing both together. This allows the counsellor to form an alliance with each person, and to hear any information that the client does not want the partner to hear, but does want to share with the counsellor. Of course, it is necessary for the counsellor to reinforce the confidentiality aspects of these individual sessions. If, however, the partner of a client does not wish to attend for sessions, the counsellor will then need to work with the individual. The counsellor should warn the client that, in these circumstances, very often the partner resents and feels excluded from the therapy, and may persistently ask what happened within the sessions (Roberts, 1996).

Begin by **exploring** each person's presenting distress, being careful not to form an alliance with one or other of the couple. Here, the relationship is your client, not any one individual.

In relationship disputes, pick through the arguments on the surface, to get to the basic anxiety that lies beneath the presenting row. For example, if a couple argue about who is to cook the evening meal, or to make the sandwiches for work, it is more likely that the real issue is that one of the couple feels uncared for, or that the relationship lacks the appropriate nurturance. Street and Smith (1988) feel that such issues are more about fears about personal identity, which manifest in superficial bickering, which in turn can impede sexual closeness and intimacy.

The balance of power in a relationship needs to be explored. Is it an egalitarian one, or does one or the other of the partnership have the major proportion of control? Maybe the power comes from outside the relationship, for example from the mother of the husband who is unable to let her son be an independent married man, so she continually rules him and his new family from outside. Power is the predominant issue in abusive relationships: and a very controlling man who dominates and isolates his wife from her family and friends is as abusive as a man who hits his wife (Jukes, 1990). Here the counsellor needs to encourage the couple to recognise the imbalance of power. An abusive partner will be in denial of the responsibility for any violence. He may deny that it happened, claiming he cannot remember, or offering excuses that it was her fault for provoking it, that she deserved it, or that he was unable to control himself. For the violence to stop, the client needs to conceptualise that there is no excuse for violent behaviour, and he must take responsibility for his actions.

Counsellors working in General Practice need a good knowledge base of sexual issues, and an understanding of the basic therapeutic techniques proposed by Masters and Johnson (1970). The counsellor must be able to explore sexual behaviour in an open and non-judgmental way, remembering that whatever method of sex the couple may choose is OK providing they are both happy and consenting. The counsellor should start exploration by asking questions of an intimate nature to establish the sexual history:

- What was your sexual experience prior to your relationship?
- What was your masturbatory experience?
- Have you always experienced sexual difficulties in your current relationship?
- What made things change?
- What made you decide to ask for help?

It helps at the early stages of couple counselling to place a prohibition on sexual intercourse, allowing only hugs and kisses. In long-term relationships, hugs and kisses are often dropped from the repertoire as couples start taking each other for granted. This intervention reinforces the importance of closeness without sex, as does sensate focus (Masters and Johnson, 1970). The sex ban allows the 'pressure to perform' and the 'putting up with it even though I do not feel like it' feelings to be removed. It is also a paradox intervention, and many couples who have not been having sex very often find themselves gleefully disobeying like naughty children after being told not to!

When the counsellor is faced with a client who cannot choose between two women, the counsellor again needs to adopt a non-judgmental stance that will aid the client to explore both rela-tionships in depth. A force-field analysis (Egan, 1994) would be the most valuable in this situation, allowing the client to explore the facilitating and hindering forces of each relationship. The client will be very confused, and may feel he loves both women in differing ways and may vacillate between the two from session to session, as Roger did. It is important for the counsellor to be supportive during this process, and to be aware of any bias that may underpin her questioning. It is not for the counsellor to decide which woman may be best (although she would not be human if she did not have a preference), but for the client to make his own choice in whichever direction it may be.

When exploring with clients their own perception of the diffi-culties within the relationship, explore with them the relationships of their families of origin. We base our knowledge and experience of marriage on those of our parents, which shape our expectations of how we feel things should be. Two people coming from totally different backgrounds will have totally different expectations of the roles they should play, and this can lead to confusion and conflict. If one (or both) partner comes from a damaged, turbulent or unhappy background, she may well be acting out her distress in her own marriage. Transgenerational transmission means that people repeat their pasts rather than remembering to change them, thus men who watched their fathers beat their mothers are most likely to beat their own wives. Mixed racial, cultural or religious partnerships also bring their own set of problems resulting from differing expectations of roles and responsibilities and this can cause some people to have acute identity crises.

Lucinda's family of origin was Asian, and arrived in England from Bangladesh before she was born. Lucinda, however, felt herself to be English and was proud of her cockney accent. She loved her family, and was a good daughter, but she felt uncomfortable with their strict cultural values that did not seem to fit in the Western environment in which she was reared. She only ever defied her parents twice: once when she was nine when she refused to wear her sari, and again when she refused to marry the man she had never met back in Bangladesh. She ran away and married Jeremy, her college boyfriend, instead. Her husband was a white, middle-class Welshman. His father left his mother when he was seven years old, so he and his mother and sister were all the family that he knew. Lucinda's parents disapproved of her marriage to Jeremy as he was not Asian, but once the deed was done, they forgave her rather than lose their daughter. Jeremy's mother, on the other hand, thought Jeremy was extremely lucky to get a girl as beautiful as Lucinda, and welcomed her into the family unreservedly.

Difficulties had struck their relationship within two years of their marriage. Lucinda went to the counsellor desperately worried about their financial situation and her loss of sexual desire for Jeremy. They had several large credit-card bills that they could not afford to pay, and she feared that their house might be repossessed. When the counsellor explored the backgrounds of this young couple, he found the fundamental differences in their belief systems. Lucinda's family worked consistently long hours, seven days a week, in their own shop. They never bought anything for the house until they had saved up for it. Jeremy's family, alternatively, struggled financially much of the time, so many of their household goods were bought on hire purchase. Credit cards were no big deal, Jeremy argued, although he admitted that he had spent too much and now they had insufficient income to cover all their debts. Lucinda hated living in debt, and her respect for Jeremy was lost, because he had not cared for her enough to protect her from debt. She saw him as an irresponsible spendthrift. This then caused her to focus on other differences, like their eating habits. She was a vegetarian and extremely slim. He ate convenience foods, like burgers and sausages, and was progressively putting on weight. She found him disgusting and stopped having sex with him. He felt hurt and betrayed, and spent more money to comfort himself. 'I can't leave him till he sorts this financial mess out,' she cried. 'My parents will never forgive me, after all the fuss I made about marrying him, if they knew the mess we were in financially!' Jeremy had no incentive to sort out the financial mess, because he knew that if he did, she would leave him.

Many clients, even those who have been married for years, have insufficient or incorrect knowledge about sex. Providing information and instruction helps the clients to **understand** their difficulties and put them into perspective. It is important not to form an alliance with the non-dysfunctional partner, or to be critical or impatient with the dysfunctioning one. Provide affirmations for even small successes, and support and encouragement when there are failures.

To facilitate the couple's understanding of the symmetrical behaviours they get locked into, gentle challenge and a repertoire of therapeutic techniques will enable the counsellor to break the spiral. For example:

Jennifer and John had been married for five years, have one small son, Tom, and were continually arguing.

Jennifer: It's all John's fault! He's so irresponsible! I work all day, do all the taking and fetching Tom to the childminder's, organise the food, the money, the housework. I do it all! Since John's given up work to do this degree, all he does is go to lectures or the library, and sit in front of that damned computer. If I go out to the shops and ask him to mind Tom while I'm out, he is plonked in front of the computer, and Tom is getting up to all sorts of mischief because his dad is not taking any notice of him. I can't even ask him do a simple thing like mind his own son for half an hour!

John: I don't know what she expects from me! We both agreed it would be a good idea for me to do this degree. I'm doing it for us, anyway, to improve my earnings potential for the family. But it is so hard, it doesn't come easy to me like it does to the other students. I really have to struggle to keep up with them. And instead of supporting me like she said she would, all she does is nag that I haven't done this or I haven't done that. It's got that as soon as she sees me, she starts nagging. I dread being at home now, because all I get is nag, nag, nag!

Counsellor: Do you feel you nag John a lot, Jennifer?

Jennifer: Yes, I suppose I do. But I get so frustrated and angry with him that he won't help me. I can't do it all, I just want him to help.

Counsellor: So you nag him because you need help?

Jennifer: Yes, I can't do it all on my own.

Counsellor: Does the nagging work?

Jennifer: No, it doesn't! He still won't do anything!

Counsellor: So if you nag to get help, but nagging doesn't work, could you explain why you keep doing it?

Jennifer: [*pause*] Well . . . I . . . I guess I don't know, it's just a habit I have got into.

[*At this stage, Jennifer looks deflated and John looks triumphant, so it is necessary for the counsellor to redress the balance to prevent an alliance forming.*]

Counsellor: John, you said at the outset, you and Jennifer made an agreement that she would support you through your degree?

John: Yes. We knew it would be hard, so she agreed that she would allow me time to study.

Counsellor: So the agreement was to give you time and space to study. Did you agree that you should abrogate responsibility for the family? That Jennifer should become, in effect, a single parent for the duration of your degree course?

John: Well, no, of course not.

Counsellor: Well, can you see, John, that because you have found the course so hard, that is essentially what you appear to have done?

John: Well, I suppose, if you look at it like that. I didn't mean to leave everything to Jennifer. I just get so absorbed . . .

Counsellor: Do you agree, therefore, that maybe Jennifer had a grievance that she could not communicate to you?

John: I guess so. [*He doesn't look so triumphant now, and Jennifer looks stronger.*]

Counsellor: Maybe we could spend some time in our session working out between us how you can apportion time appropriately between family duties and studying, Would that be helpful?

The counsellor needs to be careful that the client does not feel criticised or battered, so these kinds of challenges need to be conveyed with the warmth of soft eye contact.

There are some useful skills to be used with couples with communication difficulties. For example, if one of the couple dominates the conversation, not giving the partner sufficient time or space to say her piece, then it is helpful to hand each of them a clock or stopwatch in turn, allocating a fixed period of time for speaking, like two or five minutes, during which the other must not interrupt. This is quite a learning exercise for the dominant partner. Many couples listen to each other, but do not *hear* what has been said, usually because they are too busy formulating their next response. Here the counsellor can encourage accurate listening by asking the client to repeat in her own words the feelings that her partner has just expressed. This can then be confirmed or denied by the original speaker. Sometimes, a couple's communication pattern becomes unnecessarily derisory or critical; they get into a habit of putting each other down. This pattern is not always readily identifiable by the couple, as it becomes an automatic rather than a thought-through response. Bubenzer and West (1993) suggest a way of making this more overt by using what they call the penny game. Both are given the same number of pennies, say 20 or 30. Then, whenever the person feels put down by the other, he passes a penny over to his partner. No comment or discussion is allowed as to why the penny is passed, it is just accepted that this how that person feels. What is interesting in this exercise is that usually although one of the couple will complain more about being put down than the other, when the pennies are counted at the end of the session, the numbers are roughly equal.

Another useful brief therapy tool that can lead to establishment of homework tasks and client **action** is the magic wand question (Cade and O'Hanlon, 1993), which is a version of the miracle question:

Counsellor: I would like you both to answer this question separately. If I had a magic wand, and could wave it and instantly make your relationship better, what changes would be made? What would you be doing differently? Perhaps Joan would like to answer that question first?

Joan: Well, for me the biggest problem in our relationship is that he doesn't participate in the family. He works long hours in the week, so the children have gone to bed by the time he comes home. At weekends he has his head stuck in paperwork, or is watching the sport on the telly. He never wants to do anything with me or the children. So if you had a magic wand you would make him a family man.

Counsellor: What would you be doing differently?

Joan: Me? Well I suppose that if he enjoyed being with us, I would look forward to him coming home, instead of feeling angry and resentful. I would be pleased to see him, and have his meal ready for him, and we could talk together about our day. I would enjoy his company like I used to before the children came along.

Counsellor: OK James, what is your answer to that question?

James: Well, I would like to feel important to Joan again. I haven't felt she had any time for me since we had the children. Her total topic of conversation is about what the children have or haven't done. She seems to have pushed me out somehow. Before we had the children, she was an interesting and stimulating person to talk to, and she was interested in me. Now she is only interested in what I don't do, and is constantly nagging and argumentative. So if you had a magic wand, I would like you to bring back the old Joan, the one I used to know.

Counsellor: What would you be doing differently?

James: Well, I would get home earlier in the evening for a start. At the moment I dread going home, so I don't leave work until my desk is totally clear, although there are some things that could wait until tomorrow. I would want to spend more time with her and the children, because she would be interested in me and we would talk about things other than what the kids had for tea or what they did at school.

Counsellor: So, what we have is a situation where you, Joan, feel angry and resentful that you are rearing the children on your own; that James does not participate in the family. You, James, also feel resentful and pushed out by Joan's preoccupation with the children, feeling that she has no time for you, and no interest in what you do. For your homework this week, I would like you to move toward your goals. I

would like you, Joan, to each day read some of the newspaper, or watch the news on television, to find a topic that you might like to talk to James about when he comes home from work. You are not to discuss the children with James until after you have asked him about his day, and talked about your chosen topic. I would like you, James, to come home from work each day in time to help Joan bath the children and put them to bed. Perhaps you could do the bathing and read them a story while Joan is preparing the meal. That way you can also build up a relationship with the children without Joan being there. Joan, you will not eat your evening meal with the children, but will wait until you and James have tucked the kids up, and then have a quiet meal together. Is this something you would both be willing to try?
[*They look nervously at one another.*]
James: Well, I will certainly give it a go.
Joan: Yes, so will I.

For couples experiencing sexuality difficulties, homework tasks should focus on reducing the pressure and performance anxiety of the couple, which is why a sex ban is very often so successful. Encouraging couples to be intimate with one another without sexual intercourse can be a learning curve for some people who feel that intimacy is only about sex. Teaching couples to bathe or shower together, to give mutual massage or sensate focus also encourages intimacy, as do hugs and kisses and talking about sexual matters when they are not in sexual situations.

I would work with the couple in exactly the same way if the couple are opposite sex or same sex. Some therapists argue that if the therapist is not gay, then there is a limit to their understanding of the difficulties portrayed. I disagree with this point of view. You do not have to break a leg to know it hurts, and skilled time-limited therapy is about good empathic skills, lack of prejudice or preconceived ideas, and an open approach. Any client can be helped to some degree.

A General Practice environment provides a safe place for people to review discrepancies in the perceptions of how their relationship should be, and in so doing removes a lot of psychosomatic presentations to the GP.

Recommended reading

Fisher, B. (1992) *Rebuilding. When Your Relationship Ends.* San Luis Obispo, California: Impact.

Forward, S. (1986) *Men Who Hate Women and the Women Who Love Them.* New York: Bantam.

Norwood, R. (1985) *Women Who Love Too Much. When You Keep Wishing and Hoping He'll Change.* London: Arrow.

Notes

1 This concept of serial monogamy suggests that maybe marriage for life is out of date, and perhaps 10-year renewable contracts would be a preferable replacement!

2 Less often, men will admit to being the victim of a woman's violence. This admission is more likely to materialise in the course of a counselling contract, however, and is rarely confessed to a GP, especially a male GP.

9

Counselling People with Eating Disorders

Since working in General Practice, I have been surprised to discover how many people have difficulties with food. These are not necessarily people with specific eating disorders, but are people experiencing difficulties in controlling what they eat, how they eat, whether they eat, or difficulty in controlling the consequence of eating – their weight. What seems to be occurring is that the client has become trapped into a pattern of eating or not eating that becomes habitual. These people are not necessarily emotionally disordered, but have a conditioned behavioural pattern that needs to be unlearned, or the food-related problem is a symptom of some other form of distress. There are other people, however, who attend with deep-seated eating disorders who have associated personality difficulties. Such people need more in-depth therapy than time-limited work can offer. This chapter, therefore, describes the latter type of problem which will need a secondary (or sometimes tertiary) referral, whilst the procedures for time-limited work focus on the former type of food-related problem.

Eating disorders are predominantly a Western cultural phenomenon. There is a Western idea of what a feminine body should look like from the glossy magazines, and much is included to help girls look like the ideal. There is also much criticism of what a feminine body should not look like compared to this abstract concept of perfection. The paradox is that it is disembodying to try to conform to an abstract concept. Thus if you live in a culture where an idealised body shape becomes institutionalised as ours has become, then there is a manifest form of institutionalised abuse.

Anorexia

Anorexia nervosa is a serious mental illness, of which 20 per cent of sufferers will die (Pearce and Crisp, 1994). An anorectic is a person unable to give herself the nourishment that her body needs so she slowly starves herself to death.[1] She has a very distorted body image, so that when she looks in the mirror, what she sees is fat and flab whereas others see her as skeletal. The psychopathology of anorexia is not about eating, however, it is about weight, pivoting the emotional development of puberty into a reversal of the maturation process. Anorectics have unresolved adolescent issues that make them wish to regress into a childlike state. The loss of weight makes them suffer with amenorrhoea, and as a consequence become asexual. (The anorectic has to have missed at least 3 menstrual cycles for formal diagnosis of anorexia.) Anorexia is about the avoidance of puberty for girls (mean onset age is 17.5) who are emotionally incompetent. Thirty per cent of these girls have been sexually abused.[2] As anorexia usually reflects conflict within the family, family therapy is commonly the most successful form of treatment. Pearce and Crisp (1994) recommend that successful treatment requires 40–50 sessions spread over three to four years and concentrated in the first 18 months. It is therefore not a condition considered appropriate for time-limited therapy.

Anorectics are thought to be extremely narcissistic, manipulative and clever at pretending to significant others (and their therapists) that they are eating when actually they are hiding or removing their food. However, it is not known if this is really a consequence of changes in the brain brought about by starvation which are considered to reduce the capacity for complex thought. The issue is one of control: when an adolescent feels so out of control of what is happening around her, one thing she can control is her food intake. This feels empowering to her in a distorted 'I'll show them' way. She will find relationships scary, but if one is formed, the anorectic tends to be very ambivalent, needy and insecure, and will adopt a childlike role within it, preferring the relationship to be non-sexual. She wants a father, not a lover. Anorectics are generally unwilling and resistant clients and can produce strong negative feelings in their counsellors. Such is the extent of their self-loathing that their suicidal wish is not just to kill themselves, but to do so slowly and painfully.

Bulimia

Bulimia is more common than anorexia, affecting three out of every 100 women at some time in their lives, and used to be thought to be almost exclusive to women. It is now considered that up to 10 per cent of cases are male. Bulimia usually involves some form of binge eating where the client eats a large amount of food, and then, feeling uncomfortably stuffed and disgusted with herself, will take herself off and vomit. Seventy-five per cent of teenage females want to reduce their body fat after puberty, but with some girls it gets out of hand. It often starts as a form of weight control following dysmorphophobia (distress about bodily fat), and one may find that the person abuses laxatives or undertakes excessive exercise in addition. However, the client is unlikely to lose weight because of the initial bingeing. The self-loathing, here again, is indicated by the extremely pejorative regimes and may involve some other form of self-harm like cutting. People with bulimia have an ambivalence over intimacy, so one tends to find them in relationships which mirror the problem: that the bulimic will be needy, gobbling up the partner one minute, and then pushing him away (vomiting him out) the next. Bulimics are not usually anti-sexual, like the anorectic; in fact for some vomiting can be erotic and arousing.

> Josephine was a 22-year-old artist from Paris living in the UK. She left France to escape her mother's constant attentions that she endured when living in her own country. She was an only child, and although culturally the French are very much more food-orientated than the English (one of the attractions of living in the UK), Josephine found that she could not cope with her mother's exhortations about her eating. She became bulimic as a young teenager when she found that she was putting on weight, but could not persuade her mother to reduce her food portions or to buy less fattening foods. Food left on the plate would be considered insulting, when her mother would chastise her with comparisons to all the starving people in the world who were unable to eat the food that she was privileged to receive. This led to feelings of guilt when she felt full in addition to her worries about her flabbiness. As soon as she was old enough, she left home to go to art college, but would persistently receive food parcels from her mother. On visits to her parents, meals would last 2–3 hours when course after course was brought out for Josephine to eat. On graduating, she came to the UK to live, but found she was unable to break the pattern of eating, feeling guilty, and vomiting that she had established over the previous eight years. The enamel on her teeth had started to disintegrate and she was unable to form any stable kind of relationship. She finally decided to ask for help.

Binge-eating

Bingeing (also called comfort eating) is extremely common in people feeling unhappy or discontented with their lives. It is a regressive form of oral gratification that mimics pacifying an unhappy infant through the mouth with food or drink. Thus people find themselves eating very large amounts of food (like chocolate and other seretonin-stimulating carbohydrates) in a short space of time, or perpetually grazing through the fridge. This symptom of unhappiness becomes a stressor in its own right as the client then worries about the eating, but feels powerless to stop it.

Compulsive eating and obesity

Fifty per cent of women over 30 years are over 30 per cent heavier than their recommended weight. So where does binge-eating end and compulsive eating begin? The borderline is smudged, but it is mostly about control and compulsion. A compulsive eater is as addicted to food as a drug addict is to heroin. But where there is hope for the drug or alcohol addict in abstention, that is not possible for the food addict. Also, the more the person eats, the more weight he gains, the more sedentary he becomes.[3] He embarks on a cycle of food increase and burns fewer calories, turning to more food because he feels so bad about how much he weighs. Often in relationships, obese people are very needy and vulnerable, but their weight provides a form of protection or armour against the scary world and gives an illusion of power. The cliché of being fat and happy has been empirically disproved (Hudson and Mountford, 1992): most large people experience very low levels of self-esteem, although may be less anxious and depressed than normal-weight people. It is common for an obese person to become inert and inactive. Marriages are set up around this inertia. Thus the partner of an obese client might argue that he likes his wife like that and would not want her to change. In reality, if he truly loved her for her own sake, he would encourage her to lose weight, because he would know she is more likely to live longer.[4] However, her fatness makes him feel safe and secure in the knowledge that she will always be where he can find her.

Ellen was five foot one and weighed 19 stone. She ignored the continual exhortations of her GP that the strain she was putting on her heart would kill her. She just liked cooking for the family, and she liked eating, and she saw no reason for being any different. One day she overheard her daughter and friends discussing her daughter's wedding plans for the following year. The friends were teasing her daughter about her mother's size, saying that there would be no room for her and her fiancé in the wedding photos if Mother were in them too. Another asked if Mother was going to have her dress made from a parachute. Ellen could tell by her responses to these remarks that her daughter was upset and embarrassed. She felt guilty that, in not taking care of herself, she was letting her daughter down. She resolved to diet. She joined Slimming World and set herself a goal of reaching 10 stone for the wedding in 13 months' time. Ellen's determination and persistence with her diet impressed everyone as the weight slowly but steadily started to reduce. In six months she had reduced to 12 stone. Her husband, however, had become very irritable and argumentative. He complained about the money she needed to spend on new clothes as the sizes she wore started to reduce. He complained about her being less cuddly and said he found her less sexually attractive. He complained about her being obsessed with dieting, called her anorexic, and demanded that she stay at home with him on the evenings she went to Slimming World. Ellen felt angry and resentful at his lack of support, and they began to row on a regular basis. She knew how much better she looked now compared to six months before, as she kept a photograph of herself in her swimsuit attached by a magnet to the fridge. Her husband's complaints therefore gave her greater resolve that she was going to reach her goal. At the end of 10 months, Ellen was a slim nine stone, and wearing a size 12. She was ecstatic, but her marriage was in a dangerous state. When they eventually went to counselling, her husband admitted that he did find her with her new weight more sexually attractive than he had ever done before. But the scary part was, so would other men. He was convinced that a slim Ellen would leave him for someone else.

Obese people are also more prone to neurotic disorders and phobic avoidance syndromes compared to those of normal weight. Social phobia (as discussed in Chapter 4) develops from fears about rejection leading to humiliation and shame (Kalucy and Crisp, 1974).

Assessment

There is a lot of embarrassment and shame around the misuse of food, so clients are often very reluctant to discuss it. So you may notice that a client is either over- or underweight, but she will argue that it is not a problem. This form of denial is difficult, as there are obviously some people who really do not care whether their body is too fat or too thin. However, it is unusual to come across a client who is totally satisfied with her body exactly the way it is; usually there is some part that is too big or too small, too lumpy or too emaciated, too high or too droopy.

To ascertain whether the food-related difficulty is becoming a serious problem, the counsellor needs to check out her self-perceptions. Once again, start with the very general and move to the more specific:

- What is your diet like?
- Do you feel you eat well?
- What is your relationship with eating?
- Do you find yourself overly thinking about what you are next going to eat?
- Do you take an avid interest in buying food or cooking for others?
- Do you eat to fixed time schedules or do you eat when you are hungry?
- Do you feel you eat enough/too much?
- What do you see when you look at your body in the mirror?

The body image question is really important, because if the image is distorted – e.g. a thin person seeing fat and flab, or a fat person seeing ordinary weight – the client is already moving into a difficult psychological position that you are unlikely to shift within six sessions. Clients do not always tell the truth on these issues at first, especially when it comes to vomiting, so although the policy is always to believe what a client says with unconditional positive regard (Rogers, 1961), it may be necessary to gently query incongruous information. For example, watch out for a person with discoloured teeth (as stomach acid dissolves the enamel and dentine on the teeth, especially the maxillary incisors) or unpleasant breath, fingernail degeneration, calluses on or near the knuckles of the index and next finger, a hoarse voice, wounds that will not heal, or swollen salivary glands at the throat. These tell-tale signs of regular vomiting can be remarked upon in a non-threatening way. Similarly, adolescent girls who develop eating disorders tend to wear very baggy dark clothes which hide their shape, even in the heat of summer. Bulimics tend not to lose much weight, as some of their ingested food has been processed, although they will have a loss of stomach muscle tone and some menstrual disturbance. Anorectics will exhibit sunken eyes, hollow cheeks, fine body hair and emaciated arms (particularly the biceps). Their bones become brittle and break easily, they have a slow heart rate and they constantly complain of feeling cold. People who abuse laxatives may complain of stomach pains and may have swollen fingers. All people who abuse their eating will complain of feeling tired all the time, and commonly experience an irritable bowel.

TLT procedures

As in other cases, **explore** the feelings that are being expressed, and hear the relationship with food that is not being acknowledged. When a food-related difficulty is encountered, take the client back to early infant and childhood experiences that she can remember, and discuss her relationship with food at this time. This is when eating patterns are set, and they are revisited at times of distress.

> Barbara had struggled with her weight ever since her children were born. Although not drastically overweight, she felt uncomfortable with the fact that she was two dress sizes bigger than she used to be before having the children. Barbara recognised that it was cakes, pastries and biscuits that were her weakness. She was constantly baking for the family, but would eat the majority of her produce herself.
>
> *Counsellor*: Were you overweight as a child?
> *Client*: No, not at all. My mother used to tell me that I had hollow legs. I would eat everything that was put in front of me, and I never had to consider my weight.

Counsellor: Did you have to eat everything on your plate, or would it have been OK to leave some?

Client: Oh, no! I wouldn't have been allowed to leave any. I was born immediately after the war, so there was still rationing in my early years. Food was considered so precious that Mother would have considered wasting any terrible.

Counsellor: And when rationing ended?

Client: Well I was about five then. I remember Mother was always baking. There was always the smell of home-made cakes or biscuits when I came home from school. I didn't get on very well at school; I was quiet and shy and didn't mix well with the other children. But if I was feeling unhappy, Mother would sit me on her knee and give me a freshly baked biscuit, still warm from the oven. I can almost taste it now.

Counsellor: So the message you learned as a child was to eat everything that you are given, and unhappiness can be consoled by food?

Client: Why, yes. I suppose you are right. And now, when I am feeling a bit down, I take myself off to the kitchen and create something nice for the family's dinner. It cheers me up.

Counsellor: Just like your mother used to cheer you up; you have become a mother to yourself. You eat so as not to be unhappy. What makes you unhappy, Barbara?

Client: Well, I haven't got much to feel unhappy about, although my weight does get me down.

Counsellor: Ah!

Client: Gosh, I see. It's a circle, isn't it? I eat to stop feeling down, yet I feel down because I eat too much. How can I break the circle?

Counsellor: What would you suggest?

Client: Well, I really don't need to bake so much, because my girls don't really eat it. So I bake for four, yet only two of us will eat it. And then with Mike being at work, he doesn't tend to eat as much as I do.

Counsellor: So who are you baking for, Barbara?

Client: Well, if I really analyse it, it is me really. My mum always baked, so I feel that to be a good wife and mother like she was, I have to bake too. But people don't seem to set so much store to home cooking these days, do they?

Counsellor: If you reduce the amount of baking that you do, will that make you a bad mother?

Client: No, of course not.

So here the counsellor, in exploring the eating routines and rituals of the family of origin, establishes the unspoken beliefs and assumptions about the power of food. It was not a coincidence that Barbara developed this pattern of behaviour after becoming a mother, as she started unconsciously repeating her mother's nurturance behaviour. But it had become out of step with contemporary views which focus more on healthy eating, and where people (even Barbara's own daughters) are more weight conscious. Breaking the food codes of a different generation can be very empowering for the client. As she develops insight and **understanding** in her eating habits, she will be better equipped to change them. Fairburn and Cooper (1988) suggest that the focus needs to be on altering the client's beliefs about the importance of her shape and weight. However, she also needs to gain insight into the family dynamics which led her down this path in the first place.

For the client's **actions**, to break the cycle of malnutrition, whether it is from eating too little or too much, I recommend a new diet as homework. The client should eat little and often, say, every two hours between their main meals. This should be something small and light like a piece of fruit, a wholemeal roll (without fat spreads) or low-fat yoghurt. Meals should also be small, but should consist of a high proportion of complex carbohydrate (rice, pasta, potatoes or wholemeal bread), fresh vegetables and fruit. White meat and fish for carnivores, beans and pulses for vegetarians. Red meat, cakes and pastries, convenience and snack foods should be avoided. Vitamin supplements and/or a tonic also helps. This diet is successful in several respects. First, if the client is not eating enough, or is vomiting regularly, the body will not be getting sufficient vitamins and minerals, which creates internal stress. This diet tops up on healthy nutrition. Second, for the non-eater and for those who are overweight and go on starvation diets, the metabolism will have slowed down to starvation mode, thus making energy-saving adjustments to cope with the insufficient fuel provision. Eating this frequently with a lot more high-fibre foods will speed the metabolism up, which in turn burns calories. Third, if the problem is overeating, the client fills up on non-fattening foods and does not feel hungry. Fourth, by not having long gaps between eating, and thus no low blood-sugar levels, the client's energy levels are increased and as a consequence their work performance increases. I find that clients rarely stick to this diet rigidly, but adapt it to their own lifestyle. However, it is very successful in getting clients to think about and plan what they are going to eat, rather than eating on the run and grabbing what is available.

Keeping a food diary is another good way of encouraging people to change their diet. It has long been recognised that diary-keeping is a poor way of undertaking scientific research as the participant inevitably changes the behaviour that is being observed. People often do not realise how much (or how little) they eat until they see it written down.

For people who are overweight, it is useful to encourage them to reduce the speed at which they eat food. It takes about 20 minutes for the message of fullness to pass from the stomach to the brain, in which time the stomach can be really overloaded and feel uncomfortably distended. Slowing-down strategies help the client to be more cognitively aware of their eating, and this aids reduction. Such strategies are:

- putting cutlery down between mouthfuls
- chewing food a certain number of times before swallowing
- not preparing for the next mouthful before the last mouthful is swallowed
- drinking a glass of water before starting a meal, and drinking another glass at intervals throughout the meal
- conversing while eating
- eating small bite-sized pieces
- not eating while reading or watching the TV

Although these strategies seem very simple, some clients find them very hard to do. For if a man has spent 40 years eating his food in a certain way, say, if he bolts down large mouthfuls in quick succession, this is a very difficult habit to break.

People with deep-rooted eating disorders need long-term in-depth psychotherapy. Many people, however, can be successfully helped with time-limited therapy if they have food-related anxieties and phobias.

Sam was 15 and had suffered with anorexia for the last four years. Her childhood had been difficult because of her parents' divorce and her relationship with her mother was stormy. Sam had spent one year in an adolescent unit for girls with eating disorders, leaving there 18 months previously when her weight had reached a menstruous level. She was sent to the counsellor for assessment when she told her GP she was again experiencing difficulties with food. Sam was not interested in any form of counselling or help, and was only there to 'shut her mother up'. The counsellor recognised that this was not appropriate for TLT and arranged for a secondary referral. Three weeks later, another girl, Sandy, also aged 15, was brought to the GP by a worried mother. Sandy had been vomiting after her meals. The GP referred Sandy to the counsellor. Within another two weeks, another girl, Pat, was sent to the GP by her mother because of vomiting. The GP remarked to the counsellor, when discussing Pat's referral, that there seemed to be a bulimic epidemic. The counsellor soon began to pick up distinct similarities in the stories told by both Sandy and Pat. They did not have particular difficulties at home, other than the usual generation gap arguments. However, they both started vomiting as a way of losing weight, and found that it had very soon become an addictive ritual that they couldn't stop. They were both distressed by the situation, and felt out of control. It soon became clear to the counsellor that Sam, Sandy and Pat all went to school together and were quite close friends. As Sam's psychological condition worsened, she had convinced her friends Pat and Sandy that they were both overweight and needed to diet. She explained to them that the quickest way of losing weight was by vomiting. They both tried and were continually encouraged and reinforced by Sam. However, both Pat and Sandy had sufficient psychological strength to realise that they were getting themselves into difficulties and were willing to accept help. Sam, on the other hand, thought Sandy and Pat were weak and stopped speaking to them. After a couple of sessions each with the counsellor, plus a couple of weeks on the new eating regime, both Sandy and Pat had stopped vomiting. Sam was referred for psychiatric help.

Recommended reading

Crisp, A. (1980) *Anorexia Nervosa: Let Me Be*. London: Academic Press.
Fairburn, C. (1995) *Overcoming Binge Eating*. New York: Guilford Press.
Hollis, J. (1989) *Fat is a Family Affair*. Minnesota: Hazelden.

Notes

1 Only one in 20 sufferers is male. Men are more likely to develop a drinking disorder. It is as if women want to gain control through the way that they eat, and men want to lose control through their drinking. Which, of course, is the reversal of power and control between the genders in our society. If the anorectic is a man, however, his most likely form of weight loss will be through exercise. This is because there is almost a cultural admiration for someone able to demonstrate such stamina and willpower.

2 Crisp, personal communication, 1994.

3 Although the numbers of obese men and women are roughly the same, it tends to be only the women who seek help.

4 It is fair to say, however, that people who perpetually diet and gain weight (yo-yo dieting) have a higher mortality risk than those who stay obese.

10

Counselling Adults Abused as Children

There are many ways that adults suffer from the consequences of their childhood. Physical and sexual abuse immediately spring to mind as they have been brought into contemporary public consciousness. But some adults suffer from their childhood even though on the surface it appears they had reasonably safe and secure upbringings. These people may have suffered emotional deprivation, social neglect or scapegoating. They may have been loved too little, not loved at all, or been scorned in a step-parenting situation. On the other hand, they may have been loved too much or over-indulged by obsessive, intrusive or achievement-orientated parents. Such children grow into adults with very little ego-strength to cope with life's crises. They can manage the day-to-day events that life brings, but when a life event occurs (whether it is positive or negative) or they are put under the strain of chronic stressors, they crumble readily and end up at the doctor's surgery.

When I first started working in General Practice, and a client presented with an abusive childhood – particularly either sexual or physical abuse – I would immediately discuss with the client referral to the secondary health team. My opinion at that time was that people needed a lot longer than six sessions to deal with a lifetime's worth of damage. However, I do not tend to discuss secondary referral with these clients now until we start on the ending of our short-term contract. There are two main reasons for this change of view. First, many of my secondary referrals to the psychiatric/mental health service for longer treatment care were refused. The psychiatrists did not have the resources to deal with such people who were basically functioning on a day-to-day level, but were just exhibiting a lot of emotional distress, or dysfunctioning on an interpersonal rather than a social level. For the few that were considered to be candidates for NHS psychotherapy, many were still turned down, either because they had experienced life events within one year of referral, or they were considered to be insufficiently 'psychologically minded' (!). In these early days, therefore, the number of refusals for longer-term psychotherapeutic work conditioned me to exercise caution as to whom I referred, especially as such adults had already experienced rejection of one form or another all their lives, and here were the mental health services reinforcing their feelings of abandonment.

The second reason for changing my view of referrals for abuse was that it soon became very clear that this was not what the clients wanted. They were glad of the opportunity to discuss their trauma within the confines of the doctor's surgery, and as my presence became generally known, many seized the opportunity to come along and talk about it. They felt safe and secure, doing so in familiar surroundings. But they did not want to extend the time they spent on the work, nor did they want to go off to psychiatric out-patient units to continue the work. Thus many rejected my suggestion of referral to mental health teams, and I even found that on occasion my suggestion that it might be more appropriate damaged the speed at which trust was established in our own working relationship.

This chapter examines the issues raised for adults with damaged childhoods, and considers how TLT can give life-long helping skills in short-term work.

Sexual abuse

The incidence of child sexual abuse is conservatively considered to be 12 per cent of girls and 8 per cent of boys (Baker and Duncan, 1985). Sexual abuse may involve incidents of sexual penetration, oral sex, fondling, indecent photography, voyeurism, exposure to pornographic material or masturbation. It is unhelpful to categorise types of abuse into mild or severe, as each individual experiences their psychological trauma differently irrespective of the classification of the event (BPS, 1990). Although it is possible for sexually abused adults to grow up into able, well-functioning, non-abusive adults, such abuse is also highly likely to lead to adult disturbance for which many never seek professional help.

Clients who experienced sexual abuse as children tend to exhibit common behavioural patterns as they develop into adulthood. As children, they become sexually aware earlier than other children, and often embark on their own sexual career at an early age. They may go through a phase of sexual promiscuity as the emotional development is accelerated (Dale, 1992). It is as if they are per-petuating the abusive situation. They choose unsuitable partners to have long-term relationships with, many of whom behave like or subconsciously remind the client of the abuser, or who may have been sexually abused themselves. The experience of sexual dys-function is common, with sexual associations relating back to the abuse; for example, a total lack of sexual desire, sexual arousal linked to violence or force, or flashbacks of the abuse when having sex, causing the person to link the abuse with the present partner.

These damaged adults also suffer with recurring depression throughout their lives with no obvious precipitating event. They often feel strong emotions of guilt and self-blame; that they were responsible for the abuse and that they should have said no. If the client was a boy who was anally penetrated, this may also (but not always) precipitate behaviour of a homosexual orientation as the client repeats the pattern of the abuse. The real confusion about a man's sexual orientation following abuse in childhood is dealt with fully by Etherington (1995).

It is common for the clients to feel very angry with their mothers, whether the mother knew about the abuse or not (and assuming that the mother was not the abuser), for not protecting the child from the abuser. What of the silent, colluding and allowing mothers? What can the client say to her? What would be the consequences of an angry backlash? Thus there is a powerful and pervading responsibility in not speaking. So, as adults, the family system often follows a Karpman triangle (Karpman, 1968) where the victim (the client) persecutes the would-be rescuer (the mother). If the abuser was the mother, this hits the child hardest, and produces the most severe form of psychological damage, as the one person in the world who is supposed to love and protect you is your mother.

What is interesting about the symptomatic behaviour, however, is that the common presentations occur whether the client can remember the abuse or not. If the clients can remember, they will describe their psychological splitting from themselves in order to cope with the trauma. They will describe how they left their bodies in their minds, and watched the events take place from afar. It is this splitting which also allows people to totally forget their trauma as it buries itself in the unconscious. I believe that this repression (psychogenic amnesia) is actually very functional. Repressed material will emerge naturally when the person becomes psychologically able to deal with it. If not, it is probably best left where it is.

Geraldine lived alone in a flat above a shop where she worked weekends. She had two other jobs, cleaning, one in the early morning and one in the evening of the week days. With these three jobs she earned just enough to keep herself, her car, and pay all her bills, but with very little to spare. Her arrangement with her landlord, which allowed her to live in this flat, was that she had to do a minimum number of hours working in the shop. However, as time went on, her landlord/boss demanded that she work longer and longer hours, with the threat that she would lose her flat if she refused. Geraldine had no friends and her mother, who lived nearby, was her only companion. Geraldine suffered repeated bouts of depression, and could never maintain satisfactory long-term relationships with men. As she crumbled under the stress of working too many hours with little time for herself or her mother, Geraldine's GP sent her to the counsellor.

As the counsellor helped her explore her present dilemma, he asked about her upbringing. It transpired that Geraldine's father had left the family home when she was five years old. She had two sisters, one a year older, the other a year younger, neither of whom would have anything to do with their mother and nothing to do with Geraldine because she maintained the relationship with their mother. Geraldine therefore felt the sole responsibility of her mother as she became elderly, as well as her mother being her only companion.

Geraldine's memory of her childhood was short and sketchy. So as she and the counsellor picked out the pieces of her past like a jigsaw puzzle, a picture was beginning to emerge to Geraldine for the first time. Her father had left the family home when a relative found him having sex with the eldest daughter. Geraldine could also fleetingly remember her father pulling down the knickers of his youngest daughter. She also knew that he would choose her alone to go with him for rides in his car, but had no recollection of what had transpired or whether abuse had taken place.

With the counsellor's help, Geraldine understood that on the balance of probability she had been sexually abused by her father, as had her two sisters. As she had no recollection of the events, the counsellor worked on an 'as if' policy which allowed her to work through her distress. She also felt that again, on the balance of probability, her mother knew of the abuse, but did nothing about it in order to keep the family together. It was a relative that had blown the family apart at the discovery. In much the same way, Geraldine did not challenge her mother on this, to keep the remnants of her family together. Her sisters, however, could remember their abuse and could not forgive their mother for it. Nor could they understand where Geraldine was coming from.

Working on her childhood difficulties enabled Geraldine to understand how she perpetuated her own abuse in the relationships she chose and why she allowed her boss/landlord to treat her in an abusive way.

False memory syndrome

Much has been written lately on the pros and cons of false memory in abusive situations. This has developed from the lobbying of people who have been challenged with or accused of abusing members of their own family. FMS applies only to people who, prior to therapy, had no memory at all of the abuse (Toon et al., 1996). It does not apply to those who have had partial recollection of abusive situations. Therapists have been accused of 'planting' suggestions of abuse in the heads of their clients (the Karpman triangle again!); that there is a new form of over-zealousness by which therapists see all adult damage in terms of sexual abuse. This reminds me of the rigidity of Freud who saw all neuroticism in terms of sexual fantasy and the desire to be seduced, never considering that it might actually have happened. Alternatively, it is argued that therapists implant ideas of sexual abuse in their clients' minds to prolong the therapy for financial gain.

From my own experience, I know that there are people who have been abused who, to outside appearances, have lived very ordinary lives. They function relatively normally and choose to do nothing and say nothing about their abuse. Going to therapy, even in a short-term contract, may change all that. For the first time they talk about it, cry about it and rage about it. It is at this stage that the client is most likely to want to go off and say something to other members of the family, or even challenge the abuser. I would not encourage the client to do so, but the counselling is about encouraging the client to take charge of her own feelings, becoming autonomous rather than reactive. From the outside, it looks to friends and relatives as if the person has been changed by the therapy, and this may be a time when the therapist becomes blamed. It also happens that in reviewing one's past in a deep and meaningful way, as occurs in therapy, people remember things that had hitherto been forgotten. We have known for many years (Bartlett, 1932) that our method of remembering is fragile. As fragments of memory of past events emerge from the unconscious, our brain weaves them into a solid fabric of an event, providing a cognitive structure. The fragments will be true, but the woven interplay may be false. The counsellor will help the client sort the wheat from the chaff with questions and challenge, but at the end of the day the accuracy of forgotten memories cannot be validated without external verification. What is important to remember, however, is that 'false memory syndrome' does not exist *per se*. It is not a researched and proven phenomenon that has basis in fact. It is a theoretical concept brought about by those who argue that they have been wrongly accused. It is therefore preferable for the counsellor to maintain an open non-judgmental stance and, as always, to believe the client.

Physical abuse

Parents who are angry, aggressive, dominant and desire the complete and absolute obedience of their child may use violence as a means of breaking the child's will. If they succeed, the child grows into an adult who is meek and inadequate with a broken spirit. She will be compliant, malleable and unable to meet her own needs. In her desperate desire to be liked and approved of, she will go to enormous lengths to meet the unreasonable demands of those who are important to her. Her fear of parental authority will be ever-present, even when she is a middle-aged adult and the parent is elderly.

Alternatively, the parent may lash out at the child because he is unable to control his own frustrations and has not learned how to communicate or negotiate adequately. Such a child may grow into an adult seething with frustration, anger and resentment, with an equal inability to communicate or keep her own anger in check. Under situations of stress, or circumstances similar to those that occurred in her own upbringing, the child becomes an adult who is likely to lash out at her own child. Thus the battered child becomes a child-batterer. Such transgenerational transmission is obviously dangerous as violence has a tendency to escalate.

Emotional abuse

Too many children experience covert damage as a consequence of their parents' own psychological damage. The most obvious example is children of those who have some form of mental ill-health. In a situation where the adult is unable to meet their own needs, they are equally liable to be unable to meet the emotional needs of their children. Children of alcoholics, drug abusers, workaholics, all suffer emotional deprivation as a result of their parents' addiction. This includes adults on long-term prescribed psychotropic medication. Thompson (1992) describes in detail the kind of abuse and deprivation that people experience emotionally, covering a range of parents who are over-critical, demanding, manipulative, overbearing, intrusive, suicidal or just plain cold. She elaborates: 'through denigration, resentment, criticism and judgement; through humiliation and cruelty of any description; through coldness and the withdrawal of any warmth, caring and support leading to feelings of abandonment, isolation and bereftness; for whom one parent meted out abuse or was responsible for neglect and deprivation and where the other parent stood passively by' (Thompson, 1992: 225). Such children grow into adults who are insecure, inadequate and needy.

> Susan was the consequence of her mother's affair with an American GI during the war. Her mother married a local man when Susan was two. He was reasonably tolerant of her until her half-sibling was born. When her stepfather had a child of his own, his attitude to Susan changed. He became cold, and would never speak to her, conveying messages of instruction only through her mother. When he came home from work she was sent to her room, and was not allowed into his company. At weekends she was pushed out of the house to play, and was only

allowed in the house for meals. If it was raining she was allowed to go into the garden shed and had to stay there alone. At the rare times she was in his presence she was forbidden to speak and had to keep absolutely still as if in a catatonic trance. She had to eat her meals alone in the kitchen while the rest of the family ate in the dining room. Another sibling was born, and she pleaded with her mother to be allowed to help with the baby. Stepfather flew into a furious rage at the suggestion and screamed that under no circumstances was she to be allowed anywhere near his son. As Susan and her half-brothers became older, they would secretly whisper together in their father's absence about his unfair treatment of her, and occasionally one would risk trying to appeal to his better nature. But any such thought of including Susan in his family caused him to fly into a terrible rage.

By the time Susan was a teenager, she was the household cook, cleaner, and gardener. She still was excluded from the family and had little pleasure in life. Her stepfather forbade her to work as she had to keep the house, but she managed to sneak off and work for a couple of hours each day at the local supermarket, which gave her enough money to buy the one or two new things that she had ever had in her life. It was there that she met David, a trainee manager who was attracted by this thin, pale, socially inept girl with a haunted expression. When her step-father heard of their plans to marry, he flew into another rage forbidding her to marry or to continue working, and confined her to the house, locking her in her room. David, however, was not intimidated by the stepfather, and challenged him openly and publicly at his place of work. In the face of his colleagues' and superiors' opinion as they heard how the stepfather treated Susan, he agreed to release her from the house on the proviso that she left the home and never saw her mother and step-brothers again. She indeed did not see her mother again as her mother died of cancer six months later. Her stepfather did not inform Susan of her mother's illness or her death.

Assessment

These are the most common presentations of people with a history of childhood damage:

General abuse:
> recurring depression without obvious cause
> difficulty in establishing and maintaining relationships
> sleep disturbance
> fear of being overwhelmed by emotion (e.g. unexploded bomb)
> no self-worth
> inability to trust
> recurring suicidal tendencies

Sexual abuse:
> fear of intimacy
> nightmares/flashbacks

sexual dysfunction
genital-urinary problems
bowel problems
Physical abuse:
    inadequacy
    being compliant/whining
    continual anger or rage
    old wounds (e.g. healed broken bones) causing physical discomfort
    damaged hearing or eyesight from head blows

Counsellors need to be mindful that there is also a correlation between the following disorders and childhood abuse: eating disorders, self-mutilation, substance abuse and compulsive behaviour.

Geraldine, Susan and Richard to be discussed in the next section, all worked in TLT taking six sessions and a six-month review. None of them opted for referral for further psychotherapy.

TLT procedures

Children learn injunctions at an early stage of abuse. These injunctions, like *protect the family, don't be selfish, don't make a fuss, don't tell*, keep the child behind a wall of secrecy. By telling the counsellor the details of the abuse – very often in such detail as would not be told to anyone else – the childhood injunctions are transformed into adult evaluations. However, as such injunctions are so strongly embedded in the client's psyche, they may not be so easily removed. The client may become angry with the counsellor for suggesting he break the secret code, or may remove himself from the counselling for fear of the negative consequences. For this reason, during the first and second sessions, the counsellor needs to **explore** the feelings of the client as an adult, and keep the details of the abuse low-key.

When you feel trust has been established, explore with the client the consequences of breaking the secret by telling you about the abuse in detail. When the client is ready, debrief in minutiae, stopping the client if she is speeding through it. If the client starts to describe it as an observer, bring her back into the child by asking for elaboration on feelings and sensory perceptions. Remember that splitting was functional for the child, but the dissociation is causing a malfunctioning adult. Grounding helps the client to become more integrated, but it will be a very painful experience. The counsellor should not try to obliterate the pain, but should acknowledge it and move it on to a place where it does not hurt so much. In validating the pain, the counsellor can encourage growth in spite of it.

Telling the story produces powerful emotions for the client and for the counsellor (who may feel like an abuser or a voyeur). The balance between the right amount of prompting to tell the story and recognising when the client has gone as far as she can is a fine one, and mirrors the intensity of the client's ambivalence (Dale, 1992). This debriefing often produces a process where the client gets worse before she gets better, as all the pent-up emotions are released. Clients should be made aware that progress is never a straight line, but has peaks and troughs, two steps forward and one step back. This also needs to be conveyed to the significant others of the client who may find her mood swings difficult to handle.

Affirmations are very important when the story has been told, particularly ones that reinforce the client's **understanding** that it was not his fault, and he was not to blame. The feelings of shame, guilt and responsibility are pervasive, especially if the client experienced sexual arousal or orgasm during the abuse. It is important therefore not to say to the client you *must not* feel guilty. Say, rather, that you are *bound* to feel guilty given the way you were victimised. Encourage the client to acknowledge repeatedly 'I was the child, she (the abuser) was the adult.' For, as Thompson (1992) pointed out, it is not until a client is absolved from the blame for how he turned out as an adult that he is freed to take responsibility of himself in the present and start the process of healing. The client needs to be aware of himself as a victim in the process. However, the counsellor has to treat these affirmations very sensitively as the client may still have strong warm feelings for his abuser. In this situation, the client needs to be given permission to love the abuser but to hate her behaviour.

As part of our unconditional positive regard, we therapists believe what clients tell us, and we validate and reinforce how they feel about that. A client not knowing or not remembering whether she has been abused as a child experiences a great deal of psychological anxiety. It helps in these situations for the counsellor to suggest to the client that they work on an 'as if' basis. Continuing the work as if the abuse had occurred allows the client to step away from the stress of something that is uncertain, and to work on concrete issues. It soon becomes clear that whether the abuse occurred or not is secondary to dealing with how a client is responding to his past.

> Richard came to the counsellor in a great deal of distress. He had been to a hypnotist, and during the course of the sessions he had visualised himself as a child in a rape situation. The hypnotist had brought these images out of his unconscious, but nothing further had happened. The

hypnotist had not helped him to deal with the images and he still was not sure whether they were true. But these images kept flashing into his mind and he was deeply disturbed by them. The counsellor talked Richard through the flashbacks in detail:

Counsellor: Bring your image into your conscious awareness, Richard, and tell me about it as if you are describing a photograph. What do you see?

Client: I see a little boy curled up lying on the ground. His hands and feet are tied, and he has a dirty scarf wrapped around his mouth.

Counsellor: How old is the child?

Client: I'm not sure. About six or seven I would say. He looks small.

Counsellor: What is he wearing?

Client: He has a thin cotton T-shirt with a little pattern on the front. It is yellow. The pattern is a rabbit – like Bugs Bunny. He has short green cotton trousers, but they are pulled down exposing his bottom.

Counsellor: Can you see Bugs Bunny in that position, or are you remembering him?

Client: I remember the T-shirt, it was one of my favourites.

Counsellor: This child is you then?

Client: I think so. It looks like me, but part of the face is covered up.

Counsellor: The hair is the right colour and style?

Client: Yes, I am sure it is me.

Counsellor: Now describe the surroundings.

Client: It looks like a yard of a farm or a cottage. There are some trees nearby and a little clearing amongst the trees. I am lying on bracken in the clearing.

Counsellor: Did you know of anywhere like this when you were a child?

Client: Why yes! There was a place, a sort of small-holding, near where we used to play as children. It was away from the housing estate where we lived, and it was a sort of run-down. I used to meet up with my pals and would run over there and call out to the old man who lived there. He used to live with his son. There weren't any women in the house. They always looked so scruffy and dirty. We used to laugh at them and call them names.

Counsellor: Do you recognise the place in the picture?

Client: Yes, I do, it is close to this cottage amongst the apple trees. There was a clearing amongst the trees where we used to sit and talk and eat the apples we had stolen from the trees when the old man wasn't around.

Counsellor: Can you see anyone else in the picture?

Client: No I can't, but I seem to know it wasn't the old man, it was his son who was there with me. And I know he put something into my backside. I don't know what, but I just know it happened.

Counsellor: How do you know this?

Client: I don't know how I know. I don't really remember, I just sense it. And there is something else I sense but can't really remember. Something to do with sweets. Yes! There they are in the picture! The boy is clutching them between his tied hands.

Richard could never really remember whether this picture fragment was a real event, or whether it was a dream or a fantasy. He could not piece together anything more than this image brought out in a hypnotic trance. But by using an 'as if it had happened' approach, he had something to work with and on. His distress reduced and he concentrated on dealing with the consequences of it.

Part of the client's understanding has to be to realise that she is going through a grieving process as the adult mourns for her lost childhood. All the common manifestations of grief occur, so as in bereavement situations, much of the process is repeated exploration and facilitating understanding rather than direct **action**. However, some homework may be appropriate to aid the client's progress. For example, I recommend the workbooks at the end of this chapter at the first session. This enables the client to read about other people's stories and discover that she is not alone in what has happened to her and how she feels. There are useful exercises in the book, like writing about the abuse, and it helps if the client does this before having to speak about it as it helps her to formulate her thoughts. There is also a section for the partner of the client, who may feel totally bewildered and pushed out of the process.

The client may move on to wanting to tell others of the abuse outside of the session. It will help if the consequences of this can be thoroughly explored within the session as very often the reaction received from outside is not what the client had anticipated. Sometimes, the counselling can lull the client into a false sense of security. He may feel reassured because the counsellor has believed everything he has said, and has validated his sense of humiliation. He may mistakenly assume that partners, siblings or parents may react in a similar way – and, of course, they don't.

Should the client challenge the abuser? This is a difficult one, and the consequences should be thoroughly reviewed beforehand. Some clients have no wish to do so because their abuser is now elderly or frail and to cause them distress would make the client feel guiltier. It would invoke even more distress in the client if the abuser flatly denied the abuse and called the client a liar. The denial of their own reality can throw clients backwards in their therapeutic process. Other clients, on the other hand, may be so full of anger and the need for revenge that they will be unable not to challenge their abuser. Or they may choose to avoid the person, which can have equally disruptive consequences for the family system.

Gender issues are a vital consideration in working with people who have been abused as children. If the counsellor is the same gender as the client's abuser, this will inevitably invoke transference responses. If the client is a man he may prefer to see a woman counsellor whom he will stereotypically perceive as nurturing and less likely to criticise him as unmasculine (Etherington, 1996). If the client has a preference for gender of helper, this should be noted in any referral letters sent to other agencies.

Sexual, physical or emotional abuse in childhood has damaging consequences in adulthood. Although it is usually considered that only long-term psychotherapeutic work can be of any real value, some clients get enormous benefit from the intense, focused work of TLT.

Recommended reading

Bass, E. and Davis, L. (1990) *The Courage to Heal*. London: Cedar.
Forward, S. (1990) *Toxic Parents*. New York: Bantam Books.

11

Counselling Individuals within Dysfunctional Families

Very often the counsellor becomes increasingly aware that the client seated in front of him in such great distress is the wrong client. It should be the spouse/mother/father/teenage child, etc. (or all of them), who are creating havoc and are scapegoating the presenting client. Family systems operate with fascinating complexity. Each member of the family forms a part of the system and is affected by it. Even excluded members and dead members of the family have an influence upon it. It is not within the scope of this book to review the literature on family therapy. However, any counsellor working in primary care will soon discover that a basic knowledge of family systems is essential. Barker (1992) provides a good all-round overview of the topic. Of course, the seriously dysfunctional family should be referred on to the family psychiatric service for family therapy. However, it may be that the referral will not be taken up by the family therapy service, or the family may be unwilling to attend a specialised unit. The ball then ends back in the court of those in primary care, who must do what they can. This chapter will review some of the complexities that families are faced with, and examine specific difficulties that can have an effect on the rest of the family, like ripples in a pond.

Families with young children

In Chapter 8, we discussed how a couple wishing to start a family might find that it is not as simple as they might have anticipated, and how infertility can place a heavy strain on a relationship. We also addressed, in Chapter 7, how some couples have to bear the burden of losing their much-wanted baby. But for the majority of couples, starting and rearing a family is a relatively straightforward process. However, some find that rearing young children is an extremely stressful task as, for example, the children start playing up and misbehaving. Or it may be that just having children creates a strain on the relationship. Research also shows that between 7 and

15 per cent of children experience some form of psychiatric disorder (Hart, 1994). Not all of these will require psychiatric referral, but children with conditions such as depression, anxiety, post traumatic stress, hyperactivity or school phobia are most likely to be presented to the general practitioner. Early identification and easy access to the practice counsellor can therefore help enormously in family situations.

Truancy and school phobia

Conforming to the norm is very important to children and young adolescents. They are greatly influenced by what happens to most people and how most people behave. As they grow up, they are constantly monitoring what is going on in their own lives in comparison to those who live around them, that is their friends and relatives. As they monitor the relationships within their own family in relation to those of others that they see, they soon pick up on differences that make them feel separate, different or insecure. It may be that a girl notices that her parents are always arguing so she feels it must be her fault; or a boy notices that Dad is never there to watch him at the football match like the other kids' dads so it must be because he is not good enough; or Mum is always doped up on tablets from the doctor so a daughter feels she has to be mum to the younger brothers and sisters; or Dad goes out to the pub every night so his son lies awake waiting for the row when Dad falls in through the front door. Children very often do not have the verbal capacity to communicate their distress over such situations, even if they felt that there was someone they could tell who would listen to them. So they start acting out their distress, and one such way of acting out is by not going to school.

When children do not attend school, the majority do so with parental consent. This may be because of illness, or to look after other siblings or sick relatives, or parents may simply be of the opinion that they did not like school so they do not see why they should force the child to go. But some children absent themselves for other reasons. They may feel out of place in an academic environment because they are having difficulties in learning. This may be due to problems like undetected dyslexia, Asperger's syndrome (mentioned in the next section), bullying or bereavement. If the reasons for their learning difficulties are not picked up, they may join a school subculture where smoking behind the bike sheds and bunking off school to go to machine arcades becomes the norm. Rebelling against authority becomes part of the culture, although very often the ring-leaders of these gangs have learned very little respect for authoritarian figures within their own family, and the rest of the gang have just followed suit. Experimenting with tobacco, alcohol, sex and drugs is part of the rebellion as it is in defiance of parental and authoritarian prohibitions. Robinson (1989) has shown that boys who join this subculture can maintain their levels of self-esteem by belonging to the 'in-gang', whereas girls who do so have a huge drop in their feelings of self-worth.[1] This is because, stereo-typically, girls are supposed to be good, passive and obedient, and this cultural expectation is too pervasive to be ignored.

There is a small minority of children, however, who do not attend school because they run off to do more exciting things or to be out with their friends. These children are too afraid to go to school and just want to stay at home with (usually) Mum. These are the school phobics. This is not a true phobia in the sense that the children do not have an adverse reaction at the sight of school as an arachnophobic would to the sight of a spider. But they have a very real fear of going to school and develop tummy aches, panic attacks and tantrums at the very mention of them going. It used to be thought that these children had a severe form of neurosis that made them feel inadequate in a school environment, but this thinking has now changed. School phobia is now thought to be a symptom of some form of family dysfunction: that the child's anxiety about being away from the home may be a justifiable one given the home set of circumstances. This is one example where seeing the child alone would be insufficient to cure the presenting symptom.

Attention deficit hyperactivity disorder (ADHD)

Some children are severely hyperactive and aggressive. They show an inability to maintain their concentration for even short periods of time. They are impulsive, disobedient and drive their parents to distraction. They also disrupt their classrooms and any social clubs to which they may belong, once again by being inattentive and unfocused. The consequences are not only underachievement educationally, but a lack of friendships and social activities, from which they are excluded. The loneliness seems to make them more aggressive and disruptive.

There seem to be two theoretical problems with these children. First, they have an inability to focus their attention for a sufficient length of time to complete the usual developmental tasks for their age. Second, they lack the behavioural inhibition that stops all children from being totally impulsive. Some of these children will have identifiable neurological damage or a recognised chronic illness. But many show no known aetiology. Longitudinal research into this disorder is still fragmentary, but preliminary studies suggest that the difficulties reduce with adolescence and adulthood. This is particularly the case with the hyperactivity and impulsiveness, although the inattention may persist into adulthood (BPS, 1996).

A qualified psychologist or psychiatrist should make the diagnosis of ADHD, so referral to an appropriate child agency is essential. It is important not to label a child as ADHD when he manifests high levels of exuberance, naughtiness or hyperactivity that do not affect the social or educational achievements appropriate for his developmental age. Links between behaviour and food additives also need to be investigated, as many children are affected by highly coloured and flavoured food products.

Asperger's syndrome

Asperger's is a form of autism that affects the way a person communicates and relates to others. Usually, the person has a normal or sometimes above-average IQ. Such children have an inability, in a social framework, to consider how others may be thinking or feeling. In particular, they find it hard to understand non-verbal signals like body language and facial expressions. This prevents friendships from forming, so the child is often found isolated in a school environment. There is limited capacity for abstract thought, restricted imagination, and often preoccupation with certain subjects. These children may also be considered to be clumsy, lacking co-ordination, so they fail in sporting activities, another reason why they tend to lack friends at school. They may have an inability to follow instructions in a social situation, so may be perceived as disobedient and wilful. The children will have sufficient self-awareness to recognise their own deficiencies, and this can lead to acting out, aggression and self-harming behaviour. As with autism, it is possible for these children to have a savant-like exceptional talent in music, art or mathematics. This syndrome is very often overlooked by educational and medical professionals alike, so it happens that a frustrated and distraught mother ends up seeing the counsellor for help with her stress and advice in parenting skills. Once again, this syndrome needs the help of a specialist in learning disability, and will therefore need a secondary referral.

Adoption

Very often couples feel that the answer to their childless distress is to adopt. At last they have a beautiful new baby and they shower their love and caring on the new child. However, as the child grows up, he may not behave in the way that the parents had anticipated. Perhaps he is rude, argumentative and aggressive, or withdrawn, passive and compliant. These children can mature into insecure and inadequate adults who will tell the counsellor that they always knew they were different, even before they were told about their adoption. Why should this be? There is an assumption in our society that so long as a child's needs are met in respect of warmth, food and love it does not matter to the child who his carer is. However, psychologically, the child knows that the carer is not his mother. He has lived with his mother, inside her, for nine months. He was an extension of her as she was an extension of him. He knows her smell, her touch and her sound, and he knows she has gone. As basic attachment theory teaches us, he feels abandoned. His distress is on a pre-verbal level, so even as an adult he cannot express it, but the feeling is still there.

> Dean had been adopted when he was six weeks old. Although his adoptive mum had another (her own) child, a daughter, Dean was always her favourite. She gave him everything he wanted. Dean grew into a spoilt, demanding child. He was aggressive and always in trouble. He used to have stand-up rows with his mother and his father, but he was wilful and they always gave in to him. His parents had told Dean at an early age that he had been adopted and that he was chosen especially to be their son. As he grew older, he had no wish to meet his real mother. He openly admitted that he loved his adopted mother, but still spent most of his life in conflict with her.
>
> When Dean reached 20 years, he was in and out of work, never staying too long in one job, always resenting having to take orders from his employers. He had run up enormous debts with a finance company for a car that he could not afford, but had persuaded his father to stand as guarantor. Dean was constantly rowing with his mother about work and money. He had met a girl he really liked and hoped to settle down, but found himself aggressively jealous and possessive, and after an inconsequential row, he hit her. Her condition of continuing the relationship was that he got help.
>
> Dean was uncomfortable with the counsellor at first, because no one had ever listened to him or talked to him in that way before. But he soon found great relief in being able to open up. They talked of his adoption:
>
> *Counsellor*: Have you ever wanted to meet your real mother?
> *Client*: No. Despite all her nagging and that, I wouldn't want to hurt our ma. She's been real good to me, like, and given me everything I ever

wanted. I do love her, you know, but she just gets on my nerves all the time, that's all.

Counsellor: How do you feel about your real mother?

Client: Why should I have any feelings about her? I don't know her.

Counsellor: You don't love her then?

Client: [*getting louder*] Why should I love her? She didn't love me when she gave me away, did she?! She didn't care, did she? She just gave me away to strangers!

Counsellor: You sound really angry, Dean.

Client: I am angry. All my life I've known I was different. That I didn't fit in. I didn't have any friends at school 'cos I was different. I used to stay on my own most of the time. I didn't need them anyway! I had one friend, Billy, but even he had his real mum. No one at school had been given away by their mums like my mum had given me away.

Counsellor: Did the others know about it at school? Did they used to tease you about it?

Client: Oh, no. I never told any of them. Only Billy knew and he wouldn't have said anything to the others. It was just *I knew*. I knew I was different.

Counsellor: You're really angry with your real mum for giving you away and making you feel different from the other children?

Client: [*quieter*] I'm really angry with her for not loving me enough to keep me.

Counsellor: So, you are really angry with your real mum, but you punish your adopted mum with your anger. You have displaced your anger on to her.

Client: I suppose you are right. It wasn't her fault my mum gave me away. All our ma did was to pick up the pieces.

Step-parenting

In Chapter 8, I mentioned the contemporary trend of serial monogamy rather than marriage for life. The unhappy consequence of this trend is that as adults move from one relationship to another, they leave behind a trail of displaced and sometimes unwanted children. As mentioned earlier, children very often feel guilty when they hear their parents argue, and this is reinforced when the parents split up. They also feel deeply hurt by the parent who has left, despite the contact maintained. So separation and divorce produce in children feelings of hurt, abandonment and guilt. Yet, all too soon in some cases, the parents are introducing a new adult, a stranger, for the child to accept as a substitute parent. The child is in a no-win situation. If she readily accepts her new stepfather, she feels that by default she is denying her own father. If she does not accept the new stepfather, her mother will feel upset and let down and it will create tension in the household. Children also use their hurt to get paybacks for the situation. They soon notice the absent father who appeases his guilt by buying unusually expensive presents or giving sums of money. They feel the pressure of the caring parent who is trying to balance work, childcare and a new relationship and so they start playing up, demanding later nights out, outings or expensive clothes under the threat of going to live with the absent parent if demands are not met.

The pressures increase more than the sum of the parts when two sets of stepchildren are involved: for example, the children of the mother may live in the household, with the children of the stepfather also staying at weekends. This creates for the two sets of children enormous tensions, resentments, rivalries for attention and affection, demands on time and money, jealousies, plus the confusion of differing value and discipline systems. The parents are torn between trying to put their own children first, being fair to the children of the partner, and trying to balance the testing time of a new relationship with the hurts of the past marriage and divorce they are still suffering.

Kylie was just 14 years old when she took an overdose of paracetamol. She had seen someone do that on television, and they had died, and she wanted to die too. When she woke up in hospital she cried because it had not worked. Mum was crying too. But Mum did not want her any more, not really. She had Graham now. Graham had moved in with her and Mum the week after Dad left. Kylie had cried all that week because she wanted her dad back, but Mum had told her off. Mum had said she had to stop crying because Graham would think she didn't like him. Well, she didn't! She didn't like the way he kept looking at her with that funny half-smile on his face. She didn't like the way he kept brushing her breasts 'accidentally' in doorways or on the stairs. And when she found him leaning against the doorframe watching her get dressed for school one morning, she complained to her mum. That caused an awful row between them. From then on, Graham was horrible to Kylie. He was always shouting at her, complaining about her to her mum, and stopping her from going out. Mum would always give in to him, saying 'He is only trying to protect you, Kylie, he really cares about you.' But Kylie could tell by the way he looked at her that he didn't care at all. She was just in the way. They were always arguing about why Kylie wasn't spending more time with her dad. She didn't care! She would rather be with Dad anyway. But he had no room for her in his little one-bedroom flat. And anyway, he was starting to see someone else and didn't have much time to spend with her. The only person who cared about her was her older sister who was married and living nearby. She cared about Kylie, and Kylie was glad of the money her sister paid her for babysitting. Her sister wanted Kylie to go and live with her – they had a spare room. But Mum would have none of it because then Dad would not have to give her money for her keep. Mum and her sister had an awful row, and Mum said she would send Kylie to the social services to be put in care rather than allow her to go and live with her sister. When Kylie was forbidden to visit her sister, Kylie took an overdose.

Adolescence

Some parents dread their offspring reaching adolescence, usually manifested between the ages of 13 and 17, and commonly earlier for girls than for boys. This transition between dependent childhood and adult autonomy can be as difficult for the teenager as it is for the parent. For the teenager, it is a time when their hormones are all over the place and sexual exploration is exciting yet scary. Future work and career prospects seem overwhelming as they feel that they are having to make decisions that will affect them for the rest of their lives. Sometimes they feel all grown up, and are irritated by their parents' injunctions about their childishness; other times they feel that their parents are not so available in protecting them and are expecting too much of them. The parents are going through their own transitionary phase, so they have their own emotional turmoil to deal with in regard to their middle age. In addition, they have to cope with the unpredictability of their child (their 'baby') who behaves like a child but demands to be treated as an adult.

High youth unemployment has placed additional pressures on young adolescents. The need to achieve academically is now being greatly encouraged by parents (who fear having to support a long-term unemployed young adult), teachers (who want to keep up their school's success ratings), and the state (who want youngsters to remain in education to keep unemployment statistics down). This is fine for those teenagers who can fit into an academic system. But many cannot. Many are not academic enough and hate the school system. They may have practical talents, but these are not so readily accessed, as the national curriculum pushes the formal academic qualifications and employers still generally ignore GNVQs. This leaves unacademic youngsters feeling displaced, demoralised and unmotivated, and they will often take their anger and resentment out on their parents. This is especially so for young men, as research shows that girls are currently achieving more academically than boys. One researcher (Willis, 1984) suggests that high youth unemployment has personal ramifications for boys in that not obtaining the status of full-time work undermines working-class masculinity. This, paradoxically, strengthens the position of young working-class girls who see unemployed young men as a less attractive prospect as husbands and fathers, and therefore prefer to set up on their own as a single-parent family rather than tie themselves down with a young man who is a financial liability. This somewhat biased view of the desires of young girls overlooks the desire of well-educated girls (irrespective of class) to establish themselves in a career before considering whether and if they want to marry or to have children. But this chauvinistic approach to the goals and wishes of young girls is pervasive and still held by many fathers. This can create tension in a household, and very often a gender split between mother and daughters and father and sons.

Sue and Sid Johnson had seen the counsellor for four sessions, and the relationship was settling down well. They were arguing less, and Sue was feeling less disgruntled about her role as a full-time worker outside the home and full-time skivvy within it. Sid worked at home and was always shouting at Sue about her vacuuming before she was going to work when he was trying to make business phone calls. In the sessions, they negotiated appropriate times for certain duties, and reluctantly Sid starting occasionally helping with household chores. They identified that Sid's way of relieving the stress and tension from his job was to shout and bawl, but Sue had a tendency to take it personally. All she wanted was to be organised and to have some peace and quiet. Sid worked in continual chaos, and his business papers were often spread all over the house. They negotiated business and home boundaries within rooms.

Suddenly, the GP sent their daughter, Emily, to see the counsellor. Emily turned up with a very pale and worried-looking Sue. Emily also looked pale, her cheeks hollow with a porcelain-like opaqueness. Emily now weighed only five stone, Sue announced anxiously, and the GP thought she was anorexic. After hearing Sue's outline of her daughter's resistance to eating and continual exercising, the counsellor asked Sue to leave the room.

Emily shared with the counsellor the trauma of living with two parents who had been engaged in verbal warfare for the last three years. She was in the middle of her A levels, and didn't think she could cope with the work. Even when Mum was out at work, she found it difficult to study at home. Dad was always shouting down the phone, which was constantly ringing. Then, as she would try to settle to a book, he would pop his head around her door and ask her to make him a cup of tea, or get his lunch, or pop to the shops for some cigarettes. She then found herself frantically rushing around the house clearing up after him or else there would be another row between him and her mother when she got home from work. She even found herself following her brother, picking up after him when he came home from school for the same reason. Then she decided to take over the household cooking. If tea was ready for Mum for when she came home from work, she would be less tense and there would be fewer rows in the house. It also allowed Emily to control the portion that she served herself for meals, which was increasingly becoming less and less. Her father was overweight, and she was frightened that one day he would have a heart attack, the way he carried on. So by doing all the cooking she could also make sure that the meals were as low in fat and calories as possible. She had heard that exercise was good for stress, and she knew she was stressed because of all the headaches she now got, especially if her parents were arguing. So she took up jogging first thing in the morning, her runs getting longer and longer. The exercise made her feel good, but her headaches and tension would return not long after she returned home. With all the time it took to run, clean the house, run errands for Dad, and shop and prepare meals, the time she had available for lectures and study reduced. She found herself skipping classes, which in turn increased her stress and worry about her approaching exams. Feeling so out of control, she could hardly bring herself to eat anything. The counsellor asked her what she saw when she looked in the mirror. 'A scarecrow,' was the reply. 'Little more than an overdressed stick insect.' This was not likely to be anorexia, the counsellor thought, as her body image was not distorted. Emily confirmed the counsellor's thoughts. 'It's not that I want to be thin, or lose weight or anything, because I know I am too thin and need to eat more. It's just that I've got that I can't be bothered any more. No matter what I do, I can't stop the rows, so I can't bring myself to do anything any more.' Emily has stopped eating to make her parents stop rowing.

The demanding parent

Being a parent is very difficult, and we are not taught the skills with which to do it. We rely on our own upbringing and a few tips from health visitors and the like to guide us through. But if we have had a damaged childhood ourselves, our frame of reference for bringing up children is very distorted. On a conscious level, we may remember unhappy things that happened to us as children, and may make a pact that our children will never experience anything similar. Or, on the other hand, we may remember good things that happened and consciously repeat them. But things happen on a subconscious level too, and parents under stress can snap into behaviours that can be damaging to the emotional and psychological development of the child. This has been covered in more detail in the last chapter, but it is worth reiterating here as parental behaviour so profoundly affects how people behave as adults.

What commonly happens is that rather than the negative parental influence diminishing as the child moves into adulthood, it perpetuates. So the counsellor will often be faced with an adult client unable to escape the demands, criticism, taunts or disapproval of her parents. Even as she moves into her thirties and forties, Mother will still be there, in the background, making demands for visits, for attention, intruding in personal affairs or interfering in child-rearing practices.[2] Or it may be a mother who cannot allow her son to be a man ('you may think yourself a man but you will always be my baby, and don't you forget it'). This is what Gorodensky (1996) calls

Mama's Boy Syndrome. The woman makes the stereotypical mother-in-law who is jealous of her daughter-in-law taking her son away. So she makes life difficult for her by complaining about and criticising to her son the housekeeping or child-rearing skills of his wife. Mother will demand that her son make frequent visits to her home, trying to draw him away from his own home. If she is divorced or widowed, the emotional pull becomes stronger on the son, who feels torn between helping his mother because she is all on her own, and spending time with his own family doing jobs in his own home. Daughter-in-law's resentment will increase as she watches the emotional blackmail as the mother rivals for his attention, and she feels continually criticised. Such resentments will inevitably lead to friction between the son and daughter-in-law and threaten their relationship. Mother, however, would not mind this, because if she can get rid of the daughter-in-law ('I told you she was no good when you insisted on marrying her!') maybe Mother could have the grandchildren and then she would feel needed again.

If the adult child's sanity survives through middle age, the next hurdle is the demanding elderly parent. Now frailer and needing more help with her physical needs, Mum can become a constant worry. The adult child is trying to balance the demands of work, her own home-life, and trying to take care of the needs of her mother. Mother will want to be taken shopping every day or so, as she will never want to buy too much at once as a constant reminder of her frailty ('I may not live that long you see, dear'). She will need her washing and ironing done, and she will also need help to clean the house. She will want to be taken out on Sundays for a drive, or she will want to be taken to the OAPs' club or bingo in the week. ('I can't get about like I used to, dear, so if you don't take me then I will see no one from one week's end to the next.') She will want to be taken on holiday with the rest of the family, and if her daughter insists on leaving her behind, you can guarantee that Mum will have a fall while she is away and will need to call her back. If the daughter does try to assert herself over Mum's demands, she turns on the tears and the frailty act in an instant. Yet the daughter knows deep down Mum is as strong as an ox and the way things are going she is going to outlive her daughter. But she also knows that her mum is elderly, so she just cannot take the chance, in case something does happen to her because then she would not be able to live with the guilt. This leaves the daughter feeling well and truly trapped and resentful, with an equally resentful husband who has been waiting for the much-promised time when the children grew up and left home so they could do what they wanted. As the couple move into their own retirement transition, they may be faced with caring for an elderly parent who is unable to live her life except through them.

The demented parent

Demographic changes have demonstrated that people are now living much longer, and it is becoming increasingly more common for people to live until their eighties and nineties. The ageing process produces changes in cognitive function, often due to vascular degeneration. Six per cent of people over 65, and 20 per cent over the age of 80 are affected by dementia. Research has shown that people experience dementia and die sooner (Rodin and Langer, 1980) when their need to keep in cognitive control is taken away from them. Thus a person who can physically cope with living independently, and staying in control of his own life, is less likely to experience dementia than someone living in a residential or nursing home where everything is done for him, and all decisions are taken away from him.

Alzheimer's disease is a severe form of senile dementia in which the brain cells start to atrophy and dry up. It produces a severe memory loss in which sufferers may not even know who their sons and daughters are. They also have a tendency to be argumentative, aggressive, and to wander off (often in their night-clothes) in a state of bewilderment. The only true methods of diagnosis of Alzheimer's disease are by post mortem or brain scan, which can highlight the atrophy of the cerebral tissue (Rosser, 1993). Unfortunately, Alzheimer's is increasingly becoming used as a generic term for anyone who starts showing any signs of cognitive dysfunction, like memory loss or confusion. In the elderly, this may be senile dementia, where the symptoms are not as severe as Alzheimer's. Or it may be that the person is either grieving, depressed, stressed, on psychotropic medication, or has an undetected head injury from a fall, all of which also produce senility-type symptoms.

Living with an elderly parent who is demented can be highly stressful. They can become unpredictable and argumentative, and challenges to their behaviour will not be accepted readily; they still see themselves as the adult, therefore in charge, and their carer as the child. They often start collecting things from around the house, like a magpie, and storing them in secret cupboards or hideaways. They may forget to buy or prepare food. There is also some distorted perception, as they do extraordinary things, like toasting a tissue under the grill, or spreading gravy browning on their toast. Like a young child, they need to be watched carefully, as the carer can never really be sure what they will get up to next. Social services will not really become involved in their care until they become a danger to themselves or others, and a long period of time can go by before they get that bad. In the meantime, the carer, who may be an elderly spouse or a not so young sibling, struggles to care for someone who is forgetting who they are. Respite care can be emphatically refused by the elderly person, who has no concept of the stress he is causing, or that the carer has anything else to do in her life other than look after him.

Assessment

How can you assess a dysfunctional family? Well, in a sense, they leap out and hit you as the client tells her story. The client may feel inadequate, withdrawn and guilty as the family heaps their blame on to a willing victim. There may also be, deep down, a bubbling anger, for her sense of justice knows things are not right.

If the client is a child, is he acting out the problems of the parent or caregivers? For example, the child may be playing up because the parents are constantly arguing or are splitting up. Check to determine if the behaviour is in response to an inability to achieve in classroom activities. Is the child finding it too difficult, or too easy, to achieve normal developmental tasks? If an educational psychologist has not assessed the child, determine if such an assessment can be made. Assess the child's interaction with his peers: is he isolated, or is she being bullied? The counsellor also needs to be mindful of abusive situations that fill a child full of prohibitions against telling the truth. Can she say if she is the victim of emotional, sexual or physical abuse? Is she showing signs of withdrawal, inappropriate sexual language or sexual behaviour? Be careful, however, not to rush in on the assumption of abuse without being very sure. For example, one counsellor called the social services because a child had talked about it being rude to lick bottoms. It turned out to be an innocent remark about the behaviour of dogs. But the investigation by the social services nearly destroyed the family, and made the father nervous of ever getting close to his daughter again.

If the client is elderly, do not make the assumption that memory loss or occasional confusion is the onset of dementia. Check out for depression first. Remember that depression is a normal part of grief, and the elderly are likely to experience more grieving situations than younger people. If the client is depressed, medication should be discussed with the GP and considered cautiously. The elderly often respond to psychotropic medication with confusion, memory loss and abstract behaviour (Munos, 1994), and then others accuse them of being senile. Neill (1989) suggests assessing for dementia by asking if the person has noticeable problems in:

- working out how to do basic tasks
- remembering recent events
- keeping in touch with conversation
- knowing where he is
- knowing the time
- correctly naming persons seen regularly

Here, as with children, the counsellor needs to be mindful of the elderly being physically, emotionally, financially or sexually abused (SSI, 1996).

Other clients need to be assessed as part of unveiling their stories. It may be that the client is so demoralised and lacking in self-worth that she really does believe, as her family make her believe, that anything that goes wrong is all her fault. If the family collude with her in thinking and feeling that is the case, then that family is dysfunctional. For example:

> Jean's life was in total chaos. She lived in a large house jointly owned by herself, her husband and her parents. Her mother was a dominant matriarch who had ruled her family with an iron rod until four years ago when she was 72. At that time, Mother still took the salaries earned by Jean and her husband, George, away from them for household expenses and gave them pocket money. When her mother started to develop dementia, Jean gathered sufficient assertiveness to insist that she now took over the financial considerations of the home. Mother eventually agreed, but became increasingly more angry and aggressive because she no longer had total control. Jean's father, who had been a passive, insignificant shadow behind his forceful wife, had a stroke. After two weeks' hospitalisation, he was sent home, with the nursing staff pointing out that he would probably need 24-hour care.
>
> Jean had three children. The eldest had bought a home of her own, but it was just around the corner, so she still went to Jean's every evening for a meal and company before going home. Her second daughter was married, and had a small child with another on the way. When Jean had an accident at work, which permanently damaged her back and led to her medical retirement, her second daughter saw it as an ideal opportunity for Jean to look after the child while she went to work. The daughter and her husband bought a house for themselves, again near Mum, but it was in such bad condition that it needed complete refurbishment. So they moved in with Jean and her parents while George started doing up the house for them. His son-in-law initially helped him, but then the son-in-law had a car accident that seriously damaged the structure of his leg. He was going to be incapacitated for a long time. Jean's youngest child, John, was 14 and had for several years suffered with obsessive compulsive disorder.

This involved him running up and down stairs 87 times and other compulsive rituals of which Jean was the focus. John's psychiatrist blamed Jean for John's disorder because Jean was constantly losing her temper and shouting at members of the family.

Jean and George would also continually argue, because Jean had nowhere else to dump her anger and frustration. He was a quiet passive man, like her father, so Jean picked on him. George worked long hours, and then, after his evening meal, would go off to his daughter's house to decorate so he kept himself out of the way most of the time. Jean was therefore, single-handedly, caring for an aggressive mother with senile dementia, her stroke-victim father, her two-year-old granddaughter (and the threat of another baby on the way), her semi-crippled son-in-law, and her son with obsessive compulsive disorder. She also tried to keep the house clean and would cook for ten every night. And they all complained when she got angry. Her second daughter would scream at her, 'You've got a real problem, Mother! Why don't you go and see someone and get your head sorted!'

Of course Jean was angry. Her house was living chaos and everyone was blaming her for it. Yet without her, the whole system would grind to a halt. Her son's obsessive disorder developed as a result of the chaos, yet even his therapist was joining in the system by blaming Jean's anger. And, because of years of being at her mother's beck and call, Jean had insufficient personal self-worth to see otherwise. She was unable to say no to any members of her family except her husband, whom she had chosen because he made no demands on her anyway. For there to be any help for Jean, therapy had to involve other members of the family otherwise they would vehemently resist any changes Jean wanted to make in her own life-style.

The other scenarios mentioned in this chapter show similar family dysfunctions. Dean was angry and blaming his mother for his adoption. But when his mother was brought in to the sessions, the counsellor found that she was overly intrusive in Dean's life and well-being. She still treated him like a little lad who was throwing tantrums to get his own way. She also clearly resented the girlfriend, whom she saw as a rival for Dean's attention and affection. Mother was therefore constantly disparaging about the girlfriend and their relationship. Her biggest fear was that Dean would leave home altogether, and her hold over him would be broken, so she would encourage the financial indulgences and dependence in order to prevent him from having sufficient income to do this. Dean realised the hold his financial difficulties had over his ability to control his life. He had found a nice girlfriend and wanted to settle down. Mum realised that if she could not accept the girlfriend, she would lose her son altogether. They finished after four sessions, but the counsellor took the view that Mum would continue to snipe at the girlfriend behind Dean's back whenever she got the opportunity, because of her obsessiveness with Dean. The counsellor tried to raise the issue of the mother's relationship with her own husband, but she was not willing to allow that to be addressed.

Kylie's mother attended the session shortly after Kylie's suicide attempt. At this session she was very concerned for her daughter. Mum acknowledged that her relationship with Graham was not a good one, and that she had made a mistake. On one level she said she had felt jealous of Graham's initial attention to Kylie, yet on the other hand she insisted that his feelings for Kylie were only fatherly. She had not realised how desperate Kylie had felt until she had taken the overdose. Mum knew she now had to go to a solicitor and sort her relationship out. At the next session, however, as the memory of Kylie's OD faded, her mum had changed her mind. She felt her relationship was not that bad. Anyway, she argued, she was entitled to a life of her own. When Kylie grew up she would leave home and her mum would be left alone, and she could not bear that. When the counsellor reminded her of Kylie's desperation, Mum dismissed it as a cry for attention. She blamed everything on Kylie's sister who had ideas above her station and stirred up trouble between her mother and Kylie. It was all right for the sister, Mum continued, as she had a man of her own, but she was trying to get rid of the man in her mother's life. She must be jealous. The counselling ended after five sessions. Kylie accepted Mum's need to maintain a relationship with a man of her own choosing, and her mother begrudgingly agreed that Kylie should go and live with her sister.

Sid and Sue Johnson were horrified that their arguing, which for them had almost become a way of life, had caused their beloved daughter to go to such lengths to stop them rowing. Emily was unable to talk to her parents at home, because they immediately resorted to the pattern of blaming each other. When the three went to counselling, they had to stop and listen to each other. In particular, Sid had to realise that his little girl was an adult in her own right, and was not there at his beck and call to run his errands for him; that she was entitled to her own space. Sue had to learn that although it was right that Emily should help in the home, it was wrong for Sue to allow Emily to take over all the domestic chores to appease Sue's anger because Sid would not help. This made Sue realise that she was creating in her children another generation where it is assumed that the women undertake all the domestic chores, whilst the men (their son) did no chores at all, like his father. This family resolved their difficulties in just three sessions, after which Emily had regained her appropriate weight.

TLT procedures

The work will start with the presenting client alone. **Explore** the issues being presented, and hear the problems within the family that are not being identified. This might be the first opportunity for the scapegoated client to be heard in her own right, so this exploration and understanding phase may take longer than with other clients. Action will be delayed, other than small homework tasks that allow the counsellor to test the dysfunctional family hypothesis. Such families will fiercely resist the client making even minor changes, and will decry the counselling as a subversive influence. Family members may even impose their point of view on to the counsellor by writing letters, telephoning, or even attending the counselling session uninvited. The counsellor should make his boundaries clear in relation to all such attempts. No discussion of the client's progress should be made with the family of the client. Unexpected attendances, even if the counsellor feels it would be a good idea to see that family member at a later date, should be refused. The family needs to learn about boundaries from the counsellor's example. The counsellor and the client should always make it clear to the family that they are in charge of the counselling work, and family members will only be invited by mutual consent.

The client will need two or three sessions on her own to discuss her family dynamics, and how she responds to them. Affirmations should focus on her accepting responsibility only for her own behaviour, and not for the behaviour of others. Very often, in these kinds of families, emotional blackmail is a very overt method of manipulation. But they also become masters at more subtle methods of making the scapegoat feel guilty and responsible for non-compliance with unreasonable demands. Double-bind messages are common. For example a mother will deride her son for being over-weight but will buy him cream cakes for his tea. There will be a high level of intrusiveness into the life of the adult children. Autonomy and personal space will not be accepted. The client will need to learn that such things are basic rights, and even if he is unable to assert himself sufficiently at the early stages to demand these rights, he will soon feel less guilty for aspiring to them.

Once the relevant family members are brought into the sessions, it is important that everyone feels listened to and heard. More malignant members of the family will seek to exert influence, either by being absent, thus treating the process with contempt, or by attending and being either disruptive or overwhelming. The counsellor will need to be a very tactful referee, making sure that each member has equal time to have a say. She will also need to be constantly vigilant against being drawn into the family system by allowing the scapegoated client to assume responsibility for the problems of the family. For example, in Jean's family, they all complained about Jean's outbursts of anger, that would erupt with unpredictable ferocity. However, they were less willing to accept that she was overloaded and needed help because she was in constant physical pain from her back injury. Her daughters were equally resistant to the idea that they should be getting on with their own lives away from Jean and George, rather than relying on them still to cook for them, decorate for them, and provide continual childcare over and above normal grandparenting arrangements.

Some of the skills used in systematic family therapy can be very useful to the counsellor. For example, gossip questions are a very useful tool. In this case, the counsellor may ask the teenager, 'What does Mum feel about Dad constantly working late?' Mum will already have said how she feels, but may hold things back from embarrassment. Asking another member of the family to assess the feelings of others will often reveal family secrets or hidden alliances. Such gossiping can also be less threatening to a family than asking the questions directly. Another useful intervention is one already mentioned in Chapter 8, and that is the paradox intervention. Telling a family that they cannot change, or that they need to change very slowly because of potential damaging consequences, can have profound and rapid effects.

If the presenting client is a teenager, the counsellor may be viewed as another authoritarian adult. The counsellor must respect the teenager as an equal, and insist that family ground rules are negotiated fairly. Parents worried about sex, violence and drugs represented graphically in the press often try to over-protect the teenager by laying down rigid ground-rules in respect of going out, coming-home times, and friends that are considered unsuitable. They will try to enlist the counsellor on their side by emphasising their love and desire to give the teenager the best possible start. The counsellor has to achieve a difficult balance of appreciating the love and fear of the parents, whilst affirming that loving means trusting and letting go. Quid pro quo arrangements of expecting both the parents and the teenager to make concessions are the most successful.

When one of the family members is elderly, especially if dementia seems to be an issue, the elderly person should be allowed sufficient time and space to have his say. Not many therapists include people with dementia in therapeutic situations, although there are a few initiatives of this sort throughout the country. However, as with geriatrics, it is not the most favourite presenting disorder; adult survivors of sexual abuse or eating disorders are more the flavour of the month (if you will excuse the pun). There are also some basic existential anxieties for the elderly that may need to be addressed. Modern technology means that our society has changed faster over the last generation than it has in the previous three or four generations. Thus an elderly person may remember a time when there were no cars or planes, let alone space travel. Religious values, child-rearing practices and home economics were vastly different in their childhoods. They were taught their beliefs and have held them firmly for many years, so they find it hard to understand why others should have a different point of view. Sometimes the very pace of life is too confusing for them. They know that death is looming, but they fear more the onset of Alzheimer's where they may lose their dignity and respect in the eyes of others. So the counsellor will need to give the elderly person much more time to explore, to the point of rambling, as he catalogues a very long list of life events and how things were. When people become old, the one thing they are not given by society is time and respect, so they will value counselling sessions enormously.

Counselling children also needs special consideration. As their behaviour is moulded and shaped by their parents, they are very often not given time to express how they feel, or to join in in-depth discussions. When a young child is crying or throwing a tantrum in Tesco's, you often see the stressed mother scold or spank the child for his behaviour. Yet, when you think about it logically, shopping in the supermarket can be a stressful experience, and I often feel it would be lovely to throw a tantrum in the supermarket aisle.[3] So the child is doing naturally what we as adults have been conditioned, to our cost, not to do. However, children learn at an early age that they are not allowed to express emotions that are viewed as negative: for example it is considered unacceptable for a child to express irritation or anger or to feel depressed. Boys are still told by numerous fathers that it is unmanly to cry. Although the custom of children being seen and not heard is less predominant in contemporary society, it still exists in many people's child-rearing practices.

Bullying at school has resulted in some young people attempting and even succeeding in committing suicide. Press coverage of these events has forced schools to take bullying seriously, and some schools have adopted in-house counselling schemes either using a professional counsellor or by training the children to counsel each other. These schemes, and initiatives like Childline, have highlighted the importance that people are now placing on letting children seek help from the oppression of others, even their own parents. Increasingly, children are going to the counsellor at the doctor's for help with a particular problem.

For some children, sitting alone with an adult in a strange room, talking about personal things can be an awesome experience (some adults feel this too!). But many open up very rapidly and are very frank and matter-of-fact about their domestic situations. If you do find that the child is having difficulty in expressing himself, ask him to write it down as homework, either as a story or in poetry. One lad brought me a folder full of poems about his unrequited love, which I felt could have been publishable. Others write the story of their troubles as if it is happening to someone else. Others draw pictures of their distress. Whatever they bring, it opens up a new medium of communication, especially in younger children whose command of language is insufficient to be fully expressive. As Carolin (1995) reasoned, the primary emotions are always there in their faces, their gestures, their body language: 'the blues of sadness, sorrow and grief; the scarlet of anger and rage; the yellow of anxiety and fear' (Carolin, 1995: 207), plus the greens of jealousy and envy, the greys of rejection and abondonment and the black of depression.

It is important to reinforce the confidentiality ethic to the child, as they are used to professionals reporting events back to parents. They need to be clear that the counsellor will not tell their parents what they have said unless they expressly ask her to do so. Counsellors may also find that they need to shorten the length of the counselling session, as 50 minutes is a very long time for a young child to concentrate.

Some children, however, are very comfortable with counselling, as their parents have encouraged them to talk about issues that affect them. I will end this section with such an example.

Joe was nine years old. He lived with his dad, Alan, who was a teacher. Alan and his wife had separated three years before, and she now lived in Spain. Alan and Joe were very close, and Alan always took the trouble to talk to Joe about the situation of this single-parent family. Alan had started seeing another woman, who also had a child, and although they were not living together, they frequently stayed in each other's homes for weekends. Alan asked Joe to see the doctor when Joe started playing up at school, and getting angry at home. The GP referred Joe to the practice counsellor.

Joe showed no trepidation about his counselling experience. He sat on the comfy chair, swinging his legs that could not reach the floor, pouring out his problems to the counsellor. Yes, he was angry with his mother for abandoning him. He could only see her two or three times a year and he felt lonely without her. He also felt different from his friends as, although there were a few with separated parents, all the other children lived with their mothers not their fathers. He was also angry with his dad who did not have so much time for him now that the new lady was on the scene, and he feared losing Dad, too. He felt jealous of their closeness and often caused trouble just to get Dad to notice him. The only one he felt close to was the new lady's daughter, Jenny. She was in the same situation as him, and she knew how he felt. He even called her his sister, because he always wanted to have a sister. The only thing was that she could see her dad every other weekend, whereas he could not see his mum that often.

When Joe attended for his third session, he looked at the counsellor squarely and said, 'My dad should be talking to you, you know, not just me. He still gets angry with my mum, and then he shouts at me. It's not fair! When I get angry he punishes me. When he gets angry he still punishes me because I shout back. He needs counselling too.' The counsellor asked if he could tell his dad how he felt. He immediately jumped off his chair and headed for the door. 'He's in the waiting room. I'll get him and tell him now.' Joe fetched his bemused father and told him all he felt about his father's anger. Alan looked somewhat embarrassed, but let his son have his say. He agreed with Joe's assessment that he was still angry with his former wife. He admitted that he did have a tendency to displace his anger, even though he tried not to. He then apologised to Joe for assuming that all Joe's bad behaviour was due to jealousy, and accepted his part in it. Alan decided to book in for some counselling sessions on his own. He left with a triumphant Joe hugging him tightly.

Recommended reading

Crabtree, T. (1980) *Living with Teenagers*. London: Macdonald Futura.
Forward, S. (1990) *Toxic Parents*. New York: Bantam Books.

Notes

1 Personal communication.

2 These paragraphs describe a demanding mother in a matriarchal family system, but the situation can be the same, although less often in my experience, in patriarchal families.

3 Now I know that you are thinking that we cannot all have tantrums in supermarkets. However, if we did, there would be no unstaffed check-outs, no trolleys with ineffective wheels and supermarkets would be more ergonomically designed.

12

Counselling People with Medical Conditions

Increasingly, GPs are beginning to realise that even patients with an identifiable physical illness also suffer emotional distress as a consequence of that illness. GPs are therefore choosing to refer such people for help with the emotional side of their illness, thus facilitating a more holistic approach to patient care. Research shows that counselling can greatly reduce the distress of those suffering chronic ailments (Taylor and Aspinwall, 1993). This however provides a greater challenge to the counsellor in TLT as the duration of the counselling may be dictated by the prognosis or duration of the illness rather than the number of sessions available to the client. It helps the counsellor in her work with her client if she has an understanding of the nature of the client's illness, and some of the process of medical care. It is also important for the counsellor to keep abreast of the current prognosis in a potentially fatal illness, as this can change from session to session. This chapter will review some of the more common medical illnesses that counsellors are likely to face. However, one can never anticipate how an individual will respond to the diagnosis of a chronic complaint (which Daines et al., 1997 liken to finding an elephant in the living room) so the following are likely to be the tip of the iceberg.

Multiple sclerosis (MS)

MS is a degenerative disease of the central nervous system that can be extremely varied in its effect on the sufferers. Some have it for 30 or 40 years with very little effect other than occasional wobbliness. In others it produces rapid degeneration of the organs in the body. They experience an inability to function in ordinary daily tasks, becoming first wheelchair-bound, then bed-bound, with eventual death. Some sufferers also experience a personality change, like hypomania, as the disease affects the brain; others may become deeply depressed. The average life expectancy is more than 35 years after the first onset of the disease. Common symptoms include movement and co-ordination problems, double vision, numbness, bladder dysfunction and weakness.

At the diagnosis stage, fear of a disease that one has insufficient knowledge about produces tremendous stress. However, the unpredictability of the disease is the biggest stressor, as a person who is experiencing remission from unpleasant symptoms lives with the looming prospect of not knowing what will happen tomorrow. Because of the incurability of the disease, the person soon picks up a sense of hopelessness from their medical practitioners (Segal, 1991), which can lead to bouts of severe depression and often unspoken anger.

Much of the emotion expressed in counselling focuses on fear, and anger at the medical profession for being so inadequate at combating this disease. This applies not only to the sufferers but also to the families who can do nothing but watch their loved one suffer, degenerate and die. People fear that stress or over-activity will make MS worse. They may decide, or even be encouraged by members of the family, to stop doing things that they are still capable of doing in case it makes matters worse. Thus the client is in danger of falling into a self-perpetuating spiral of fatigue and inactivity.

Some marriages cannot stand the test of time and break up, often when the person loses mobility. This is partly caused by the spouse's fear, who had not envisaged being a full-time carer of an invalid, especially when children also have to be cared for. It is also partly a desire of the sufferer who does not want to become a burden on the ones that they love. Sometimes a sufferer will stop wanting to have sex because of the illness; others will be incapable of doing so. Some have such rapid personality changes that they seem impossible to love and care for.

Chronic fatigue syndrome (CFS)

Also known as ME or 'Yuppy flu', this is a debilitating condition which is still not fully understood by the medical profession, and indeed in some circles is still not accepted as a recognisable complaint. There are several hypotheses as to how this condition comes about: either it is the aftermath of a viral infection such as myalgic encephalomyelitis or Epstein-Barr virus infection; or it is a derangement of the immune system; or it is a form of depression (which does not, however, respond to antidepressant medication). My own hypothesis is that it could also be a form of stress burnout, as virtually all the clients I have seen with this complaint previously led very over-active, full lives which ground to a sudden halt following a viral infection. Common symptoms include fatigue, muscle weakness, depression, headache, sleep difficulties, tender lymph nodes, and mental confusion. Exertion of any sort has repercussions on the client for days after, and some clients may become bedridden. The medical profession suggests anecdotally that if recovery is not made within a five-year time span, then recovery is unlikely.

Cancer

Cancer is treated with universal dread because of its history of disfigurement and inevitable death. Nowadays, early medical treatments have a good success rate, but the fear of the disease persists. A lot of this is to do with the severity of the treatments: surgical mutilation, radiation burns, severe sickness and loss of hair from chemotherapy are a lot to go through with no guarantee of success at the other side. Thus some researchers have suggested that people greet the diagnosis of cancer with the same reaction as a death sentence (McIntosh, 1974).

Cancer sufferers experience fear, anxiety and depression. These may be mixed with feelings of guilt or anger, as some people believe that the disease is a punishment for past injustices. Or there may be a behavioural-disease link that increases the feelings of personal responsibility, for example with smokers who have lung cancer. There was a similar suggestion that women who had early sexual activity were more likely to contract cervical cancer. Counselling is also sought from people following surgery for help with their altered body image, especially following breast or testicular surgery. Loss of sexual desire in these cases is also common, and during treatment patients may experience some loss of cognitive functioning.

Fallowfield (1991) points out that while the medical profession is quick to pick up on the physical aspects of cancer, the emotional distress of the patient is largely ignored. Oncology centres usually provide some form of counselling service, but of course, oncology centres are not a universal service.

Lack of knowledge contributes to a lot of the distress and fear, together with the stigmatisation and fear-reaction of others. Many cancer sufferers notice that some family and friends withdraw from them. This may be for a number of reasons, like fear of contagion, or an unwillingness to witness the pain and suffering. But this withdrawal can make the sufferer feel rejected and abandoned.

It may not only be the cancer sufferer who attends for counselling, but the partner or spouse who comes in his own right for help in coming to terms with the illness of his wife, as Peter did in Chapter 7. He may be looking for emotional support in order to get through the ordeal, but he may also be looking for guidance as to the processes involved, wanting to know what to expect and how to respond.

Diabetes

Diabetes Mellitus is a disorder of the metabolic system responsible for the storage of glucose, the main energy source derived from food. Insulin is the hormone produced by the pancreas that regulates the level of glucose in the bloodstream. Glucose is a critical source of energy used by all the organs of the body, and is the only energy source of the brain. There are two types of diabetes: type I is insulin dependent, and type II is non-insulin dependent. Those with non-insulin dependent diabetes are commonly middle-aged and over-weight with blood sugar levels that are higher than normal. They can maintain their levels of glucose through diet and weight reduction, so rapid changes in glucose levels are less likely than for those with insulin-dependent diabetes. For insulin-dependent people, the onset of the diabetes is usually in childhood or adolescence and require insulin injections to maintain their normal body chemistry. They are more at risk from sudden changes in glucose levels that can invoke hyperglycaemia or hypoglycaemia, which can lead to coma and even death.

The most likely time people will go to the counsellor because of their diabetes is at diagnosis. The message from the medical practitioner that they can lead 'normal' lives with this chronic disease feels unreal when they are required to test their blood sugar and inject themselves repeatedly throughout the day. They cannot go out without an armamentarium of syringes, insulin, blood testing equipment, and high-sugar foods. They are on a perpetual low-fat, high-carbohydrate diet, with food-binges having disastrous results. They have to constantly monitor themselves, and their significant others are constantly monitoring their behaviour, fearing a glycaemic episode. This does not feel like a normal life. In fact it feels like intense pressure and people are likely to get very low at the prospect.

Diagnosis of diabetes in children and adolescents can cause acting out, social withdrawal, feelings of isolation and 'differentness' (as discussed in the last chapter). Linking up children and teenagers to others with the same problem, either informally or through a self-help group, allows the youngsters to share coping strategies, removes the feelings of alienation, and provides an opportunity for the expression of emotions which they might not otherwise have.

Those who are less successful at maintaining their metabolic levels are more susceptible to anxiety and depression. The hormones produced at times of anxiety and stress also counteract the action of insulin, making it harder to maintain the appropriate levels. And, of course, those who are feeling anxious, stressed or depressed are less likely to be motivated to monitor and maintain appropriate levels, thus placing themselves at risk. The most common emotional responses are frustration and anger at the unfairness of developing this problem. This anger is displaced on to the medical staff, who deal with the medical aspect efficiently but often allow no opportunity for the expression of the emotions.

Diabetes places extra pressure on relationships, irritability and lethargy being common complaints of partners (Shillitoe, 1991). Sexual dysfunction is also a common complaint, in particular impotence in men and loss of sexual desire in women. Diabetes does knock a person's feeling of self-worth, because you cannot have a good sexual relationship if you do not feel good about yourself.

There is one group of insulin-dependent suffers called 'brittle' patients whose diabetes causes the most medical concern. Interestingly, these are predominantly young women who are in their early twenties or thirties, are overweight, have family or emotional problems, and are totally nonchalant about their metabolic maintenance (Tattersall and Walford, 1985). As such they have glycaemic instability and hospital admission is not uncommon. This has a manipulative effect on their nearest and dearest:

> Alison was a bubbly 25-year-old who had developed insulin-dependent diabetes when she was eight years old. She was sent to the counsellor by her GP because she was in emotional turmoil within her relationship, and was abusing herself by not monitoring her metabolic levels. The GP expressed her exasperation with the client to the counsellor: 'I keep telling her that there is no way she is going to live to old bones with this kind of behaviour, but she just shrugs and says that we all have to go some time.'
>
> Alison described to the counsellor a typical co-dependent relationship between herself and her lover. He was a man 20 years her senior with whom she worked. He lived with his wife for a while, and then would leave her to live with Alison. Then after a turbulent few weeks he would return to his wife again. This pattern of behaviour had been going on for some years, but Alison's behaviour was becoming more and more volatile and irrational as she increasingly failed to maintain appropriate levels of insulin. Her weight had doubled since she had known him. Alison's childhood had also been one of continual emotional turmoil. Her mother and father had huge fights, often in front of Alison and her siblings. Her father was an alcoholic, and would frequently beat her mother, and would lash at her or her sisters if they got in the way. Alison had one vivid memory of her father trying to run them all down in their car when her mother had dramatically left the house with her children after a fight. The only time that Alison felt any love or caring from her father or mother was when she had problems with her insulin levels and went into insulin

shock. When she came round, if dad was sober, he would be there for her, showing her tenderness and kindness. Subconsciously, Alison had incorporated this as a manipulative repertoire in her adult relationship. She had chosen an older man, looking for a surrogate father, who was just as emotionally damaged as she was. She stopped monitoring her metabolic levels when she found that this man was concerned about it, and made a fuss for her to look after herself. The more he worried about it, the less she cared about glycaemic instability because at least he noticed her then.

HIV and AIDS

Human Immunodeficiency Virus (HIV) is transmitted through body fluids, most commonly blood and semen, and is the causative factor in the development of AIDS (Acquired Immune Deficiency Syndrome). Those most at risk are people who have unprotected sexual intercourse (irrespective of sexual orientation), drug users who share intravenous needles, and haemophiliacs. The incubation period for the infection of HIV is some three to six months after exposure to the virus before obtaining a positive HIV antibody test. An HIV seroconversion illness may occur after infection, which is a flu-like illness with muscular pains, fever and night sweats. This will last about the same length of time as flu. The mean incubation period into development of AIDS for an adult is 8.23 years, although for some people it has been anything up to 20 years. Death occurs from AIDS because the immune defence system breaks down in the destruction of specialised white blood cells, and thus is unable to fight viral attack. Thus death is most likely to occur as the result of opportunistic infections like pneumonia, tuberculosis, skin cancer or toxoplasmosis rather than from AIDS.

It is important for a counsellor to be clear about the distinction between people infected with HIV and those with AIDS. All people with AIDS are HIV positive, but not all HIV positive people have AIDS.

Clients who are HIV-positive experience feelings of loss of control as the time-bomb ticks slowly away. Fear and anxiety are common, not only in the sufferers, but also in those near to them. There is still a lot of fear and ignorance regarding HIV, and many people treat the victims of the disease as if they have the bubonic plague rather than a sexually transmitted disease. Testing for HIV requires counselling both before and after the test to allow the client to evaluate the implications appropriately and to reduce the risk of suicidal ideation. This may be carried out at the surgery, but is more likely to be conducted at a specialised unit.

Coronary heart disease (CHD)

Heart disease is the single most common cause of death in the UK, and accounts for 40 per cent of deaths in men and 10 per cent in women (Bennett and Hobbs, 1991). Those who experience a heart attack and live often report feeling a changed person thereafter. The trauma of the crisis as medical staff go into action, the physical pain, and looking death head-on makes people re-evaluate their lives and change their priorities. Fears for the future, guilt about past life-style and anxieties over current chest pain and breathlessness are the primary feelings. Similarly, the spouse or partner may be in a constant state of anxiety, exhorting the person to limit their levels of exertion. This can make him feel angry at being mollycoddled, when all he wants to do is to demonstrate how well he is doing now. Counselling has been shown to reduce much of the emotional distress experienced by people with heart disease (Hill, Kelleher and Shumaker, 1992). As high proportions of people with CHD are type A personality (see Chapter 5), they will be experiencing a great deal of frustration and anger at having their usual working activities curtailed. They will also feel frustrated because they will be unable to cope with the demands that they had previously made on themselves. This lack of activity for a type A is extremely stressful. Counselling will therefore need to introduce stress management relaxation training to help the client cope with his new situation.

Angina pectoris is a tight, gripping pain in the front of the chest. People with angina are again commonly found to be of type A personality with high levels of anger, hostility and neuroticism (Bennett and Hobbs, 1991). Angina attacks, which can last anything up to an hour, can be triggered by extremes of emotion, stress and anxiety. Continual worrying about the possibility of an angina attack can be self-fulfilling, so cognitive thought stopping can aid this self-defeating behaviour. Counselling again needs to be focused on adopting new life-styles in terms of diet, exercise and smoking.

Psychosomatic illness

Throughout the chapters in this book, the link between emotional distress and physical symptoms has been repeatedly made. Most clients do realise that their physical symptoms are exacerbated by their emotional state. However, some clients remain in total denial as to the contribution that their psychological condition makes toward their physical well-being (Henderson, 1995). Such people may be those who have been experiencing dis-ease for many years (Brown and Smith, 1985), often from late childhood or early adolescence.

The most common psychosomatic complaints are of gastro-intestinal difficulties. Such clients repeatedly present to their GPs with a wide range of physical symptoms. The concept of irritable bowel syndrome (IBS) was developed for these people who have a constellation of bowel complaints, but on examination have no demonstrable anatomic abnormality. There seems to be two forms of IBS: the first is where people suffer with constipation, chronic pain (sometimes referred to as spastic colon), abdominal distension and flatulence. The other form is where the person experiences constant diarrhoea and therefore becomes extremely debilitated. Nausea and/ or vomiting may also occur. Such people become very anxious and plan their lives around the availability of toilets. Interestingly, once given the label of IBS, these clients act as if their problem has been legitimised as a recognisable disease rather than accepting that it is, in fact, a psychosomatic complaint brought about through stress. IBS sufferers can experience great relief from their symptoms following psychotherapy (Guthrie, Creed and Dawson, 1993).

In a similar vein, anxious patients experiencing adrenalin surges feel chest pain when hyperventilating in a panic attack, and are convinced that they have a heart problem. Repeatedly worrying about a weak heart increases the incidence of the experience of panic, which increases the incidence of pain, which reinforces the belief in heart disease. Sanders (1996) suggests that such people have difficulty with the expression of emotions. Either they are unable to find the words to express their feelings, or they believe that their emotions are unacceptable or dangerous, or they feel they can only get their needs met through their illness (as in Alison's case above), or they feel that physical illness is the only acceptable expression of weakness. All cases of chest pain should be checked by the GP as a way of providing reassurance for both the client and the counsellor. Some clients, however, have developed a fear of GPs themselves because of the way they have been labelled and treated by the medical profession:

> Ethel was in her late fifties when she went to see the counsellor. 'I don't know why that new doctor has referred me to you,' she said. 'I've seen all the special psychiatrists over the years and they have all told me I am a hopeless case.' Ethel looked considerably older than her years, had a stooped posture, a dishevelled appearance, and her cheek twitched nervously as she spoke. 'I suppose you've read all about me in my notes.' She indicated with a shaky hand the thick pocket of medical notes on the desk. The counsellor replied that he had not read any notes, so Ethel would have to tell him about herself.

Ethel related a story of a very unhappy childhood because of her mother's behaviour towards her. Her mother, now diagnosed as schizophrenic, was living in an institution. Ethel married early to escape her mother's tyranny. Shortly after her first child was born, Ethel became deeply depressed and her GP prescribed Valium. She took it for 10 years, then when her father died, she had a complete breakdown. 'They gave me some new tablets, but didn't tell me that I couldn't eat cheese,' she said. Ethel was hospitalised and underwent electro-convulsive therapy. She was sent home and put back on Valium, and had been experiencing panic attacks ever since – nearly 20 years. 'I no longer take Valium,' she said. 'I got myself off that years ago when I saw on the telly how addictive they were. I had a bad time but I did it! But I guess I'm always going to be a bag of nerves. I heard that nurse in the hospital. She told someone else that I was a psychopath.'

Intrigued by the story of the hospital admission, the counsellor later went through the medical notes to find that, at the time of her bereavement of her father, Ethel had been prescribed a MAOI antidepressant (Nardil) in addition to her Valium. By her own admission, Ethel had not been told she could not eat cheese. She obviously had done so, and had a severe hypertension reaction, which was interpreted in the medical notes as a 'psychotic incident'. She was admitted to a psychiatric hospital and was immediately taken off all medication. As her addiction to diazepam was of a 10-year standing, she experienced severe withdrawal, which was interpreted as a 'second psychotic episode'. She was given six doses of electro-convulsive therapy. As suddenly as she was admitted to hospital, she was discharged home with a renewed supply of Valium. Someone, the counsellor presumed, had realised the error. It was, however, too late for Ethel who had heard the nursing assistant describe her as a psychopath. She had internalised this label, presuming she had inherited her mother's madness.

Assessment

Assessment of the psychological difficulties of a person with a medical condition requires some understanding of the condition *per se*. For example, the counsellor may assess a client to be depressed, but is that a primary symptom of the condition (as in the case of CFS), or is it a secondary condition (as in the case of a person with cancer)? If it is the former, the counsellor and the client must discuss realistic goals for the counselling contract, as the removal of the symptom involves removal of the complaint.[1] If the depression, or anxiety, or whatever is presented, is secondary to the physical ailment, then reduction may be considered a goal worth working towards.

Assessment of the psychosomatic complaint is harder. How much of the presenting problem is a real physical disorder evoked through stress, and how much is hypochondriasis? As Sanders (1996) points out, not all clients will feel that referral to a counsellor is appropriate. Some may feel angry or betrayed by the referral. It is as well in this situation to remind the client that the purpose of the assessment is to enable you both to review whether the counselling is appropriate. Too much focus on emotional issues at this early stage, Sanders warns, may be inappropriate and unhelpful for a client whose emphasis is on the medical rather than the psychological. Care needs to be exercised with psychosomatic issues, however, as physical illnesses can sometimes be mistaken for psychological disorders (Cooper, 1973).

Even clients with seemingly straightforward medical agendas may have underlying issues that counselling can address:

> John was in his late twenties when he was referred to the counsellor. As a child John had Crohn's disease, a chronic bowel complaint, which plagued him until he had had an ileostomy when he was in his late teens. Although he had had an external catheter since then, he had never really come to terms with it. He blamed his catheter for his inability to maintain relationships, feeling that women thought it dirty and disgusting. He had, since his operation, embarked on a self-destructive life, abusing alcohol and hard drugs. He made repeated suicide attempts during bouts of recurring depression.
>
> When John met his counsellor, he had just finished a detoxification programme and had not touched drugs or drink for three months. His goal was to try and get his life in order by coming to terms with his catheter. 'You have had the bag for 10 years now John, and you say you still cannot accept it,' the counsellor mused. 'Yet you talk about it in a very matter-of-fact way, and you don't seem that embarrassed about it. Your self-destructive behaviour, however, seems to me indicative of something else. You said you had a relatively happy childhood other than your illness. If you hadn't told me that your upbringing was OK, I would have been asking you if you had been sexually abused as a child.' John's eyes flashed with rage. 'Sexually abused!' he stormed. 'Of course I was sexually abused! What else would you call it? All my childhood I've had to lie in different positions while doctors shoved things up my arse. If that isn't sexual abuse, I don't know what is!'

John's catheter was not the real issue; the abuse of his body was – however well intentioned – and the catheter was a symbol of the abuse. The counsellor allowed him to express his rage at the medical profession in a way that he had never been allowed to do before. Being constantly ill as a child, he had always been coached by his parents to be grateful to the doctors for all they were doing for him. Even though he had been 'cured' of Crohn's disease, he did not feel grateful; he felt abused and violated. John only took four of his six sessions, leaving with optimism after forming a new and promising relationship.

Ethel took all of her six sessions, although both she and her counsellor knew that she did not really need the last one. She was now a transformed woman. When the counsellor had gently explained to her what really had happened to her at the psychiatric hospital, and that none of it was her fault, she came to realise that she was not mad. She was not like her mother. She started walking with a more upright posture, had her hair cut and styled, and bought some new and fashionable clothes. She enrolled in an assertiveness class. By the end of her sessions, she looked calm and graceful, even though she still had a bit of a nervous twitch, and her hands still occasionally shook (which may have been extra-pyramidal effects induced pharmacologically). Ethel had found herself.

Alison was not helped by TLT. She attended two sessions during which she discussed her relationship and her childhood. She could see the comparisons. She knew the doctor was worried about her abuse of her insulin levels, and was enjoying the attention. She tried the same thing with the counsellor when she cheerfully told the counsellor of her personal neglect of her metabolic levels. She wanted the counsellor to exhort her to be careful and take care of herself, but the counsellor was impassive and non-judgmental. Alison started to try and manipulate the counsellor by not turning up for booked appointments, then phoning, saying she was feeling unwell and asking for another appointment. When Alison failed to turn up for the third booked appointment she was refused another. Alison was not ready for therapy.

TLT procedures

Much of the counselling referred to in this chapter will be grief and loss work. This may be for the client who is grieving for the loss of his own life on being given a terminal prognosis, the loss of an active life on the prognosis of a chronic illness, or the loss of a body organ. Or it may be the spouse who is the client experiencing anticipatory grief (see Chapter 7), distress or even resentment at the prospect of being a carer for a disabled partner. So much of the work will be **exploring** feelings that the medical practitioners often do not give clients the opportunity to express.

The skills required for a counsellor helping anyone with a (particularly) life-threatening illness need to be a balance between being supportive, yet keeping the client in a reality frame without being overly pessimistic. Deep-seated fears need to be acknowledged and validated. A discussion of death in a matter-of-fact way relieves the tension of the client and allows her to discuss openly what death means for her. People often think about issues of money and property at times of death, but they may not make the space to express their hopes and wishes in other spheres of their life. For example, the client may want to discuss what she would like to happen to her loved ones after her death. Who will care for the children? Will I want my husband to meet someone else after my death? Would I want another woman living with my husband in my house?

First, cover the physical illness in detail, giving the client plenty of time to discuss his symptoms. Sometimes the client may tell the counsellor of symptoms which, for one reason or another, he has not told the doctor. The client should be encouraged to discuss this with the doctor. For example, headaches are a common presenting symptom in situations of anxiety, stress and depression. But if the headache is accompanied by visual disturbance, vertigo, vomiting, or is so intense that it keeps the client awake, then the client needs to be referred back to the GP. Similarly, the various symptoms of IBS have been discussed, but if bowel disorder is accompanied by bleeding or weight loss, refer back to the GP. The counsellor should never be tempted to make an analysis of what symptom is important and what is irrelevant. If the client expresses reluctance, the counsellor could offer to mediate by talking to the doctor for the client. This offer is usually seized on readily, although confidentiality on non-physical aspects needs to be emphasised.

> Doreen was convinced that she did not need to be on the medication for hypertension, but whenever she went to the doctor's she could feel herself getting more and more panicky. 'He doesn't listen to me,' she cried. 'He hardly even looks at me when I'm in his room. He just grunts when he sees me, roughly takes my blood pressure, which is always sky high, and then prescribes more tablets. I'm sure that I don't need to take these pills, and I don't like taking them. I'm sure it is just coming to the doctors that sends my blood-pressure up!' The counsellor offered to speak with the doctor for her, and Doreen readily agreed.
>
> The counsellor tactfully spoke to the doctor about Doreen being nervous about coming to the surgery. The GP was slightly surprised, but suggested that a 24-hour monitor would prove it one way or the other. After the monitor, it was found that, if anything, Doreen's bloodpressure was slightly on the low side. She was taken off her medication, and no longer had to attend the surgery for regular check-ups.

Once the physical side has been covered in great detail, move the client on to talk about the emotional side of her problems. Introduce the topic gently in case there is some resistance to the idea that her physical difficulty is exacerbated by emotional worries. For example: 'You have had many difficulties to face with all these hospital visits and tests, and it has been hard for you to come to terms with the fact that you have emphysema. How do you think other aspects of your life affect your illness?' The object of this question is to move the client on from the tracking exploration of their physical difficulties, to the **understanding** of how their emotional responses have consequences in physical symptoms. As clients develop a mind/body link, they are able to move into strategies for relieving some of their own symptoms. People with psychosomatic complaints have secondary gains in their illness. The task of the counsellor, therefore, is to move the client on to understanding what these gains are.

As mentioned in the assessment section, the counsellor needs to have some knowledge of the physical complaint from which the client is suffering. Look up the condition in a medical textbook (there are always plenty in the surgery), and look up the medication in MIMS (Monthly Index of Medical Specialities held in all practices) to check for possible side-effects and interactions. It is important to know, for example, if impotence is a common side-effect of the medication before heading down a path of psychosexual therapy. If the client reports to the counsellor an unusual symptom occurring while on medication, encourage the client to return to the GP to discuss it. It may help if the counsellor makes the appointment for the client to reinforce how important checking out the symptom is deemed to be.

Talk with the GP regularly about the client's medical process and progress so that you are clear what you are dealing with. For example, a client may tell you that the doctors have found a lump in her brain, but they are not sure whether it is benign or malignant. However, when speaking to the GP, the doctor may be absolutely clear that the lump is malignant, but is just unsure how aggressive the metastasis is.

Refer patients with chronic complaints to support groups and national organisations. There is an organisation for virtually every physical complaint you can think of (like the ME Association or the British Diabetic Association) and these groups offer invaluable support and information on up-to-date research. There are also national groups for various forms of surgery, like the Breast Care and Mastectomy Association, the British Colostomy Association, and the Cancer Aftercare and Rehabilitation Society. These groups have local offices and will provide telephone helplines and maybe local support meetings. There are also support associations for the carers of people with disabilities, who can offer advice and support and help arrange respite care.

For a client in constant chronic pain, there are pain clinics to which the person can be referred. These clinics will provide appropriate medication, teach physiotherapy exercises, biofeedback and relaxation techniques for pain reduction, and may provide a Tens machine for the client to borrow.[2] The counsellor can help by encouraging the client to take control by exploring what he can do in terms of diet and life-style to reduce his pain level as well as reviewing any emotional difficulties that increase his tension and consequently increase his level of pain.

It may be necessary in some cases to undertake domiciliary counselling sessions. Home visits may be required because a client is physically incapable of attending the surgery. They may even be at the bedside of a client who is bedridden or dying. Some counsellors have difficulty with this, because in these situations, the counsellor cannot control the environment. There may be fears of breaking boundaries of space or confidentiality. Here counsellors have to follow their own philosophy about what they feel to be appropriate. Some bedside-counselling sessions may occur to allow the client to say that he is scared of dying just before he dies or to decide where he wants to die. The client may even ask the counsellor for permission to die, because his loved ones are desperate for him to hang on. Counsellors should take all cases of death of a client to supervision to deal with their own issues of loss and the confrontation of their own death (Levy, 1993).

For potentially terminal illnesses, repeatedly check with the GP before seeing the client for an updated prognosis, as these can change rapidly. Never lie to a client about his prognosis. It is hard to tell a client that he has only days or weeks when he is thinking in terms of months. But the counsellor cannot collude with an extended fantasy, as the client will have things he will want to do or say to his nearest and dearest, or there may be places he will want to visit, and at such a time procrastination is a luxury he cannot afford. Remember, GPs also find it difficult to realistically tell a client how long they have got left to live, partly because sometimes they are not really sure, and partly because, for the GP, the death is a form of professional failure. GPs are human, and it hurts to lose a patient. Unfortunately, GPs do not have any supervision arrangements.

Recommended reading

Donaghue, P. and Siegel, M. (1992) *Sick and Tired of Feeling Sick and Tired: Living with Invisible Chronic Illness*. New York: Norton.

Wilber, K. (1991) *Grace and Grit*. London: Macmillan.

Notes

1 Some physical ailments have been dramatically improved in short-term counselling work. For example, a woman suffering with Sjögren's Syndrome found herself fundamentally improved after a six-session counselling contract in which she spent her time discussing her unhappy marriage. However, removal of the illness should never be expressed as the goal of the counselling contract, as the focus should be on the psychological, not on the physical. Everything else can be treated as a bonus.

2 A Tens machine is a small unit which can be attached to the body with electrodes. It pumps a small electronic pulse into the person, and this has been found to help relieve pain.

13
Counselling People with Mental Health Difficulties

Throughout this book, there have been illustrations of client presentations that may not be suitable for counselling in a time-limited setting. For example, in Chapter 4 it was recommended that those presenting with puerperal or manic depression or learned helplessness should be referred on to secondary mental health care. Similarly, those with severe post traumatic stress disorder (Chapter 6) or anorexia (Chapter 9) need greater input than six sessions will allow. This chapter will look at other presenting problems that will be more appropriate for referral. However, this does not mean that these clients should be instantly dumped if considered unsuitable. This would only increase the feelings of abandonment and rejection that many of these clients already have as a major issue. Indeed, some very useful work can be undertaken within a time-limited boundary while waiting for the secondary referral to be taken up (which in some cases may be six months or more). Some would argue that counselling is not appropriate for any of these clients, especially those who are psychotic or demented. But even these clients have their lucid times, and no developmental work is wasted. As Daines et al. (1997) have argued, counselling is not contra-indicated for mental illness providing the appropriate level of work is undertaken. Of course, the counsellor has to be mindful of the risk of violence to herself or to others, but compared to those who abuse drugs or alcohol, the risk of violence from someone with a mental illness is small (Monahan, 1992).

> Edwina was new to the area when she asked to see the counsellor. She complained that her ex-husband, her father and her nephew had sexually abused her three daughters. When the counsellor discussed Edwina with the social services, he found that she was well known to them. Edwina had presented this problem to many health workers. The children had been thoroughly investigated on a number of occasions, which was now considered to be abusive *per se*. It was thought Edwina was exhibiting a form of Munchausen's Syndrome by proxy, but she refused to attend for psychiatric help. The goal of TLT was to get her to accept that help. She did, and also did some useful work on her broken marriage.

Obsessive-compulsive disorder (OCD)

These clients have a deeply entrenched fear of being out of control and have a need for perfectionism. They are overwhelmed with intrusive thoughts, often about dirt, contamination and disease. They may also experience thoughts about violence in relation to either harming others or themselves in order to prevent contamination. They therefore indulge in rigid counting regimes of hand washing, and fear touching anything or anyone without the use of gloves or tissues. They may fear sitting in public places in case they are contaminated through the seat. They are constantly doubting what they have done, like switching off lights or locking doors, and will continually check up on themselves. Eighty per cent of clients with OCD are concurrently depressed (Lemma, 1996).

TLT can only help clients who are starting to develop this problem. It is one that can be relatively easily nipped in the bud, but deeply entrenched problems usually span many years and therefore need a much greater input to resolve. However, these clients are less likely to seek help. It is usually because they are driving someone else mad that they come to the attention of the GP. The common pharmacological treatment is clomipramine, which is a tricyclic antidepressant that relieves much of the intrusive thought processes, but relapse rates are high. The referral should be to a specialist in cognitive behavioural therapy, which has the greatest success rate with this problem. TLT can best help with the depressive part of the disorder.

Substance abuse

I expect you are puzzled as to why I would include a section on substance abuse in a chapter on mental health issues. The reason is that a client who is a substance abuser exhibits many symptoms of mental ill-health. For example, a regular speed (amphetamine) user will become manic and paranoid. A user of hallucinogens (e.g. LSD) may flash back into a trip during a session. Heroin users are seen as devious, manipulative and deceitful. Even long-term users of 'soft' drugs, like cannabis, can develop angry, aggressive and paranoid personalities. And iatrogenic addicts (benzodiazepine users) are thought to have dependent personality disorders and can suffer permanent physical damage in the form of akathisia and tardive dyskinesia.

Clients with addictions to hard drugs, alcohol, benzodiazepines or solvents need specialist intervention over a protracted period of time to see them through their detoxification regimes. For example, clients with long-term alcohol dependency require expert assessment of physical (hepatitis, pernicious anaemia, liver cirrhosis) and mental (dementia, Korsakoff's syndrome) damage. Hard-drug users can have similar physical and mental damage. Referral therefore needs to be to the many specialist units established for their holistic care. However, as these clients have a 20 times increased risk of suicide (Gunnell and Frankel, 1994), the TLT counsellor can help contain their distress whilst waiting for a place at a unit. The counsellor needs an accurate knowledge of the effects of the various substances used by the client, particularly their psychological effects. These clients are often viewed by therapists as manipulative, deceitful and difficult, so any counsellor feeling wary or nervous should not embark on a time-limited contract but should leave them to the experts. TLT can offer support for crises and can help explore why the addictions took hold in the first place. Clients can also learn about the physiological and psychological aspects of dependency, which will help with their detoxification.

> Ethel was helped into the counselling room by her husband, who supported her as she slumped into the chair, then he left. She was very wobbly on her legs, and had a shuffling gait. Her hands trembled as they rested against the arm of the chair. Her hair was now so thin and wispy, she had taken to wearing a wig. She had been diagnosed five years previously as having Parkinson's disease, but she did not respond to the treatment. After a recent thorough series of tests at the local hospital, it was concluded that she did not have Parkinson's after all, and that her symptoms were the consequence of 20 years of taking Lorazepam. She was sent to the counsellor for some help as the doctors were now planning to wean her off her medication.

Personality disorders

People who have paranoid, schizoid, narcissistic or borderline personality characteristics need long-term input from the mental health services because of the intractable nature of their difficulties (Lemma, 1996). They are characterised by dysfunctional, anti-social and non-compliant behaviour. Anti-social or sociopathic clients are those who are considered to present the greatest risk to others in terms of violence. For a full description of how they present themselves see Beck and Freeman (1990) or Hoyt (1995), as accurate assessment of personality patterns enhances clinical effectiveness.

These clients are described in the literature as having personality disorders, although this description makes the assumption that we know what normal personalities are. Derksen (1989) prefers to refer to their disturbed relationships or interpersonal style rather than a disorder of their personality. By the nature of their problems, they have difficulties with trust, and therefore self-disclosure, which makes insight therapies very difficult. Daines et al. (1997) warn that for those who have a tenuous grip on reality, regression in therapy can become pathological and can result in a further disintegration or acting out of destructive feelings both inside and outside of the counselling sessions. For example, a paranoid person who is unaware of the delusion may lash out in perceived retaliatory behaviours. Anyone who says he hears voices telling him to kill needs to be taken seriously and an immediate referral made to the psychiatric service.

> Simon found his own way to the counsellor without the referral from the GP. He had heard that this counsellor was an older woman, and that was what he wanted. He would not have gone if the counsellor had been a man. He needed to talk about sex. He could pretend that they were his experiences. She would listen to what he had to say, and would ask him to elaborate in more detail. He knew what she would do because he had been to counsellors before. He liked the warmth and intimacy of a counselling engagement, and he liked having her undivided attention. He would watch her expression as he described the various sex acts in vivid detail. Then he would go back home and masturbate at the memory.

Self-harm

One of the aspects of a person with a borderline personality disorder may be deliberate self-harm, such as cutting wrists or arms with knives or razor blades, scraping the skin with a cheese grater, or burning with cigarettes. This is an intentional behaviour pattern, which has the function of expressing feelings that the individual might be otherwise unable to express (Favazza, 1989). Self-harming is also addictive. People with this problem are thought to be ego-syntonic, but if they have come for help with their problem, it is likely that they are in fact very distressed by their own behaviour. TLT counsellors who may wish to contain these clients until secondary referral takes effect should take a very matter-of-fact approach to the issue of self-harm, as showing shock, disapproval or dismay has the secondary gain of reinforcing the behaviour.

Psychosis

A person who is psychotic is unable to distinguish reality from his own perceptions. Anecdotally, it is suggested that neurotics build sandcastles in the air, whereas psychotics live in them! They present with thought disorders, paranoia, delusions, hallucinations and speech disturbance (word salad). These symptoms can occur if the person is schizophrenic, manic, depressed, has an organic brain disease, or is in a drug-induced state. Those with psychotic depression, for example, are likely to have all the symptoms of depression with delusions, hallucinations and psychomotor agitation or retardation (thoughts and movement extremely slow). Such people are likely to be suicidal or murderous so they need immediate psychiatric help. Schizophrenia is a controversial diagnosis with cultural implications. For example, there is a statistically significant higher chance of being diagnosed as a schizophrenic in the UK if the client is Afro-Caribbean than if she is white. People from ethnic minorities are also more likely to receive medication than psychotherapy for their mental ill-health (Campling, 1989).

TLT procedures

As was stated at the beginning of this chapter, a counsellor will be unable to help these clients with their specific disorder in six sessions. However, much can be done to help and contain them while they are waiting for their secondary referral to take effect, and the value of supportive work through crisis situations should not be underestimated. It also gives the client an opportunity to practise being within a therapeutic relationship and to start developing the concept of trust. Simply listening to what a person has to say about her delusions and taking them seriously can be extremely empowering for the client. It is important not to be placatory or patronising, but to show a genuine concern for the emotions that the symptoms are trying to convey. The aim is to try to understand why a person needs the delusion to demonstrate their distress (Lemma, 1996). Hoyt (1995) notes that although personality restructuring is too vague and too ambitious for people with personality disorders, what might be usefully achieved in a time-limited contract would be to try and answer three questions: how is the client stuck? what does the client need to get unstuck? how can this be facilitated? Ryle (1990) argues that people with these personality disorders need the commitment of a time-limited contract that will contain them against the emergence of destructive transference–countertransference relationships. This will protect both the client and the counsellor.

Make clear why the referral has been made, to whom, and what the counsellor feels will be achieved by the referral. Always set limits with these clients as to what your role is as far as any TLT sessions are concerned. Also set limits on what is acceptable or not acceptable within the counselling session. For example, if a client paces up and down within the counselling room, and the counsellor is fearful of violent behaviour, then this needs to be clearly stated. Do not attempt to counsel any client with whom you do not feel safe. But always be assured that with a firm belief in the benefit of TLT even the longest journey requires the first step.

Appendix 1: Leaflet for Clients

YOUR QUESTIONS ANSWERED:
A GUIDE FOR USERS OF OUR
COUNSELLING SERVICE

Counselling Service
The Surgery
Anytown
Tel: 1234567

What is counselling?

Counselling is a process that enables you to talk about your problems or your difficulties in your life. Counsellors help you, through talking, to manage your life better by changing the way you respond to difficulties.

What is the counselling process?

The model most commonly used is: explore, understand, act. The counsellor will help you tell your story to explore how you feel about a situation. This will enable you to understand your self and your life better. You may then choose to make changes in your life through action.

Will the counsellor tell me how to solve my problems?

No. The counsellor will help you explore different ways of dealing with a situation, but the choice of whether you do anything about it is yours.

Will the counsellor record our talks in the medical notes?

The counsellor works with the doctors and nurses as one of a team. The rest of the team know that you are seeing the counsellor and why. But the contents of your discussions with the counsellor are confidential and are not recorded in the medical notes.

Will the doctor know what is happening while I see the counsellor?

The doctor and the counsellor discuss the progress you are making in terms of your health and well-being. They are working together to make you feel better and to enable you to cope more effectively. They do not discuss any secrets you may share with the counsellor.

Will I have to talk about things that I would prefer not to discuss?

No. The counsellor will encourage you to talk about many aspects of your life, and will encourage you to express your feelings. But your wish not to discuss a particular issue will be respected.

How do I know that the counsellor is suitably qualified?

The counsellor used by this surgery is a Chartered Psychologist and a counsellor accredited by the British Association of Counsellors.

What happens if I don't feel comfortable with the counsellor?

Tell the counsellor, or if you would find that difficult, tell your doctor. Other arrangements can then be made to help you.

What can I expect to happen when the doctor refers me to the counsellor?

Your first appointment will be for half an hour. This will allow you to meet the counsellor, briefly tell your story, and get a feel of what it will be like. After, you may then have up to six 50-minute sessions.

How often can I see the counsellor?

Because of high demand, appointments are usually at two- to three-week intervals. At holiday time it may be longer. Longer gaps can be arranged if you prefer.

What can I do if things get worse and I can't see the counsellor for a few weeks?

Ring the receptionist and ask to be placed on the cancellation list. She will then arrange for you to be placed in a cancellation appointment. However, very little notice is provided for these cancellation appointments, which are for emergencies only.

Can I phone the counsellor between sessions?

In general, the counsellor will not interrupt a session to answer a phone call. However, it may be possible to talk briefly to the counsellor by prior arrangement with the receptionist.

What should I do if I can't attend an appointment?

Phone the receptionist and cancel your appointment as soon as you are aware that it is inconvenient. Another appointment can then be arranged for you, and your cancelled appointment can be given to someone else.

What should I do if I feel better and I feel I don't need to see the counsellor again?

Ring the receptionist and cancel your appointment, telling her that you feel better. Not turning up without informing reception wastes the counsellor's time and stops her from seeing someone else who needs to be seen. It would help if you could give a minimum of three days' notice to cancel an appointment.

What should I do if I have any comments to make about how the counselling service is organised?

Contact the practice secretary, who will be pleased to hear your suggestions.

Appendix 2: Client Questionnaire

Dear Sir/Madam,

The counselling service offered at the doctors' surgery is new to the practice, and therefore needs to be carefully monitored to ensure that we meet the needs of individuals concerned. Following your recent referral to the counsellor, I would be grateful if you would complete the enclosed questionnaire to help us with this assessment.

Please answer the questions as honestly as you can. Your name will not be recorded on the questionnaire. A stamped-addressed envelope is enclosed for your reply.

Yours sincerely

J. Bloggs
Practice Manager.

Answer the question you feel you are able to by ticking the appropriate box:

1   Have you had any experience of counselling before?

      yes   no

      ☐   ☐

    If yes, please explain

2   Would you rather have seen a male or female counsellor?

      male   female

      ☐   ☐

3   Were the number of sessions you had with the counsellor

      too few   about right   too many

      ☐   ☐   ☐

4   Was the length of the counselling session

      too long   about right   too short

      ☐   ☐   ☐

5   Was the room where you saw the counsellor

      noisy   uncomfortable   about right

      ☐   ☐   ☐

6   Was the seating arrangement

      comfortable   uncomfortable

      ☐   ☐

7(a) Do you think it was right for the doctor to refer you to the counsellor?

      yes   no

      ☐   ☐

(b) Would you have preferred some other form of treatment?

        yes   no

        ☐   ☐

        If yes, what?

8   How much do you feel the counsellor helped you? On a scale of 1–6, no. 1 being not helped at all, and no. 6 being a great deal. Please circle the number that you feel is most appropriate.

        not at all 1 2 3 4 5 6 a great deal

9   In what way did the counsellor help you?

10   Was there any aspect of your life that you might change as a result of speaking to the counsellor?

11   Was there anything about the counselling that was unhelpful?

        yes   no

        ☐   ☐

        If yes, what?

12   Is there anything about the counselling service that you would like to change, or see introduced?

13   If you had difficulties again, would you

seek counselling again	cope on your own	look for others to help you	don't know
☐	☐	☐	☐

14   If counselling was not provided within the surgery, would you

seek counselling elsewhere	go without counselling	don't know
☐	☐	☐

15   Would you recommend counselling to someone else?

yes	no	don't know
☐	☐	☐

We would like to send a further questionnaire in approximately six months' time. May we send this to you at your home address?

        yes   no

        ☐   ☐

If you do not wish to receive another, please leave your name with Josephine Bloggs at the surgery.

Return this questionnaire in the envelope provided.

Thank you.

References

Abramson, L.Y., Seligman, M.E.P. and Teasdale, J.D. (1978) 'Learned helplessness in humans: critique and reformulation'. *Journal of Abnormal Psychology, 87,* 49–74.

Adams, A. (1992) *Bullying at Work.* London: Virago.

Aebi, J. (1993) 'Nonspecific and specific factors in therapeutic change among different approaches to counselling'. *Counselling Psychology Review, 8*(3), 19–32.

Armstrong, P. (1996) 'Counselling and mind-altering medications'. *Counselling, 7*(3), 233–236.

Ashurst, P.M. and Ward, D.F. (1983) 'An evaluation of counselling in general practice'. Final Report of The Leverhulme Counselling Project (mimeo).

BAC (1992) *Code of Ethics and Practice for Counsellors.* Rugby: British Association for Counselling.

BAC (1993) *Guidelines for the Employment of Counsellors in General Practice.* Rugby: British Association for Counselling.

Baker, A. and Duncan, S. (1985) 'Child sexual abuse: a study of prevalence in Great Britain'. *Child Abuse and Neglect, 9,* 457–467.

Balestrieri, M., Williams, P. and Wilkinson, G. (1988) 'Specialist mental health treatment in General Practice: a meta-analysis'. *Psychological Medicine, 18,* 711–717.

Balint, M. (1964) *The Doctor, his Patient, and the Illness,* 2nd edn. Edinburgh: Pitman Medical.

Bandura, A., Reese, L. and Adams, N. (1982) 'Microanalysis of action and fear arousal as a function of differential levels of perceived self-efficacy'. *Journal of Personality and Social Psychology, 43*(1), 5–21.

Barker, P. (1992) *Basic Family Therapy,* 3rd edn. Oxford: Blackwell.

Barraclough, B., Bunch, J., Nelson, B. and Sainsbury, P. (1974) 'A hundred cases of suicide. Clinical aspects'. *British Journal of Psychiatry, 125,* 355–373.

Bartlett, F. (1932) *Remembering.* Cambridge: Cambridge University Press.

Beck, A., Sethi, B. and Tuthill, R.W. (1963) 'Childhood bereavement and adult depression'. *Archives of General Psychiatry, 9,* 295–302.

Beck, A.T. (1975) *Depression: Causes and Treatment.* Philadelphia: University of Pennsylvania Press.

Beck, A.T. (1983) 'Cognitive therapy of depression: new perspectives'. In P.J. Clayton and J.E. Barratt (eds), *Treatment of Depression: Old Controversies and New Approaches.* New York: Raven Press.

Beck, A.T. (1987) 'Cognitive therapy'. In J.K. Zeig (ed.), *The Evolution of Psychotherapy.* New York: Bruner/Mazel. pp. 149–178.

Beck, A.T. and Freeman, A. (1990) *Cognitive Therapy of Personality Disorders.* New York: Guilford Press.

Beck, A.T., Rush, A.J., Shaw, B.F. and Emery, G. (1979) *Cognitive Therapy of Depression.* New York: Guilford Press.

Bennett, P. and Hobbs, T. (1991) 'Counselling in heart disease'. In H. Davis and L.

Fallowfield (eds), *Counselling and Communication in Health Care*. Chichester: Wiley.

Birtchnell, J. (1970) 'The relationship between attempted suicide, depression and parent death'. *British Journal of Psychiatry*, *116*, 307–313.

Black, D. and Urbanowicz, M.A. (1985) 'Bereaved children – family intervention'. In J.E. Stevenson (ed.), *Recent Research in Developmental Psychopathology*. Oxford: Pergamon.

Bond, T. (1993) Current legal and ethical issues. Paper presented at the 2nd Counselling in Primary Care Conference, London.

Bordin, E.S. (1979). 'The generalizability of the psychoanalytic concept of the working alliance'. *Psychotherapy: Theory, Research and Practice*, *16*, 252–260.

Bowlby, J. (1980) *Attachment and Loss* (Vol. 3: *Loss*). London: Hogarth Press.

Bowlby-West, L. (1983) 'The impact of death on the family system'. *Journal of Family Therapy*, *5*, 279–294.

BPS (1990) 'Psychologists and child sexual abuse'. *The Psychologist*, *8*, 344–348.

BPS (1996) 'Attention deficit hyperactivity disorder'. *The Psychologist*, *9*(10), 435–436.

Brand, H.J. (1989) 'The influence of sex differences on the acceptance of infertility'. *Journal of Reproductive and Infant Psychology*, *7*(2), 129–131.

Breggin, P. (1991) *Toxic Psychiatry*. New York: Fontana.

Brown, F. (1961) 'Depression and childhood bereavement'. *Journal of Mental Science*, *107*, 754–777.

Brown, F. (1966) 'Childhood bereavement and subsequent psychiatric disorder'. *British Journal of Psychiatry*, *112*, 1035–1041.

Brown, G.W. and Harris, T. (1971) 'Depression and loss'. *British Journal of Psychiatry*, *130*, 1–18.

Brown, G.W. and Harris, T. (1978) *Social Origins of Depression*. London: Tavistock.

Brown, P.T. and Smith, A.E.A. (1985) 'Counselling in medical settings'. *British Journal of Guidance and Counselling*, *13*(1), 75–88.

Bubenzer, D.L. and West, J.D. (1993) *Counselling Couples*. London: Sage.

Budd, S. (1994) 'Transference revisited'. In S. Budd and U. Sharma (eds), *The Healing Bond*. London: Routledge.

Budman, S.H. (1990) 'The myth of termination in brief therapy'. In J.K. Zeig and S.G. Gilligan (eds), *Brief Therapy: Myths, Methods and Metaphors*. New York: Brunner/ Mazel.

Budman, S.H. and Gurman, A.S. (1988) *Theory and Practice of Brief Therapy*. New York: Guilford Press.

Budman, S.H., Hoyt, M.F. and Friedman, S. (eds) (1992) *The First Session in Brief Therapy*. New York: Guilford Press.

Cade, B. and O'Hanlon, W.H. (1993) *A Brief Guide to Brief Therapy*. New York: Norton.

Cain, A. and Fast, I. (1972) 'The rules of bereavement. Are suicide deaths different?' *Journal of Community Psychiatry*, *116*, 255–261.

Campling, P. (1989) 'Race, culture and psychotherapy'. *Psychiatric Bulletin*, *13*, 550–551.

Carkuff, R.R. (1987) *The Art of Helping*, 6th edn. Amherst, MA: Human Resource Development Press.

Carolin, B. (1995) 'Working with children in a family and divorce centre'. *Counselling*, *6*(3), 207–210.

Chesney, M.A. and Rosenman, R.H. (1985) *Anger and Hostility in Cardiovascular and Behavioural Disorders*. Washington, DC: Hemisphere.

Cole, M. (1988) 'Sex therapy for individuals'. In M. Cole and W. Dryden (eds), *Sex Therapy in Britain*. Milton Keynes: Open University Press.

Cooper, C.L., Cooper, R.D. and Eaker, L. (1988) *Living with Stress*. Chichester: Wiley.

Cooper, G. (1989) 'Are type As prone to heart attacks?' *The Psychologist, 12*(1), 19.

Cooper, G. (1990) 'Stress counselling at work'. *Counselling, 1*(2), 34.

Cooper, I.S. (1973) *The Victim Is Always the Same*. New York: Harper & Row.

Corey, G. (1991) *Theory and Practice of Counselling and Psychotherapy*, 4th edn. Pacific Grove, CA: Brooks/Cole.

Corney, R. (1987) 'Marriage guidance counselling in General Practice in London'. *British Journal of Guidance and Counselling, 15*, 50–58.

Corney, R. (1992) Problems of evaluation. Paper presented at the Counselling in Primary Care Conference, London.

Corney, R. (1993) 'Evaluating counsellor placements'. In R. Corney and R. Jenkins (eds) *Counselling in General Practice*. London: Tavistock/Routledge.

CPCT (1993) *The Work Specification for Counsellors Working in General Practice*. Staines: Counselling in Primary Care Trust.

Crisp, A.H. (1986) 'Biological depression; because sleep fails?' *Postgraduate Medical Journal, 62*, 179–185.

Cummings, N.A. (1988) 'Emergence of mental health complex adaptive and maladaptive responses'. *Professional Psychology, 193*, 308–315.

Cummings, N.A. (1977) 'Prolonged (ideal) versus short-term (realistic) psychotherapy'. *Professional Psychology, 4*, 491–501.

Curtis Jenkins, G. (1992) What is counselling in primary care? What are the expectations? Paper presented at the Counselling in Primary Care Conference, London.

Curtis Jenkins, G. (1993a) *Counselling in Primary Care*. Staines: Counselling in Primary Care Trust.

Curtis Jenkins, G. (1993b) *How to Start a Counselling Service in Your Practice*. Staines: Counselling in Primary Care Trust.

Curtis Jenkins, G. (1993c) *Success and Failure. Counselling in General Practice*. Staines: Counselling in Primary Care Trust.

Curtis Jenkins, G. (1996) *A Guide to Counselling in General Practice*. Staines: Counselling in Primary Care Trust.

Daines, B., Gask, L. and Usherwood, T. (1997) *Medical and Psychiatric Issues for Counsellors*. London: Sage.

Dale, P. (1992) 'Individual counselling with adults abused as children: opportunities and difficulties in working with the consequences of abuse'. *Counselling, 3*(1), 25–30.

Davies, M. (1993) 'Counselling. A statistical analysis within the primary health care team'. *CMS News*, November (37), 5–10.

Davis, H. and Fallowfield, L. (1991) *Counselling and Communication in Health Care*. Chichester: Wiley.

Day, R.W. and Sparacio, R.T. (1989) 'Structuring the counselling process'. In W. Dryden (ed.), *Key Issues for Counselling in Action*. London: Sage.

Delongis, A., Folkman, S. and Lazarus, R.S. (1988) 'The impact of daily stress on health and mood: psychological and social resources as mediators'. *Journal of Personality and Social Psychology, 54*, 486–495.

de Shazer, S. (1985) *Keys to Solution in Brief Therapy*. New York: Norton.

de Shazer, S. (1988) *Clues: Investigating Solutions in Brief Therapy*. New York: Norton.

Derksen, R. (1989) 'Suicide and attempted suicide: an international perspective'. *Acta Psychiatrica Scandanavica, Suppl., 345,* 1–24.

Dorpat, L.D., Ripley, H.S. and Jackson, J.K. (1965) 'Broken homes and attempted and completed suicide'. *Archives of General Psychiatry, 12,* 213.

Dryden, W. and Feltham, C. (1992) *Brief Counselling.* Buckingham: Open University Press.

Durel, M.A., Kranz, D.S., Eisold, J.R. and Lazar, J.D.L. (1985) 'Behavioural effects of beta blockers: reduction of anxiety, acute stress and Type A behaviour'. *Journal of Cardiopulmonary Rehabilitation, 5,* 267–273.

Earll, L. and Kincey, J. (1982) 'Clinical psychology in General Practice: a controlled trial evaluation'. *Journal of the Royal College of General Practitioners, 32,* 32–37.

Egan, G. (1994) *The Skilled Helper. A Problem-Management Approach to Helping,* 5th edn. Belmont, CA: Brooks/Cole.

Eldrid, J. (1988) *Caring for the Suicidal.* London: Constable.

Ellis, A. (1967) 'Rational-emotive psychotherapy'. In D. Arbuckle (ed.), *Counselling and Psychotherapy.* New York: McGraw-Hill.

Ellis, A. (1971) *Growth through Reason.* Hollywood, CA: Wilshire Books.

Elton Wilson, J. (1996) *Time-Conscious Psychological Therapy.* London: Routledge.

Etherington, K. (1995) *Adult Male Survivors of Childhood Sexual Abuse.* London: Pitman.

Etherington, K. (1996) 'Therapeutic issues for sexually abused adult males'. *Counselling, 7*(3), 224–228.

Fairburn, G. and Cooper, P. (1988) 'Eating disorders'. In K. Hawton, P. Salkowskis, J. Kirk and D. Clark (eds), *Cognitve Behaviour Therapy for Psychiatric Problems.* Oxford: Oxford Medical Publications.

Fallowfield, L. (1991) 'Counselling patients with cancer'. In H. Davis and L. Fallowfield (eds), *Counselling and Communication in Health Care.* Chichester: Wiley.

Favazza, A. (1989) 'Why patients mutilate themselves'. *Hospital and Community Psychiatry, 40,* 137–145.

Feltham, C. (1997) *Time-Limited Counselling.* London: Sage.

Finlay-Jones, R. and Brown, G.W. (1981) 'Types of stressful life event and the onset of anxiety and depressive disorders'. *Psychological Medicine, 11,* 803–815.

Friedman, M.J. (1988) 'Towards rational pharmacotherapy for post-traumatic stress disorder. An interim report'. *American Journal of Psychiatry, 145,* 281–285.

Friedman, S.B., Chodoff, P., Mason, J.W. and Hamburg, D.A. (1963) 'Behavioural observations on parents anticipating the death of a child'. *Pediatrics, 32,* 610–625.

Fromm-Reichman, F. (1949) Discussion of a paper by O.S. English. *Psychiatry, 12,* 133.

Garfield, S.L. (1986) 'Research on client variables in psychotherapy'. In S.L. Garfield and A.E. Bergin (eds), *Handbook of Psychotherapy and Behaviour Change.* New York: Wiley.

Gath, D. and Catalan, J. (1986) 'The treatment of emotional disorders in General Practice'. *Journal of Psychosomatic Research, 30,* 381–386.

George, E., Iveson, C. and Ratner, H. (1990) *Problem to Solution. Brief Therapy with Individuals and Families.* London: Brief Therapy Press.

Goldstein, A.P. (1962) *Therapist–Patient Expectancies in Psychotherapy.* New York: Macmillan.

Gorodensky, A. (1996) *Mum's the Word. The Mamma's Boy Syndrome Revealed.* London: Cassell.

Gotlieb, I. and Hammen, C. (1992) *Psychological Aspects of Depression: Towards a Cognitive-Interpersonal Integration.* Chichester: Wiley.

Gottman, J.M. and Levenson, R.L. (1988) 'The social psychophysiology of marriage'. In P. Noller and M.A. Fitzpatrick (eds), *Perspectives on Marital Interaction*. Clevedon: Multilingual Matters.

Gravelle, H.S.E. (1980) *Deputising Services: Prescribing in General Practice and Dispensing in the Community*. London: Kings Fund Centre.

Gregson, O. and Looker, T. (1996) 'The biological basis of stress management'. In S. Palmer and W. Dryden (eds), *Stress Management and Counselling*. London: Cassell.

Gunnell, D. and Frankel, S. (1994) 'Prevention of suicide: aspirations and evidence'. *British Medical Journal, 308*, 1227–1233.

Guthrie, E., Creed, F.M. and Dawson, D. (1993) 'Controlled study of psychotherapy in irritable bowel syndrome'. *British Journal of Psychiatry, 163*, 315–321.

Hammersley, D. (1993) *Counselling People on Prescribed Drugs*. London: Sage.

Hammersley, D. and Beeley, L. (1992) 'The effects of medication on counselling'. *Counselling, 3*(3), 162–164.

Hart, C. (1994) 'Psychiatric disorders in children'. *The Practitioner, 238*, 378–383.

Hawton, K. and Catalan, J. (1987) *Attempted Suicide – A Practical Guide to its Nature and Management*. Oxford: Oxford University Press.

Hawton, K. and Fagg, J. (1988) 'Suicide and other causes of death following attempted suicide'. *British Journal of Psychiatry, 152*, 359–366.

Hayton, A. (1995) 'A previous miscarriage or abortion as a factor in counselling'. *Counselling, 6*(3), 219–222.

Henderson, P. (1995) Counsellors in chronic illness; assumptions in mind–body work. Paper presented at the 4th St George's Conference on Counselling in Primary Care, London.

Henry, J.P. (1986) 'Neuroendocrine patterns of emotional response'. In R. Plutchik and H. Kellerman (eds), *Emotion: Theory and Research* (Vol. 3: *Biological Foundations of Emotion*). London: Academic Press.

Hill, D.R., Kelleher, D. and Shumaker, S.A. (1992) 'Psychosocial interventions in adult patients with coronary heart disease and cancer: a literature review'. *General Hospital Psychiatry, 14*, 28S–42S.

Holmes, J. (1994) 'Psychotherapy – a luxury the NHS cannot afford?', *British Medical Journal, 309*, 1070–1071.

Holmes, T.H. and Rahe, R.H. (1967) 'The social readjustment rating scale'. *Journal of Psychosomatic Research, 11*, 213–218.

Home Office (1991) *Disasters: Planning for a Caring Response*. London: HMSO.

Hoyt, M.F. (1995) *Brief Therapy and Managed Care: Readings for Contemporary Practice*. San Francisco: Jossey-Bass.

Hudson, G. (1988) 'Counsellors within General Practice: time and need for utilization, credibility and accreditation'. *BPS Counselling Psychology Review, 3*(1), 15–20.

Hudson, G. and Mountford, R. (1992) Fat and happy, fact or fiction? Paper presented at the British Psychological Society, London.

Hudson-Allez, G. (1994) 'What the client wants'. *Counselling News, 15*, 18–19.

Hudson-Allez, G. (1995) 'Issues of confidentiality for a counsellor in General Practice'. *CMS News, 44*, 8–9.

Hughes, P. (1993) Counselling in primary care: the limits of competence. Paper presented at the the 2nd Counselling in Primary Care Conference, London.

Ives, E. (1979) 'Psychological treatment in General Practice'. *Journal of the Royal College of General Practitioners, 29*, 343–351.

Jacobson, S., Fasman, J. and DiMascio, A. (1975) 'Deprivation in the childhood of depressed women'. *Journal of Nervous and Mental Disease, 160*(1), 5–14.

Jewell, T. (1992) *The Introduction of a Counsellor into Two General Practices.* Cambridge: Cambridge Health Authority.

Johnstone, L. (1989) *Users and Abusers of Psychiatry.* London: Routledge.

Jukes, A. (1990) 'Working with men who are violent to women'. *Counselling, 1*(4), 124–126.

Kalucy, R.S. and Crisp, A.H. (1974) 'Some psychological and social implications of massive obesity'. *Journal of Psychosomatic Research, 18,* 465–473.

Kanner, A.D., Coyne, J.C., Schaefer, C. and Lazarus, R.S. (1981) 'Comparison of two modes of stress management: daily hassles and uplifts versus major life events'. *Journal of Behavioural Medicine, 4,* 1–39.

Karasu, T. (1986) 'The psychotherapies: benefits and limitations'. *American Journal of Psychotherapy, 40,* 324–343.

Karpman, S. (1968) 'Fairy tales and script drama analysis'. *Transactional Analysis Bulletin, 7,* 39–43.

Kell, C. (1992) 'The internal dynamics of the extramarital relationship: a counselling perspective'. *Sexual and Marital Therapy, 7*(2), 157–172.

Kelly, D. (1992) 'Professional burnout'. *Update,* 15 June, 1163–1170.

Kolber, H. and Kolber, S. (1995) The primary care counsellor – is it possible to meet the needs? Paper presented at the 4th St George's Conference on Counselling in Primary Care, London.

Kriesel, H.T. and Rosenthal, D.M. (1986) 'The family therapist and the family physician: a co-operative model'. *Family Medicine, 18*(4), 197–200.

Kübler-Ross, E. (1970) *On Death and Dying.* London: Tavistock.

Lair, G.S. (1996) *Counselling the Terminally Ill: Sharing the Journey.* Washington, DC: Taylor and Francis.

Lazarus, R.S. (1966) *Psychological Stress and the Coping Process.* New York: McGraw-Hill.

Lemma, A. (1996) *Introduction to Psychopathology.* London: Sage.

Levenson, R.W. and Gottman, J.M. (1985) 'Physiological and affective predictors of change in relationship satisfaction'. *Journal of Personality and Social Psychology, 49,* 85–94.

Levinson, D.J. (1978) *The Seasons of a Man's Life.* New York: Knopf.

Levy, S.M. (1993) 'Humanising death: psychotherapy with terminally ill patients'. In P.T. Costa and G. Van DenBas (eds), *Psychological Aspects of Serious Illness: Chronic Conditions, Fatal Diseases and Clinical Care.* Washington, DC: American Psychological Association. pp. 185–213.

Lewis, C.S. (1973) *A Grief Observed.* London: Faber and Faber.

McGrath, G. and Lowson, K. (1986) 'Assessing the benefits of psychotherapy: the economic approach'. *British Journal of Psychiatry, 150,* 65–71.

McIntosh, J. (1974) 'Processes of communication, information seeking and control associated with cancer. A selective review of the literature'. *Social Science and Medicine, 8,* 167–187.

Malan, D.H. (1976) *The Frontier of Brief Psychotherapy.* New York: Plenum.

Mann, J. (1981) 'The core of time-limited psychotherapy: time and the central issue'. In S. Budman (ed.), *Forms of Brief Therapy.* New York: Guilford. pp. 25–43.

Markman, H.J., Floyd, S., Stanley, S. and Storasli, R. (1988) 'The prevention of marital distress: a longitudinal investigation'. *Journal of Consulting and Clinical Psychology, 56,* 210–217.

Marks, G. and Miller, N. (1987) 'Target attractiveness as a mediator of assumed attitude similarity'. *Personality and Social Psychology Bulletin, 102,* 72–90.

Marsh, G.N. and Barr, J. (1975) 'Marriage guidance counselling in group practice'. *Journal of the Royal College of General Practitioners, 25,* 73–75.

Martin, E. and Mitchell, H. (1983) 'A counsellor in General Practice: a one-year survey'. *Journal of the Royal College of General Practitioners, 33,* 366–367.

Masters, W.H. and Johnson, V.E. (1970) *Human Sexual Inadequacy.* London: Churchill.

Mayou, R., Bryant, B. and Duthie, R. (1993) 'Psychiatric consequences of road traffic accidents'. *British Medical Journal, 307,* 647–651.

Menzies, D., Dolan, B. and Norton, K. (1993) 'Are short term savings worth long term costs?', *Psychiatric Bulletin, 17,* 517–519.

Middleton, A. and Williams, D. (1995) 'The aftermath of suicide'. *Counselling, 6*(4), 307–309.

Mitchell, J. (1984) *What is to be Done about Illness and Health?* Harmondsworth: Penguin.

Monahan, J. (1992) 'Mental disorder and violent behaviour: perceptions and evidence'. *American Psycholgist, 47*(4), 511–521.

Montgomery, S.A. (1991) *Anxiety and Depression.* Petersfield, Hampshire: Wrightson Biomedical.

MORI (1992) *Attitudes towards Depression.* Research study conducted for the Defeat Depression Campaign. London: Royal College of Psychiatrists.

Morrill, R.G. (1978) 'The future for mental health in primary health care programs'. *American Journal of Psychiatry, 135,* 1351–1355.

Munos, R.F. (1994) 'On the AHCPR depression in primary care guidelines: further considerations for practitioners'. *American Psychologist, 49,* 42–46.

Murray, L. and Stein, A. (1989) 'The effects of postnatal depression on the infant'. *Ballière's Clinical Obstetrics and Gynaecology, 3*(4), 921–933.

Muss, D.C. (1991) 'A new technique for treating post-traumatic stress disorder'. *British Journal of Clinical Psychology, 30,* 91–92.

Mynor Wallis, L.M. and Gath, D.H. (1992) 'Brief psychological treatments'. *International Review of Psychiatry, 4,* 301–306.

Neill, J. (1989) *Assessing Elderly People for Residential Care: A Practical Guide.* London: National Institute for Social Work Research Unit.

Neilson, D.G. and Knox, J.D.E. (1975) 'General practitioners and marriage guidance counselling'. *Journal of the Royal College of General Practitioners, 25,* 462–464.

Nicolson, P. (1990) 'A brief report of women's expectations of men's behaviour in the transition to parenthood: contradictions and conflicts for counselling psychology practice'. *Counselling Psychology Quarterly, 3*(4), 353–361.

Nieland, M.N.S. (1993) What is postnatal depression? Paper presented at the Annual Conference of the British Psychological Society, Blackpool.

Noon, J.M. (1992) 'Counselling GPs. The scope and limitation of the medical role in counselling'. *Journal of the Royal Society of Medicine, 85,* 126–128.

Oatley, K. and Bolton, W. (1985) 'A social-cognitive theory of depression in reaction to life events'. *Psychological Review, 92*(3), 372–388.

O'Hanlon, W.H. (1989) *In Search of Solutions: a New Direction in Psychotherapy.* New York: Norton.

O'Hanlon, W.H. (1990) 'A grand unified theory for brief therapy: putting problems in context'. In J.K. Zeig and S.G. Gilligan (eds), *Brief Therapy: Myths, Methods and Metaphors.* New York: Brunner/Mazel. pp. 78–89.

OPCS (1994) *Monitor 1992*. London: HMSO.

Orlinsky, D.E. and Howard, K.L. (1986) 'The relation of process to outcome'. In S.L. Garfield and A.E. Bergin (eds), *Handbook of Psychotherapy and Behaviour Change*, 3rd edn. New York: Wiley.

Palazzoli, M.S., Boscolo, L., Cecchin, G. and Prata, G. (1980) 'The problem of the referring person'. *Journal of Marital & Family Therapy*, January, 6(1), 3–9.

Parish, P.A. (1971) 'The prescribing of psychotropic drugs'. *Journal of the Royal College of General Practitioners*, 21(4), 1–77.

Parkes, C.M. (1972) *Bereavement: Studies of Grief in Adult Life*. London: Tavistock.

Parkes, C.M. (1973) 'Anticipatory grief and widowhood'. *British Journal of Psychiatry*, 122, 615–619.

Parkes, C.M. (1980) 'Bereavement counselling: does it work?' *British Medical Journal*, 6232, 3–6.

Parkinson, F. (1995) 'Critical incident debriefing'. *Counselling*, 6(3), 186–187.

Paul, G.L. (1967) 'Strategy of outcome research in psychotherapy'. *Journal of Consulting Psychology*, 31, 109–119.

Paykel, E.S. (1979) 'Causal relations between clinical depression and life events'. In J.E. Barrett, R.M. Rose and G.L. Klerman (eds), *Stress and Mental Disorder*. New York: Raven Press.

Pearce, N. and Crisp, A. (1994) Counselling approaches to anorexia nervosa in primary care. Paper presented at the 3rd St George's Counselling in Primary Care Conference, London.

Perry, S. (1990) 'Combining antidepressants and psychotherapy: rationale and strategies'. *Journal of Clinical Psychiatry*, 51(suppl.), 16–20.

Pringle, M. and Laverty, J. (1993) 'A counsellor in every practice – reasons for caution (editorial)'. *British Medical Journal*, 306, 2–3.

Rawlinson Commission (1994) *The Physical and Psychosocial Effects of Abortion on Women. (A Report of the Commission of Enquiry into the Operation and Consequences of the Abortion Act)*. London: HMSO.

Rennie, D. (1994) Human science in counselling psychology: closing the gap between research and practice. Paper presented at the 1st Annual Conference of the BPS Division of Counselling Psychology, May.

Roberts, J. (1996) 'Perceptions of the significant other of the effects of psychodynamic psychotherapy: implications for thinking about psychodynamic and systemic approaches'. *British Journal of Psychiatry*, 168, 87–93.

Rodin, J. and Langer, E. (1980) 'Aging labels: the decline of control and the fall of self esteem'. *Journal of Social Issues*, 36(2), 12–29.

Rogers, C. (1961) *On Becoming a Person*. Boston: Houghton Mifflin.

Rogers, C. (1980) *A Way of Being*. Boston: Houghton Mifflin.

Rosenman, R.H., Friedman, M., Straus, R., Wurm, M., Kositchek, R., Hahn, W. and Werthessen, N.T. (1964) 'A predictive study of coronary heart disease: the Western Collaborative Group Study'. *Journal of the American Medical Association*, 189, 15–22.

Rosenman, R.H., Swan, G.E. and Carmelli, D. (1988) 'Definition, assessment, and evolution of the Type A behaviour pattern'. In B.K. Houston and C.R. Snyder (eds), *Type A Behaviour: Research, Theory and Intervention*. New York: Wiley.

Rosser, M. (1993) 'Alzheimer's disease'. *British Medical Journal*, 307, 779–782.

Rothbaum, B.O., Foa, E.B., Riggs, D.S., Murdock, T. and Walsh, W. (1992) 'A prospective examination of post-traumatic stress disorder in rape victims'. *Journal of Traumatic Stress*, 5, 455–475.

Rowan, J. (1992) 'Response to K. Mair's "The myth of therapist expertise"'. In W. Dryden and C. Feltham (eds), *Psychotherapy and its Discontents*. Milton Keynes: Open University Press.

Rutter, M. (1985) 'Psychopathology and development: links between childhood and adult life'. In M. Rutter and L. Hersov (eds), *Child and Adolescent Psychiatry: Modern Approaches*. Oxford: Blackwell.

Ryle, A. (1990) *Cognitive-Analytic Therapy: Active Participation in Change*. Chichester: Wiley.

Sabin, J. (1992) 'The therapeutic alliance in managed care in mental health practice'. *Journal of Psychotherapy Practice and Research*, 1(1), 31–37.

Sanders, D. (1996) *Counselling for Psychosomatic Problems*. London: Sage.

Schachter, S. (1982) 'Recidivism and self-cure of smoking and obesity'. *American Psychologist*, 37(4), 436–444.

Scher, M., Stevens, M., Good, M. and Eichenfield, G. (1987) *Handbook of Counselling and Psychotherapy with Men*. London: Sage.

Segal, J. (1991) 'Counselling people with multiple sclerosis and their families'. In H. Davis and L. Fallowfield (eds), *Counselling and Communication in Health Care*. Chichester: Wiley.

Seligman, M.E.P. (1975) *Helplessness: On Depression, Development and Death*. San Francisco: Freeman.

Seyle, H. (1956) *The Stress of Life*. New York: McGraw-Hill.

Shapiro, A.K. (1971) 'Placebo effects in medicine, psychotherapy and psychoanalysis'. In S.L. Garfield and A.E. Bergin (eds), *Handbook of Psychotherapy and Behavioural Change*, 3rd edn. New York: Wiley.

Sherr, L., Strong, C. and Goldmeier, D. (1990) 'Sexual behaviour, condom use and prediction in attenders at sexually transmitted disease clinics: implications for counselling'. *Counselling Psychology Quarterly*, 3(4), 343–352.

Shillitoe, R. (1991) 'Counselling in health care: Diabetes Mellitus'. In H. Davis and L. Fallowfield (eds), *Counselling and Communication in Health Care*. Chichester: Wiley.

Sibbald, B., Addington-Hall, J., Brennerman, D. and Freeling, P. (1993) 'Counsellors in English and Welsh General Practices: their nature and distribution'. *British Medical Journal*, 306, 29–33.

Sifneos, P.E. (1992) *Short-Term Anxiety-Provoking Psychotherapy: A Treatment Manual*. New York: Plenum.

Small, N. and Conlon, I. (1988) 'The creation of an interpersonal occupational relationship: the introduction of a counsellor into NHS General Practice'. *British Journal of Social Work*, 18(2), 171–178.

Smith, D.C. and Maher, M.F. (1993) 'Achieving a healthy death: the dying person's attitudinal contributions'. *Hospice Journal*, 9(1), 21–32.

Smith, M.L., Glass, G.V. and Miller, T.I. (1980) *The Benefits of Psychotherapy*. Baltimore, MD: Johns Hopkins University Press.

Society of Behavioural Medicine (1987) 'Psychoneuroimmunology area review'. *Annals of Behavioural Medicine*, 9, 3–20.

Spiers, R. and Newell, J.A. (1995) 'One counsellor, two practices. A report of a pilot scheme in Cambridgeshire'. *CMS News*, May (43), 10–13.

Spiller, R.C. (1994) 'Irritable bowel or irritable mind? Medical treatment works for those with a clear diagnosis; psychological treatment is essential for some'. *British Medical Journal*, 309, 1646–1648.

Spinelli, E. (1996) 'Do therapists know what they are doing?' In I. James and S. Palmer (eds), *Professional Therapeutic Titles: Myths and Realities*, Vol. 2. London: British Psychological Society Division of Counselling Psychology Occasional Papers. pp. 55–61.

SSI (1996) *Assessing Older People with Dementia Living in the Community*. London: Social Services Inspectorate, Department of Health.

Stiles, W.B., Shapiro, D.A. and Elliott, R. (1986) 'Are all psychotherapies equivalent?' *American Psychologist*, *41*, 165–180.

Storr, A. (1983) 'A psychotherapist looks at depression'. *British Journal of Psychiatry*, *143*, 431–435.

Street, E. and Smith, J. (1988) 'From sexual problems to marital issues'. In M. Cole and W. Dryden (eds), *Sex Therapy in Britain*. Milton Keynes: Open University Press.

Stroebe, W. and Stroebe, M. (1987) *Bereavement and Health*. New York: Cambridge University Press.

Stroebe, W., Insko, C.A., Thompson, V.D. and Layton, B.D. (1971) 'Effects of physical attractiveness, attitude similarity, and sex on various aspects of interpersonal attraction'. *Journal of Personality and Social Psychology*, *18*, 79–91.

Talmon, M. (1990) *Single-Session Therapy*. San Francisco: Jossey-Bass.

Tattersall, R.B. and Walford, S. (1985) 'Brittle diabetes in response to life stress: cheating and manipulation'. In J.C. Pickup (ed.), *Brittle Diabetes*. Oxford: Blackwell Scientific Publications.

Taylor, S.E. and Aspinwall, L.G. (1993) 'Psychosocial aspects of chronic illness'. In P.T. Costa and G. Van DenBas (eds), *Psychological Aspects of Serious Illness: Chronic Conditions, Fatal Diseases and Clinical Care*. Washington, DC: American Psychological Association.

Terkel, S. (1975) *Working*. New York: Avon Books.

Thomas, P. (1993) 'An exploration of patients' perceptions of counselling with particular reference to counselling within general practice'. *Counselling*, *4*(1), 24–30.

Thompson, H. (1992) 'The context of abuse and deprivation'. *Counselling*, *3*(4), 225–228.

Tolland, K. and Rowland, N. (1995) *Evaluating the Cost-Effectiveness of Counselling in Health Care*. London: Routledge.

Tomm, K. (1987) 'Interventive interviewing: I Strategizing as a fourth guideline for the therapist'. *Family Process*, *26*, 313.

Toon, K., Fraise, J., McFetridge, M. and Alwin, N. (1996) 'Memory or mirage? The FMS debate'. *The Psychologist*, *9*(2), 73–77.

Trepka, C. and Griffiths, T. (1987) 'Evaluation of psychological treatment in primary care'. *Journal of the Royal College of General Practitioners*, *37*, 215–217.

Twining, C. (1996) 'Psychological counselling with older adults'. In R. Woolfe and W. Dryden (eds), *Handbook of Counselling Psychology*. London: Sage.

Tyler, M. (1993) Understanding stress. Paper presented at the 2nd Counselling in Primary Care Conference, London.

van Dongen, C.J. (1988) 'The legacy of suicide'. *Journal of Psychosocial Nursing*, *26*, 8–13.

Waydenfeld, D. and Waydenfeld, S. (1980) 'Counselling in General Practice'. *Journal of the Royal College of General Practitioners*, *30*, 671–677.

Weisman, A.D. (1972) *On Dying and Denying*. New York: Behavioral Publications.

Weller, E., Bisserbe, J.C., Boyer, P., Lipine, J.P. and Lecrubier, Y. (1996) 'Social phobia in general health care: an unrecognised undtreated disabling disorder'. *British Journal of Psychiatry*, *168*, 169–174.

Wells, K.B., Goldberg, G. and Brook, R.H. (1986) 'Quality of care for psychotropic drug use in internal medicine group practices'. *Western Journal of Medicine*, *145*(5), 710–714.

Willis, P. (1984) 'Youth unemployment: thinking the unthinkable'. *Youth and Policy*, *4*, 17–36.

Withers, M. (1995) Brief therapies. Paper presented at the 4th St George's Conference on Counselling in Primary Care, London.

Woolfe, R. (1996) 'What's in a title?: changing patterns within psychology and counselling'. In I. James and S. Palmer (eds), *Professional Therapeutic Titles: Myths and Realities*, Vol. 2. London: British Psychological Society Division of Counselling Psychology Occasional Papers. pp. 50–54.

Worden, J.W. (1991) *Grief Counselling and Grief Therapy*. London: Tavistock/ Routledge.

Index

MEDICAL LIBRARY
AILSA HOSPITAL
DALMELLINGTON ROAD
AYR KA6 6AB